THE OPINIONS OF
WILLIAM COBBETT

THE OPINIONS
of
WILLIAM COBBETT

Edited by G. D. H. and Margaret COLE

LONDON :
THE COBBETT PUBLISHING CO. LTD.

First published, August, 1944
by The Cobbett Publishing Co. Ltd.
45 *Great Russell Street, London, W.C.*1

PRINTED IN GREAT BRITAIN BY
FARLEIGH PRESS LTD.,
BEECHWOOD WORKS, BEECHWOOD RISE,
WATFORD, HERTS.

CONTENTS

INTRODUCTION

FOR more than a third of a century—from 1802 up to his
death in 1835—William Cobbett edited *The Political Register,*
for the most part weekly, but for a short period twice a week.
In practically every number there appeared a leading article
written by him: in many numbers several such articles.
Moreover, Cobbett's leading articles were not at all like the
things that go by that name to-day. They were solid stuff; and
he thought nothing of extending a single article to ten or twelve
thousand words. It would have been easy to fill the whole of
the present volume with fewer articles than could be counted
on the fingers of both hands. Indeed, the editors seriously
considered doing this, when they had been reduced almost to
despair by the difficulty of selecting in any other way. But to
do this, though it would have given a clear impression of
Cobbett's tremendous power as a political journalist, could have
conveyed no such impression either of his range or of his many-
sided personality. Accordingly, the editors returned in the end
to their first plan, read through the whole of Cobbett's own
writings in the *Register,* and, from a selection many times the
size of this which is now presented, painfully distilled the essence
—or as much of it as they could force within the compass of so
very exiguous a container. That anyone who knows and loves
his Cobbett will be satisfied it is altogether too much to hope.
Every Cobbett-fancier will look herein for his favourite passages,
and fail to find of them more than a few; and probably every
such reader will also complain that certain of his favourite
subjects are left out. Where, for example, is any specimen of
Cobbett's voluminous writings in defence of Queen Caroline;
where any adequate account of the Gagging Acts of 1817 or the
Six Acts of 1819; where any full exposition of Cobbett's singular,
but most interesting, views about popular education, Mr. Owen's
" parallelograms of paupers ", or army reform from the stand-
point of the common soldiers' rights? Alas, they are all wanting,

or nearly wanting, because the editors found it impracticable to represent them fairly without including extracts so long as to absorb an undue amount of their allotted space. One thing after another had to be jettisoned, to their sorrow; and they fully expect to be blamed by critics who have not been under the necessity of facing their difficult task.

There is, however, a second reason why readers of this volume who know their Cobbett will fail to discover in it many of their favourite passages. It has been selected from the *Political Register* on the principle of excluding articles which were subsequently made up into books. The editors have assumed that what is most wanted is not yet another Cobbett anthology made up largely of extracts from *Rural Rides, Advice to Young Men, Cottage Economy,* and a few other volumes which any reader who pleases can readily find for himself, but rather a choice from what the ordinary reader cannot find without betaking himself to the British Museum, or some other of the very few libraries in which a complete set of the *Register* can be found. They have further limited their task in a second way. An American editor produced not so long ago a volume in which he gathered together the principal autobiographical passages from Cobbett's writings, and strung them together to make a life of the author told in his own words. We have not attempted to do over again what Mr. Reitzel has so competently done— nor should we have done so in any case, because one of us had previously both made extensive use of this same material in a biography of Cobbett and edited a small volume bringing together the autobiographical extracts relating to Cobbett's life and adventures in the United States before he came back to England and started his main journalistic career. It would, no doubt, have been possible for us to extend our search from the *Political Register* to Cobbett's voluminous journalistic writings of this early American period—to comb *The Political Censor, Porcupine's Gazette,* and *The Rush-light* in the same way as we have combed the *Register* itself. But, knowing this material pretty well, we thought better to set it aside. We had enough to choose from, in all conscience; and raking in the outpourings of Cobbett's aggressive Englishness when he found himself among the people of the United States during the earlier phases of the war against France would not have been much to our purpose.

For our purpose in this volume has been mainly that of giving a picture, fair we hope as well as entertaining, of the opinions of William Cobbett the Radical, the friend of the agricultural labourer and the journeyman, the opponent of Pitt and Castlereagh and Wilberforce, the outstanding leader of the 'lower classes' in the struggle for Parliamentary Reform, the enemy of cant and humbug and repression, and the pugnacious defender of English liberties from whatever source they were attacked. We have, no doubt, included herein a specimen or two of Cobbett's 'Toryism', from early *Registers* written before his appreciation of the conditions of popular misery and oppression had converted him into a furious opponent of 'The Thing' and all its works. We have done this, because there is a continuity between Cobbett the Tory and Cobbett the Radical, whose Radicalism never forgot its Tory origins and, to the very end, hated the Whigs the more, even after they had made themselves the instruments of a Reform of Parliament which swept Cobbett himself, at the age of seventy, into the House of Commons. There was always, in Cobbett's most Radical bellowings, some reference to "the good old times." He never wearied of saying that he "wanted nothing new", only a restoration of the ancient rights and liberties of the English people, or, when he could not have quite that, some substitute for them corresponding to the needs and conditions of his own epoch. He was a Radical, in his own estimation, only because things had gone radically wrong, and no less than radical remedies would avail to put them right. He always idealised the past, harking back now to his own country youth and now to the halcyon days before the Reformation, or before the National Debt and the Bank of England, or before Scotch 'feelosofers' and steam-engines and cotton-mills had come to trouble the land—in effect, as far back as it suited him to go in search of this or that feature of the imaginary golden age which served him as a means of reconciling his Tory sentiments with his Radical notions of justice to the common man.

We have said that it is no part of our purpose to make this
volume a biography, or any sort of substitute for a biography of
Cobbett. But, for readers to whom he may be barely more than
a name, it seems necessary to set these extracts against their
background of history, albeit in but few words. William Cobbett
was born in 1763, at Farnham in Surrey, the son of a very
small farmer who was also an innkeeper in a tiny way. He
began life as a farmer's boy and, after a spell of gardening and
an unsuccessful attempt to join the navy, ran away to London
and got employment as a lawyer's clerk. Detesting this, he
enlisted in the army (in mistake for the marines) and was sent
to Nova Scotia and New Brunswick. He rose to be sergeant-
major of his regiment, discovered that his officers were engaging
in extensive peculations of the men's pay and allowances, and,
on the regiment's return to England, procured his discharge
and attempted to expose the defalcations of his superiors. The
result was peril for himself, and in 1792 he fled to France, then
in the throes of revolution but not yet at war with Great Britain.
From France, foreseeing the outbreak of war, he emigrated to the
United States, where he set up as a teacher of English to French
emigrés, the famous Talleyrand being one of his pupils.

The outbreak of the French Wars led to acute controversies
in the United States. The Americans, remembering their own
Revolution, were for the most part disposed to take the French
side. Cobbett reacted violently to their abuse of England, and
soon plunged into pamphleteering in defence of his country's
government. He denounced in unmeasured terms, first in
pamphlets and then in newspapers which he founded, the French
Revolution, Tom Paine, Radicals and Republicans of every sort
and kind: he lauded to the skies every act and every institution
of his native country. Presently, for reasons partly political but
partly arising out of his abuse of a famous American physician,
Dr. Rush, he made the United States too hot to hold him; and
in 1800 he came back to England, to find himself taken up and
petted as a valuable auxiliary by William Pitt, William
Windham, and the Anti-Jacobins generally. He started a daily
paper, *The Porcupine,* which speedily failed; and thereupon,
with aid from Windham and others, he established *The Political*

Register. Government subventions were open to him, but he refused them, accepting only such aid as was given to him wholly without conditions. For a few years the *Register* counted as the leading Anti-Jacobin journal; but very soon Cobbett parted from Pitt, whom he denounced for his financial methods and his support of the monied interest. He gave independent support for a while to the Ministry of All the Talents, which came in on Pitt's death in 1806; but he soon parted company with them, and from this time onwards grew more and more Radical. The main grounds of his change of front were, first, that he believed the methods of financing the war were ruining the country by inflating prices and the National Debt and handing power over from the old aristocracy to the stock-jobbers and all the Pitt-pampered tribe of the new rich; and secondly that, having bought a farm of his own, at Botley in Hampshire, he began to see for himself the misery of the labourers, ground down by high prices, high taxation, and an oppressive Poor Law which was used to keep wages at starvation level.

The more Radical the *Register* became, the more its influence increased. But Cobbett himself was soon in trouble with the law; and in 1810 he was imprisoned for two years in Newgate for an article in which he had denounced the flogging of English soldiers under the eyes of German mercenaries. In prison he wrote *Paper against Gold*, in which he denounced paper-money, inflation, the ' Pitt System ', and every aspect of the new financial aristocracy which was developing out of the French Wars and the Industrial Revolution. His imprisonment ruined him: he came out of gaol in 1812 pestered by monetary embarrassments from which he was never thereafter wholly free. He came out, to denounce the war with the United States and to call loudly for an end to the war against Napoleon, but above all to clamour for Parliamentary Reform as the only means of securing a remission of taxes, the abolition of sinecures and political pensions, and a return to tolerable conditions of living for the labouring people.

The ending of the long war brought with it acute distress and unemployment and an unloosing of the long pent-up forces of Radicalism in the industrial districts. It brought a sharp fall in prices, which bore hard upon the farmers, but no corresponding fall in taxes, because of the swollen total of the National Debt. Cobbett, whose appeal had been hitherto chiefly to the farmers and agricultural labourers, began seriously to consider the plight of the workers in the industrial centres. He wrote, in 1816, his famous *Addresses to the Journeymen and Labourers,* which reached a circulation without precedent, and were read aloud at inns and coffee-houses all over the country. This big circulation was achieved by reproducing the main article from the *Register* as a penny or twopenny pamphlet, which was free from the heavy tax then imposed on periodicals containing news. In 1816, the stamped *Register,* which bore the burden of this tax, cost 1/0½d. for each issue, and was thus far beyond the means of the public to which Cobbett was setting out to appeal.

The economic unrest of 1816 and 1817 promptly provoked retaliatory measures of repression from the Government. First the Habeas Corpus Act was suspended; and then, under the auspices of the Home Secretary, Lord Sidmouth, ' Gagging ' Acts were rushed through Parliament, on the plea that plots and conspiracies were afoot to subvert the constitution. These Acts were directed largely at the press, and above all at the *Register;* and Cobbett, pursued simultaneously by pecuniary troubles and by the prospect of being gaoled under the Gagging Acts if he remained at home, fled to the United States, where he remained until the latter half of 1819. He was not, however, silenced. For two years he edited the *Register* from the other side of the Atlantic, sending home his articles by ship, and keeping up an effective long-distance fire against the Government, which pursued a steady policy of repression against Radicals and disturbers of the tranquillity of the friends of the established order. In 1819 he came back, just in time to encounter the further measures of repression on which the Government had embarked in face of the failure of its earlier enactments. He came back, moreover, to find the Government busy restoring the gold standard, without that " equitable adjustment " of the interest on the National Debt in default of which he had repeatedly declared that the gold standard could not be restored except at the cost of ruin to the people.

The gold standard was restored, nevertheless, and ruin, in shapes recognisable by the governing classes, did not ensue—though there were difficult days in the financial crisis of 1825 when Cobbett loudly asserted that his predictions had been verified. Great Britain emerged slowly from the confusion left by the war, able to bear the burdens of heavy taxation because of the vast increase in national wealth that had been brought about by the twin revolutions in agricultural and industrial production. There was, however, a heavy cost to pay. The farmers and landlords, compelled to adjust themselves to lower prices, beat down agricultural wages and reduced standards of poor relief to the lowest possible point. Cobbett's inveterate hatred of the potato, the national food of the impoverished Irish, was based on the use made of it during this period to justify low wages and restricted poor relief to the labouring households. The poor were compelled to live on a " coarser diet ", in order that the landlords might get their rents and have something left for themselves after meeting the claims of the tax-collector and the mortgage-holder. It is beyond doubt that, in the 'twenties, though national wealth was increasing fast, the economic position of the country labourers grew worse and worse.

The factory workers in the new industrial districts had more chequered fortunes, depending on the rapid ups and downs of foreign trade. Again and again, waves of mass-unemployment swept the industrial areas—in 1825-6 and again at the time of the Reform Bill agitation from 1830 to 1832. Cobbett's popularity ebbed and flowed with these movements of the course of trade. He was most in favour with farmers and labourers and urban workers when times were bad; for then his denunciations of that complex of corruption, oppression, and self-satisfied inhumanity which he called ' The Thing '* seemed to have most point, and his demand for Radical Reform commanded the most enthusiastic support. Through all these years the *Register* was a great power—by far the greatest on the side of the extreme

* See pages 255ff.

Radicals. It was at the height of its influence during the two years between the advent of Lord Grey's Whig Government in 1830 and the passage of the Reform Act in 1832 after the long struggle with the Tories and the House of Lords. In the election which followed the Reform Act Cobbett stood for both Manchester and Oldham. Defeated in Manchester by the Whig nominees, he was elected M.P. for Oldham as the colleague of John Fielden, the Radical cotton-spinner who sided with the operatives over the Factory Acts and was later to take a leading part in the contest against the New Poor Law and to give support to the Chartist Petitions.

Cobbett's orthodox contemporaries said that he was a failure in Parliament, and so he was, if voting habitually in a tiny minority be a sign of failure. It can, moreover, be agreed that Parliament was no place where Cobbett's peculiar talents could be exercised with the appearance of success. He was never happy there: he detested its rules and observances: he could never reconcile himself to the necessity of being polite to his enemies which its practices entailed. To the best of his power he used his position in the House of Commons to say to his fellow-members, not what it pleased them to hear, but what he had been saying in print for many years past. He opposed the re-election of the Speaker: he moved that Sir Robert Peel should be dismissed from the Privy Council: he vehemently opposed Irish coercion and factory exploitation: he demanded drastic tax reductions and assailed the charter of the Bank of England; and, above all else, he fought the Poor Law Bill of 1834 with every ounce of strength that was left him. He saw, in the proposal to supersede the old parochial system of poor relief by a new centralised system administered from Whitehall, with the aid of Boards of Guardians elected on a cumulative property vote, a plan to keep the poor down permanently to a starvation diet, and to deny to the destitute the rights of relief out of the superfluities of the rich which had come down to them, by way of the Elizabethan Poor Law, from the mediaeval responsibilities of the monasteries and the Church. Not that he approved of the Old Poor Law, as it was—he had denounced it often enough. But he saw in the reforms of 1834 a determined attempt to apply the notions of the hated Malthus—to shut the poor up in ' Bastilles ' where, segregated by sexes, they would not be allowed to breed and infest the country with the evil of ' over-population ', and to keep a tight hand over the poor outside the workhouses, lest, with poor relief to fall back on as a last resort, they should demean themselves too proudly towards their masters, and stand out manfully for a living wage.

Cobbett died, in 1835, before the struggle in the country over the hated Poor Law Act of 1834 had reached its height. He died, inciting the labourers and all decent men and women to resistance, almost with his dying breath. That crusade was left for his successors to take up. The New Poor Law was, more than anything else, the cause of the rapid spread of Chartism in the later 'thirties, of the bitterness which marked the social struggles of the Hungry 'Forties, and of the reverence with which most of the active leaders in these conflicts all over the country looked back to Cobbett's record. In London, Cleave and Hetherington founded the Cobbett Club, and throughout the industrial districts men still thought of Cobbett as the departed leader of the crusade against the oppressors of the poor.

It is, indeed, above all as the friend of the country labourers that William Cobbett deserves, and would wish, to be borne in mind. His greatest contest with the Whigs, even in the midst of the Reform agitation in which he was perforce their ally, was waged in support of the labourers who rose, in 1830 and 1831, throughout the Southern and Eastern Counties, demanding an improvement in their wretched lot, asking that tithes be reduced and wages raised, that poor relief be put back to a level somewhat further from sheer starvation, and that some cure be found for the monstrous evils of rural unemployment brought about by increasing population, the development of agricultural machinery, enclosure of the common lands, and the decline of rural industries in face of the advance of the factory system. These labourers, in their ' Rural War ', slew no man. They broke threshing machines, set fire to ricks, and here and there ducked an unpopular paid overseer of the poor in the village pond. The farmers for the most part sympathised with them, hating, as much as they did, the excessive burdens of tax and tithe. The urban workers were on their side; and so were Radicals all over the country. But the Whig Government, determined to prove to the propertied classes that Whigs no less than Tories could be relied on to defend the rights of property, went to the very limit of repression, sending Special Commissions into the most troubled areas to try the rioters, and refusing to intervene when the Judges at these Commissions rained down sentences of death and of transportation for life.

These events roused Cobbett to a fury of passionate resentment; and in the *Register,* while condemning destruction of property and doing his best to dissuade the labourers from it, he forcibly defended them, on the ground that their sufferings and provocations had been past all bearing. The Government, urged on it is said by the King, decided to prosecute him for inciting the labourers to revolt; and early in 1831 he was brought to trial. Defending himself, he turned his speech into a terrific indictment of the Whig Government and a spirited defence of the labourers' cause. He was able to call the Lord Chancellor himself (Lord Brougham) to bear telling witness to the fact that, so far from encouraging the destruction of property, he had warned the people of its futility. Despite the efforts of Judge and Attorney-General, the jury refused to convict. Six were for Cobbett, and six against him. He was discharged—a clear victor over Government persecution in the minds of the public, the more so because the case against him had been buttressed up with an obviously faked confession extorted from a man under sentence of death who had been induced, by a promise of reprieve, to attribute to Cobbett the responsibility for inciting him to arson.

That such methods of trying for a conviction should have been used by the Whig Government of 1830 will surprise least those readers who are most familiar with the record of the times. Ever since the French Revolution of 1789 had set the notions of Liberty, Equality and Fraternity abroad in the world, a succession of British Governments had been busy repressing Radical and working-class agitations by every means in their power. There had been, at every critical moment, a spate of repressive legislation; and circular after circular had gone out from the

Home Office urging the local magistrates to be on the alert for every manifestation of popular unrest. In these movements of repression, the employment of spies and provocative agents played an important part. Governments and magistrates alike tried to compensate for the absence of any adequate police force by employing even the most discreditable agents to keep them informed of popular doings; and it is not to be wondered at if these agents, who got best paid when they could find something sensational to reveal, were soon busy instigating plots and conspiracies in order to have good material for their reports. The names of Reynolds, Oliver, Castles, Edwards, the Bents and many other spies and informers stink in the pages of the history of the time; and it was not the least of Cobbett's services that he played a manful part in exposing these vermin and in the defence of their victims. From Oliver, the instigator of the 'Derbyshire Insurrection' of 1817, to Popay, the spy-agent of the new London police in 1833, Cobbett pursued remorselessly these agents of repression; and it is significant that much less use was made of them against the Chartists in 1839 and 1842. The improvement of the regular police service had something to do with this, and that improvement was part of a general process of administrative reform which carried many of the old abuses gradually away; but Cobbett's writings also had something to do with it, by helping to rouse popular indignation against the system.

If Cobbett himself had been asked, at almost any period of his career after about 1804, what he conceived to have been his main contribution to the cause of truth and justice, he would probably have answered with a reference to the doctrines expressed in his *Paper against Gold*, in his 'Gridiron' prophecy, and in his ceaseless writings against the 'Pitt system'. It was his habit to trace most of the evils of his time to excessive taxation, and to lay the blame for excessive taxation on the 'Money-Lords', who throve out of paper-money and the National Debt. In his view, no money was sound money except gold, or something exchangeable directly for gold. Rightly denouncing the methods by which, during the Napoleonic Wars, loan after loan was raised at increasing rates of interest and by means which allowed enormous rakes-off to the friends of the Government and to the monied classes, he held that these things would have been impossible unless the Bank of England had been relieved from its obligation to pay gold for its notes, and country banks had been allowed to rear an inflated credit structure on a foundation of Bank of England paper. So far, he agreed with the most rigidly orthodox economists; but he went on to contend that it would be a monstrous injustice to call upon the taxpayers to repay in gold values a debt which had been incurred mainly in inflated paper. He therefore opposed any return to the gold standard unless it were to be accompanied by what he called " an equitable adjustment " of the burden of the National Debt. He claimed that, if money values were to be deflated by a return to gold—as was actually done under Peel's Act of 1819—the principal and interest of the Debt should be scaled down to correspond to the altered level of values. In his ' Gridiron ' prophecy of 1819,* made at the time when Peel's Bill was under discussion, he claimed that it would be impossible to enforce the return to the gold standard without creating universal confusion, and provoking popular movements which would end in the overthrow of ' The Thing '. When, in the crisis of 1825, the Bank of England had to go back temporarily to uncovered and inconvertible paper notes, he claimed that his prophecy had been fulfilled. But the crisis passed; and the gold standard remained in being. Cobbett was shown to have been mistaken: he had failed to understand how the great enlargement of money incomes and mercantile activity arising out of the Industrial Revolution could sustain taxation and a swollen debt, or how the banks would, by developing the cheque system, find new ways of increasing the supply of money without formal departure from the gold standard. Cobbett vehemently opposed Thomas Attwood, the Chartist banker from Birmingham, who declared that the issue of money should be based, not 'on the supply of gold in the Bank, but on the needs of the productive system. The orthodox financiers also denounced Attwood as a crank; but what happened, with the growth of cheques, was not very far from what he desired.

* See page 259.

If there had really been no way of increasing the supply of money without departing from the gold standard, Cobbett would have been right about the disastrous consequences of returning to gold without scaling down the Debt.

'The Thing' meant much more to Cobbett than an ungoverned issue of paper-money, which he regarded as one of its symbols. It meant the new England of banking and mercantile wealth which was thrusting the old landowners out of so many of the historic estates. It meant the millocracy of Lancashire and Yorkshire, with its insufferably hot factories and its abominably dank and evil-smelling industrial towns. It meant the new Political Economy, with its doctrines of 'surplus population' and 'abstinence' as the source of progress, its dehumanised attitude to the relations of master and man, and its bias against agriculture. It meant the new generation of evangelical 'Saints' and Methodists, preaching a gospel of other-worldliness meant to reconcile the suffering people to their lot. It meant the boroughmongers, putting up seats in Parliament for sale to the highest bidder, and determined to defend the privilege of the "accursed hill", Old Sarum, and the rest of the rotten boroughs to return members to the House of Commons in the interest of their owners. It meant the hordes of sinecurists and placemen, in Church and State, who battened on the earnings of the people—absentee pluralist parsons, getting their parish work done by starveling curates, children appointed to lucrative public posts which were delegated to ill-paid clerks, bishops with fat incomes who lived like fighting cocks in their palaces, politicians who held high-sounding sinecure offices and handed out similar offices to their friends, corrupt army officers filching the soldiers' rations, corrupt gaolkeepers getting rich at the expense of prisoners who could afford to pay for good entertainment, and leaving poor prisoners to rot with gaol-fever.

Beyond all these, 'The Thing' meant the growth of centralised power in the hands of the Government, and a growing savagery in the use of that power against anyone who was suspected of disaffection to the established order or to the rights of property as they were understood by the rich. Cobbett had watched the criminal law getting steadily more severe; not only against political offenders, but also against poachers and petty thieves, even when they stole only because they were hungry. He hated the new Game Laws, which he regarded as proof that the old gentry had become infected with the new spirit of hatred against the poor. He hated, as signs of encroaching bureaucracy, the continuous enlargements of the powers of petty courts presided over, not by independent judges, but by magistrates, stipendiary or unpaid, who owed their appointments to government influence. He hated the new police, as agents of the growing bureaucratic power. He had, deep in his mind, a vision of an idyllic relationship between squires and farmers, farmers and labourers, in a social order in which wealth came from the land, and not from stock-jobbing or the employment of factory slaves.

All these things that Cobbett hated made up THE THING, of which " The Great Wen ", London, was the outstanding symbol, growing bigger and nastier every day. He knew the ' Wen ' better than the factory towns, and denounced it the more often; but he hated both. He knew the country best of all, and the labourers in husbandry, the ' chopsticks ', very much better than the urban artisans or the factory workers. That was why he so often lost his certainty, and gave an impression of groping, when he came to discuss industrial conditions. About the new factories he was indeed in no doubt: his most telling speech in Parliament was that which he made in support of the Factory Bill of 1833,* and he wrote much and eloquently in support of the factory workers' claims to shorter hours and better working conditions. But when it came to industrial disputes, not between millocrats and millhands, but between smaller employers and artisans, he was less at home. He was fully convinced that the workers had a right to combine and to strike if they thought fit; and he wanted to see them getting good wages and reasonable hours of work. But he was also convinced that, in general, low wages and bad conditions were not the masters' fault. Weighed down as they were by the taxes, how could they afford to pay good wages; and how could the workmen get a decent living out of their wages when nearly

* See page 184.

everything they bought was subject to oppressive taxation for the upkeep of 'The Thing'?

Cobbett's advice to masters and men—small masters and journeymen, as distinct from millowners and their slaves—was that, instead of bickering with each other, they should join forces to win Radical Reform and make an end of 'The Thing' and all its works. He advised them just as he advised farmers and farm labourers to join hands in the troubles of 1830. There is something naïve about the confidence with which we find Cobbett again and again enumerating the blessings which are certain to ensue on Parliamentary Reform.* One would imagine, to listen to him, that he supposed a popularly elected House of Commons would at once put an end to the age of mercantile and industrial development, and of new agricultural techniques, as well as to the new evils in banking and finance— in effect, to all the " vast improvements " of which Brougham and McCulloch and other popularisers of the new economic doctrines were continually boasting.

He was speedily disillusioned when Reform came. It was not, of course, the Reform for which he had contended. He had stood for Manhood Suffrage, the Ballot, Annual Parliaments, and the rest of the familiar Radical programme; whereas the Whigs, when they carried Reform, were in no mind to advance beyond the abolition of the rotten boroughs and the enfranchisement of the middle classes. As soon as the Reform Bill was produced, it was plain that the working classes were to get no share in the new distribution of political power. Cobbett, however, backed the Bill, because he saw in it the downfall of the established order of privilege—of the 'Pitt System' which, in his estimation, was responsible for the national ruin. Hating the Whigs, and seeing the prospect that the Reform Act would seat them in power, he believed that it would be in no wise possible for Reform to stop short at that point, and that they would be compelled to give in to the people. He relied on the continuance of that pressure of mass opinion without which the Bill would never have become law, because the Lords and the King would never have given way even so far. But when the

* See pages 230ff.

first Reformed Parliament met, he was soon compelled to realise that the governing classes—the old and the new combined—were much more powerful than he had given them credit for. The symbol of their union was the Poor Law Amendment Act of 1834, which the people hated fiercely, but Whigs and Tories in Parliament were equally intent on making law.

Cobbett was, in effect, a great Radical in his day, but no kindred to most of the politicians who wore with him the Radical label, and certainly no Radical in any modern sense. He by no means wished to disturb the constitution of King, Lords and Commons, but only to purge all three estates. Next to the labourers, he sympathised with the smaller farmers, and next to the smaller farmers with the old race of squires and landlords. He was continually explaining to these last how good a friend of theirs he really was, and how eager to defend them from the stock-jobbers and contractors and usurers who were busily grabbing their estates. Again and again he denounced their stupidity in not recognising the enemies of 'The Thing' as their real friends. He was no equalitarian, desirous of pulling the rich down—provided that their riches rested on claims which, as an upholder of ancient rights, he could recognise as fair. He did not want to do away with 'masters' and 'men', and to substitute for the competitive system Robert Owen's Socialist Villages of Co-operation. Quite the contrary: he believed the relation of master and man to be normal and natural, and only the new fangled relation of 'employer' and 'operative'—the terminology of the rising factory system—to be false and wrong. His 'master' was a working master, a fellow-craftsman with his men: not a grasping, blackcoated Methodist employer in a counting house, using women and children and steam-engines to take the bread out of the mouths of honest journeymen and masters.

Yet, with all this traditionalism in his blood, Cobbett was the greatest Radical of his day. He was so, because he never came face to face with an abuse that caused human suffering without putting forth all his powers to denounce it and to set it right. Of abuses which he did not meet face to face he could be sometimes all too tolerant—for example, of negro slavery. It needed actual observation to rouse him to a sense of the facts: he was stirred, not by reading about things, but only by seeing them for himself. But when he had seen them, his tenacity was limitless; and he had, above all, a way of talking about the victims of oppression as if he were their fellow-man and not a being of a remote and different order. He identified himself with the people for whose rights he fought; and in doing this he gave them courage and will to fight manfully at his side.

That Cobbett talked a great deal of nonsense, as well as much sense, is undeniable. The nonsense is so much a part of him that it cannot go unrepresented in any selection from his writings. No one now regards tea or potatoes as inventions of the devil, as he regarded them; and no one takes to-day quite his view of the motives of the advocates of popular education or of its effects. But it was true enough in his day that a potato diet was widely recommended as a means of reducing the cost of the poor and as a source of cheap labour-power; and it was no less true that there were abroad brands of educators who saw in education of the 'right' sort a means of keeping the poor contented with their place in the social order. There were Methodists distributing cheap tracts about otherworldly holiness and the need for due subservience to 'betters' in this vale of tears; and there were utilitarian Malthusian propagandists organised to teach the working classes the inexorable laws of population and orthodox political economy. Cobbett was convinced that these were the people who between them would dominate any school system which the State could be persuaded to set up; and in that matter he was not far wrong. That was what the National Schools Society and the British and Foreign Schools Society set out to do, by the cheapest mass-production methods they could devise. As against their efforts, Cobbett's notion was that he would educate the people himself, as Tom Paine had begun to educate them in the days of the French Revolution. It was not a modest notion; but modesty was never Cobbett's way. It was a notion on which he acted to some purpose, in his *English Grammar* as well as in his political writings.

Of the gross inadequacy of the following selection to illustrate the range of Cobbett's appeal or the sheer cumulative force of his writing, we have spoken already. It remains to say a word about the quality of his style. He himself disclaimed all stylistic aspirations,* and claimed that the literary craftsman, equally with any other, should be judged by the effect of his work and not by any inherent quality subject to critical judgment. But he was far from meaning by this that a man ought not to pay attention to how, as well as to *what,* he wrote. He had himself a great devotion to Swift; and unlike Swift's as his manner is, he owed Swift much. Writing at high speed, and under conditions which allowed no opportunity of polishing up, he was bound to write unevenly, and with lapses. But he recognised to the full the need to possess himself of so exact a mastery over words that, however fast he wrote, he should write well—forcibly and freshly, and with a clarity which would leave his meaning in no doubt. That he could do this, writing day after day in the " stone-floored room " which he recommended as the best place for such labours, implied a natural talent industriously improved. That his talent was natural and spontaneous, the vigour and graphic power of his earliest writings, published in the United States when his Anti-Jacobinism was at its height, put beyond question. But it is no less certain that his style went on improving with practice. He wrote best in middle age. *Rural Rides* were mostly written when he was round about sixty; and his best period as a writer began with his exile in America when he was fifty-four. In these works of his maturity, he at last gave full scope to that astonishing power of graphic and lively description with which he had again and again in his articles in the *Register* suddenly irradiated some tract of humdrum political argument.

Cobbett had the art of putting his personality across to his readers, whatever the subject on which he was writing might be. They never knew when, in the middle of a disquisition on some quite ephemeral subject, he would launch out suddenly on some personal reminiscence or on some graphic picture of the English countryside or of the manners of the Americans, or on some sudden diatribe about one of his aversions, from the stock-jobbing

* See page 42.

gentleman in the City to the *nouveau riche* who was making himself ridiculous with faked ' ruins ' on his newly acquired estate, or from the " old bishop in petticoats " (Hannah More) to the farming upstart who had bought a piano and sent his daughters to boarding school to learn polite manners and ape the ladies, instead of busying themselves about the dairy or scrubbing out washtubs in the cold of the morning, as Mrs. Cobbett was doing when he set eyes on her for the first time. You never knew what Cobbett would be saying next; and that was a goodly part of his charm. He had an art of making relevant to what he was writing about the most apparently irrelevant things; and the consequence was that he appeared always to be talking about real things and real people, and not about abstractions.

Abstract, indeed, Cobbett never could be, or wanted to be. He was a dealer only in applied ideas. When he discussed the truth of the Christian religion, then powerfully challenged in Radical quarters, the question with him soon came to be, not whether the doctrines of Mother Church were true, but whether the parsons could prove their usefulness to society and justify their temporalities by their loyalty to their Master's creed. When he argued about Radicalism, he speedily deserted the ' Rights of Man ' for the homely contention that the poor would never get a square deal until they were given a recognised right to play their part in deciding what the deal should be. Over all was the assumption, the unquestioned assumption, that what finally mattered was that the common man should be given a fair chance of happiness, on the footing that he, like his betters, would stand the best chance of being happy if he and his wife and children could be assured of good food, a sound roof over their heads, clothing that would keep out wind and wet, and a secure status among their neighbours. In such terms did Cobbett conceive of the rights of man, and show himself ready to fight for them upon all occasions.

As for his hates, which were strong and expressed strongly, who dares say that, in the passages given in the text of this volume,* he displayed in them too unforgiving a spirit? That

* See pages 45ff.

he was often much too unmeasured in his denunciation, and too much inclined to characterise as a 'miscreant' or a 'reptile' anyone who chanced for the moment to get in his way, every reader of him knows. He was, indeed, all too apt to turn the full force of his denunciation upon his friends, when they offended him, as well as on his enemies; and the innocent, as well as the guilty, were often scorched by his flaming wrath. Cobbett was egotistic and quick to resent fancied no less than real injuries. He was splenetic, and he enjoyed abusing in round terms anyone from whom he differed. But these very qualities sometimes served him, and the cause of the people, in good stead. Was he wrong to rejoice openly before the people when Castlereagh cut his own throat, or to celebrate the death of Pitt with a full diapason? *De mortuis* was a precept which he heartily pushed aside; but he spoke his mind *de vivis* with equal candour, and often at personal risk. Cobbett was born no respecter of persons; and he did much to accustom the plain man to speaking his mind about his betters. That he was often coarse,* and often bitter,† sees itself; and he said so, justifying his coarseness and his bitterness by their salutary effects. He fought, with such weapons as his nature had given him, on the side of the poor, at a time when the poor needed every weapon that could be put at their service. The consequence was that he was much abused back in his own day, and that he is much praised now, when his shafts have ceased to wound the self-esteem of the rich and powerful. No one minds hearing his great-grandfather abused for doing things which he has no call or wish to do himself: no one sets out to suppress dead men's tales of old oppressions. Yet living men may take heart of courage at the contemplation of dead men's doings; and in this sense the best of Cobbett is, we think, very much alive to-day.

*   *   *   *   *   *

As for the following selection, we have grouped it, rather roughly, under a number of heads. These necessarily overlap, and there is no great logic about them; but after a good deal of

* See page 47.
† See page 46.

shuffling, this is how the extracts have settled down. We begin with certain passages about the man himself—not auto-biographical, for we have excluded autobiography for reasons given already, but about his principles in general and his attitude to life and to his own work. Then come a couple of extracts from his Tory period, followed by an essay on the English character, written long after he had become a Radical, but serving to bring out the continuity between his Toryism and the Radicalism which grew out of it. Next comes a section showing Cobbett's reaction to the outstanding social and agricultural changes which came about during the period of the French Wars, excluding the specifically industrial changes, which made their impact on his mind only at a later date. Then follows an essay on the Royal Family, one of a series on English political institutions which he wrote for American consumption, and published only in the American edition of the *Register*—thus leaving himself free to say many things which in the England of 1816 he could not have said without the strong probability of being sent to gaol. The next section deals with the French Revolution and the French Wars, with Cobbett's attitude to Napoleon and to the war in its successive phases, and with the situation before and after the Hundred Days. Then come the extracts describing the state of the country labourers under the Speenhamland system of poor relief—a description of appalling and increasing wretchedness which, attributed to war conditions as long as the war lasted, grew worse instead of better with the collapse of war prices and the scramble of landlords and farmers to reduce the burden of the poor rates at any social cost. Here is the hard core of Cobbett's anger; for it was the plight of the country people that beyond all else turned him from a Tory into a furious Radical denouncing the oppressors of the poor.

After this, we come at last to the section dealing with the Industrial Revolution and the rise of the factory system—to the Luddites and the ' Cotton-Lords ', the curse of unemployment in the factory towns, and, in the end, to Cobbett's brief, but effective, intervention in the debate on the Factory Bill of 1833. Following this section and the one before it, we have a few extracts showing Cobbett's reaction to the new science of

Political Economy, and above all to 'Parson Malthus' and the views of his followers on the subject of 'surplus population'. These lead on to the passages dealing with emigration, actively pushed by the Malthusians as a remedy for the distress.

We turn next to the story of the Radical struggle, beginning with the liberty of the press and the constant attacks made upon it by the defenders of the established order, and proceeding thence to Cobbett's 'Twopenny Trash', as his enemies called it before he adopted the name—to those Addresses to the Journeymen and Labourers which, reissued in cheap form, first made his writings familiar to every politically active workman in the country. We wish we could give more of these; but each is long, and they are not easy to select from, and we have had to content ourselves with a goodly slice from the first and best.

This brings us to the contests and repressions which came thick and fast upon the peace of 1815. The spy system, the Gagging Acts of 1817 which drove Cobbett to take refuge in America, the Six Acts of 1819 which greeted him on his return, can be but sparsely represented here; for the story is complicated, and we have no room for lengthy narrative. It can be studied further in the volume, *The Last Hundred Days of English Freedom*, in which Dr. J. L. Hammond has brought together a number of the descriptive articles written by Cobbett in his American exile.

From this section we retrace our steps to study Cobbett's record as a Parliamentary Reformer—his struggles to enter Parliament, his pledges to the electors, his own Plan of Reform, and his views on the Whig Bill and on the two years' contest which led up to the Reform Act of 1832. Here again we have much to regret on the score of omission; and we can only say to those who miss some of their favourite passages that we have done our best.

Next, late in the day, we come to 'The Thing', or rather to that part of 'The Thing' which was closely tied up in Cobbett's mind with problems of finance. In a sense, 'The Thing' is the theme of the whole book. 'The Thing' as it appears in this section is that compound of iniquities which had its centre in the

Bank, Paper-Money, the growing National Debt, and the system of taxation which, arising from these things, branched out into the whole apparatus of pensions and sinecures, rakes-off for stock-jobbers, Government contractors, and all the hangers-on of the system, and spreading political and social corruption. At this point, Cobbett himself would, we are sure, have regarded our selection as grossly inadequate; for this medley of abuses ranked very high in his own estimate of his exposures. Those who want more can betake themselves to his *Paper against Gold,* in which they will find the processes of reasoning that underlay his *Gridiron* prophecy fully set out.

Then follow two sections, on Education and Religion, which have suffered much paring down in the final process of choice. We grieved as we lopped and lopped; but both subjects were exceptionally difficult to cover except with very lengthy extracts, for which it was impossible to find room. Fortunately, readers can get Cobbett's *English Grammar* for themselves, and can find a good deal about both subjects scattered about in his more accessible writings.

The ensuing section brings us back to the industrial workers —to combinations and the rights of combination, to strikes, and to the oft-told tale of the unfortunate Dorchester Labourers. Here again we would willingly have chosen more; but we had to spare our space for the two most important episodes of Cobbett's closing years—the 'Labourers' Revolt' of 1830 and the struggle against the New Poor Law of 1834. In the first of these, we would gladly have given more of Cobbett's great speech in his own defence against the Government in the prosecution of 1831; but we can only refer readers to the full report in pamphlet form. In the second, we have carried the story up to the last article Cobbett wrote, within a very few days of his death, adjuring the people to resist the new law and promising he would be with them in the struggle.

Such is our selection, following, where it may, a thread of historical continuity, but not adhering to any rigid chronological order. Our hope is that it will not greatly displease those who know their Cobbett, and that it will induce some who do not to wish to know him better. We append a brief note on his books, the best both of the more and of the less accessible. We would counsel those who have read no Cobbett until now to start with a dip into *Rural Rides* and, if they like that, to take *Advice to Young Men* next. Thereafter, they can safely be left to find their own way.

A Note on Cobbett's Political Register

Cobbett's Weekly Political Register (the title varied a little from time to time) first appeared on January 1st, 1802, as a stamped newspaper bearing the newspaper tax. Each issue cost 10d., of which at least 4½d. went in taxation. From 1802 to 1805 the numbers for the year were re-issued together as *Cobbett's Annual Register,* with additional material and statistics bearing on the events of the year. This practice was discontinued in 1806; and thereafter the numbers were bound up sometimes quarterly and sometimes twice a year, but with some irregularity in the numbering of the volumes. In March 1809 the price of each number was raised to 1/-. In September 1810 Cobbett began to issue the *Register* twice a week, on Wednesdays as well as Saturdays; and this practice was continued up to June 1811, the price of each issue remaining at 1/-. In September 1815 the price was raised to 1/0½d. In January, 1816, Cobbett began to publish a separate *American Political Register,* which seems to have lasted only one year. In November 1816 he began to issue, side by side with the stamped *Register,* a separate pamphlet, priced at 2d., containing only his main article, and thus escaping the tax levied on papers giving news. This developed in 1817 into a regular weekly, entitled *Cobbett's Weekly Political Pamphlet;* and the twopenny weekly continued to appear until January 1820, after Cobbett's return from America. There was an interval of four months, from April to July 1817, during which no *Registers* or *Pamphlets* were published. This was while Cobbett was on his way to the United States, and thereafter until there had been time for his copy, written in America, to be sent back to England. In January 1820 Cobbett, on discontinuing 'Twopenny Trash', offprinted from the *Register,* started *Cobbett's Evening Post,* which sold at 6d. including the stamp. This lasted until December 1821 as a regular daily newspaper. On starting the *Post,* he planned to turn the *Register* into a monthly, and it actually appeared as a monthly at 6d. from January to March 1820. Then weekly publication was resumed, at 6d., and Cobbett took the risk of being prosecuted for publishing the *Register* unstamped. In February 1821 he began to publish also a stamped edition at 1/-, containing the same matter as the unstamped edition, but enjoying the advantage of using the Post Office Mails, which was denied to the ' unstamped '. Troubles with the tax authorities continued; and there was continual bickering, though he was never prosecuted. In 1827 the method of issuing two editions was given up, and the *Register* began to appear only in a single stamped edition, at 7d. In July 1830 Cobbett began to issue a new cheap monthly paper, entitled *Twopenny Trash,* consisting partly of material reprinted from the *Register* and partly of original articles by Cobbett himself. This lasted until July 1832. Meanwhile, in October 1830, he had doubled the size of the *Register* and raised its price to 1/-, and in January 1831 further to 1/2d., at which price it remained up to his death in June 1835. His son, William Cobbett, then tried to carry it on, first at 9d. and later at 1/-; but it came to an end after a few months.

Complete sets of the *Register* are very scarce, and I have seen no set which is complete with both stamped and unstamped issues. The 88 volumes are indexed separately, or in a very few cases two together. The size and format varied a good deal from time to time, as there were a good many changes of printer as well as of price and contents.

Before beginning the *Register,* Cobbett had published in England in 1800 and 1801 a daily newspaper, *The Porcupine;** and before that he had edited successively, in the United States, *The Political Censor* (1796-7), *Porcupine's Gazette* (1797-1800), and the *Rush-light* (1800). Selections from the three American papers were included in the twelve volumes of *Porcupine's*

* The first number of *The Porcupine* was published on October 30, 1800. At the end of 1801 this newspaper was merged in *The True Briton*.

Works, which he published in 1800-1801 in both the United States and England.

A Note on Books by and about Cobbett*

Most of Cobbett's writings are now out of print, though some can still be picked up by the diligent searcher in second-hand bookshops. Of those which have been re-issued in recent years, the following are the most important :—

1. *Rural Rides.* There are many editions, including one in Everyman's Library. Of all the editions, only one is complete; and that is our own, published in three volumes by Peter Davies in 1930, the centenary of the original issue in book form. The edition of 1930 includes the *Tour in Scotland,* published in 1832 in a separate volume, the *Irish Tour* of 1833, reprinted from the *Political Register,* and much matter omitted from the earlier editions of the English tours. It has notes and a considerable biographical appendix, as well as an introduction.

2. *A Grammar of the English Language.* There are, again, many modern editions, and copies of the earlier editions are fairly easy to pick up. The *Grammar* is not only an excellent book for teaching people to write and speak good English, but also full of good Cobbett allusions to contemporary affairs.

3. *Cottage Economy.* Written for the rural householder, this is full of homely wisdom and contains some of Cobbett's best writing.

4. *Advice to Young Men.* As characteristic as anything Cobbett wrote, this is full of autobiographical material, and has been a grand quarry for anthologists.

5. *A History of the Protestant Reformation.* In part dubious history, this is a powerful plea for the rights of the poor to

* There is a fuller bibliography in G. D. H. Cole's *Life of William Cobbett* (1924).

maintenance out of the fruits of the land, and a vigorous account of the spoliations which accompanied the Reformation. It has greatly annoyed several generations of Protestants, and has given corresponding satisfaction to Catholic apologists, who have therefore kept it in print.

6. *A Journal of a Year's Residence in the United States of America.* This is Cobbett's account of the United States, and of his farming there, during his exile from England after the Gagging Acts of 1817. It was reprinted a few years ago, after it had been for a great many years unobtainable.

7. *The Last Hundred Days of English Freedom.* This is Cobbett's own account of the Gagging Acts of 1817, reprinted in 1921 from a series of articles in the *Political Register.* There is an Introduction by J. L. Hammond.

8. *The Life and Adventures of Peter Porcupine.* This is G. D. H. Cole's edition (published by the Nonesuch Press in 1927), of Cobbett's own account of his early life, with other autobiographical articles about his doings in the United States during his residence there between 1793 and 1800.

9. *Cobbett's Letters to Thornton.* This is a companion piece, also edited by G. D. H. Cole (Oxford University Press, 1937), printing for the first time Cobbett's correspondence during his residence in America with Thornton, the British Chargé d'Affaires in the United States.

10. *The Progress of a Plough-boy to a Seat in Parliament as exemplified in the History of the Life of William Cobbett* : edited by William Reitzel. (Faber & Faber, 1933.)

This is a volume in which Cobbett's articles dealing with his own life are brought together to form a connected autobiography.

Of books no longer obtainable save in contemporary editions, the most important are the following :—

11. *Paper against Gold*. Cobbett's attack on paper-money and the ' Pitt system '.

12. *The English Gardener*. Still a remarkably good book for the gardener, especially if he is interested in kitchen-gardens.

13. *The Regency and Reign of George IV*. Contemporary history, with a tang to it.

14. *Cobbett's Sermons*. Cobbett's antidote to the religious tracts disseminated by the Evangelicals, plentifully sprinkled with political and social allusions.

15. *A Treatise of Cobbett's Corn*. Maize, of which Cobbett was largely instrumental in introducing the cultivation into Great Britain.

16. *The Woodlands*. An arboricultural companion to the *English Gardener*.

17. *Surplus Population, a Comedy*. A play about the Malthusians and the Poor Laws.

18. *The Poor Man's Friend*. A series of political tracts about the rights of the poor, written for the journeymen of the factory districts.

19. *Legacy to Parsons*.

20. *Legacy to Landlords*.

21. *Legacy to Peel*.

22. *Legacy to Lords*.

These are four little books, written in the last years of Cobbett's life and dealing largely with poor law questions, with the rights of the journeymen and labourers to maintenance out of the produce of the land, and with the abuses of sinecures and pensions in Church and State.

Cobbett's sons published in 1835 a selection, in six volumes, of *Cobbett's Political Works,* taken mainly from the *Political Register.* This was fairly easy to pick up in second-hand book-shops only a few years ago, but we have not seen a copy for some time.

Among the many lives and studies of Cobbett are the following: —

The Life of William Cobbett. By G. D. H. Cole. (Collins, 1924.)

William Cobbett. By G. K. Chesterton. (Hodder & Stoughton, 1926.)

The Life and Letters of William Cobbett. By Lewis Melville. (Lane, 1913.)

The Life of William Cobbett. By E. I. Carlile. (Constable, 1904.)

There is also a pamphlet Life, by G. D. H. Cole, in the Fabian Society's Biographical Series (No. 9).

A Note on Abbreviations and on the Text

Throughout the book, P.R. means *Cobbett's Weekly Political Register,* and the volume number follows in Roman figures. T.T. means *Twopenny Trash.* A small ' c ' means ' column ', the *Register* being numbered by columns, and not by pages. We have kept Cobbett's spelling and his punctuation, which is often unlike modern punctuation. Obvious misprints have been corrected; but otherwise the text has been reprinted just as it stood, with Cobbett's own italics, capitals, and sometimes unusual constructions. Omissions in the selected passages have been indicated by asterisks. The titles at the head of the extracts are, of course, our own.

ONE

COBBETT UPON HIMSELF

Who Are You?

P.R. XII., c. 846. *Perish Commerce*—28-11-07

" **A**ND *who are you*," as the Attorney General, now Chancellor of the Exchequer, said of me, in *Latin,* when he was pleading against me, in the Court of King's Bench; " *Who are you,* that presumes to tell us we are all in error?" Why, what signifies it who I am? The only question is, *am I right*? If I am not, overset my arguments, and shew the world that I am wrong. Neither your Latin nor your gown nor your wig will weigh aught against these arguments, any more than against the decree or the sword of Buonaparté.

Cobbett's Principles

P.R. XXXVI., c. 205. *To the Earl of Aylsford—Cobbett at Meriden—1-4-20.*

MY principles, then, are as follows.—I hold, that it is the duty of us all to do our utmost to uphold a government in king, lords, and commons. That, as to religion, opinions ought to be left as God has made them in our minds, perfectly free, and that persecution on account of religious opinions is of the worst and most wicked kind. That no man ought to be taxed but by his own consent, agreeably to the law of the land. That elections ought to be free, and that drunkenness, bribery, corruption, and perjury are great and odious sins. That the affairs of the nation ought to be so managed, that every sober and industrious and healthy man ought, out of his own wages, to be able to support himself, wife and family in a comfortable and decent manner. That the law of nature, as well as the law of the land, gives every soul in the community *a right* to a sufficiency of food and raiment; and that, those who possess the land, are justly called upon to give good support to all, who are unable to labour, or who, being able, cannot obtain employment; and that this support is not a thing *given*, but a *right* to be demanded in the name of the law. I hold, further, that a false, or paper-money, not convertible into gold and silver on demand made on the issuer of the paper, is one of the greatest scourges ever inflicted upon a nation. I hold, that it is the weight of taxes, which produces all the miseries, which this nation now suffers, and that these taxes go, in part, to keep sinecure placemen and place-women, pensioners and grantees, of whose public services I can find no trace. I hold, that the Debt and other fixed expences are a mortgage (in the present operation) on the *labour* of every man, woman and child in the country, capable of labour: that, thus, in part, the food and raiment are necessarily taken from those who labour and given to those who do not labour; and this is the cause of great suffering amongst the people. I hold, that, unless a *great change speedily take place,* this nation will become feeble and contemptible as well as enslaved; and that its capital will be conveyed away to enrich and to give power to rival nations.

On his Writings

P.R. XXXV., c. 520. *To the Female Reformers of the Kingdom*—29-12-19.

AS to merit, as an author or writer, I have always despised, what is generally called criticism. I know well that those who carry on the trade of critics are a base and hireling crew; more corrupt, perhaps, than any other set of beings in the world. The only critics that I look to are the public; and my mode of estimating a writing, is by the *effect* which it produces. If there be two writings, having the accomplishment of the same object in view, that writing which soonest and most completely accomplishes its object, is the *best* of the two. I listen to nothing about *style* as it is called; or any thing else. As the man, who soonest and best weaves a yard of cloth, is the best weaver; so the man, who soonest and best accomplishes an object with his pen, is the best writer. Taking this as my standard, I know very well, that I am a very good one: but it does, nevertheless, give me singular pleasure to hear you say that you have been taught by me. Perhaps there is no pleasure so great as that which we derive from a conviction that we have produced great effect upon the minds of great multitudes of persons; and especially when we are able to reflect that, as in the present case, the effect has been produced by calm and dispassionate reasoning upon serious and important subjects. Who, besides myself, has, in our day, attempted to gain popularity by dint of fact and of argument, unmixed with any thing to amuse the human mind? If, at any time, I have indulged in a sort of jest I have been almost ashamed of the momentary triumph thereby acquired. I have rested my reputation upon the success of truth supported by dry argument. I knew well that the seeds must lie long in the ground; that the vegetation of the plants must be slow; but I knew also that the growth of them would be sure and that their nature would be durable. *" Cast your bread upon the waters,"* has always been at my tongue's end, when, many years ago, I perceived a disinclination in the People to hear, and when almost any other man would have thrown down the pen in despair. I knew, however, that I was gradually making converts, though I very seldom saw any outward proof of the fact. I waited also for the misery which I knew would be the final consequence, and which I also knew would open the ears of the nation. When that misery came, I redoubled my efforts; and the effect has been that universal conviction of the utility of my efforts, and with regard to which conviction you speak only the voice of the nation at large.

The Writing of History

P.R. XXVII., c. 66. *America*—21-1-15.

IT is often observed, that *history*, to be *impartial*, must be written long after *the date* of the events of which it is a record. This is a strange notion. It is so contrary to every rule of common life, that it naturally staggers one. If we want to keep our accounts, or the records of any proceedings in life, *accurately*, we never lose a moment in minuting the facts down as they occur. If evidence is given from a written paper, it must, to make the evidence good, have been *written at the moment that the facts occurred*. How strange, then is it, that for *history* to be *true,* it must be written a century, or two, *after* the period, to which it relates; That is to say : that, to come at the *real truth* of any national occurrence, in order to arrive at a just decision upon the conduct of a nation, you must enter upon the inquiry *after all the witnesses are dead,* and after all the springs, hidden from common eyes, and which no man has dared to record an account of in print, are wholly forgotten and are sunk, for ever, out of sight. It is said, that, at the time when the events occur, the historian is too near to the *passions* and the *prejudices* of the times, and is too likely to partake of them. But, at a hundred years after the events, what has he to refer to but *writings of the times;* and, how, then, is he more likely to get at the truth? We suppose the historian to *seek earnestly for truth;* and is he more likely to get at it, when all the springs are forgotten and all the witnesses dead, than when he has access to them all?

The real state of the case is this : the historian DARES NOT write a *true* history of present events, and a *true* description of the character of public institutions, establishments, laws, and men, in any country except America. *Truth,* in England, may be a LIBEL; libels are punished more severely than the greatest part of felonies, as my Lord FOLKSTONE shewed, in the House of Commons, from an examination of the Newgate Calendar; and, it is well-known, that in answering a charge of libel, the TRUTH of what you have written, or published, is not allowed EVEN TO BE GIVEN IN EVIDENCE. This is the real, and the only ground for pretending, that history ought to be written long after the period to which it relates.

Time of Day for Writing

P.R. LXVI., c. 338. *To the Duke of Wellington*—13-9-28.

AT what hours of the day do you write, Mr. ATWOOD? We authors should communicate things of this sort to one another. I write at this season from five o'clock to eight, and then breakfast upon Indian meal. I then return to it till twelve, when I dine; and if I intend to write any more that day, I seldom drink any thing but small beer. I am afraid that you are in the habit of writing *after dinner;* that is to say, about the time when I go to bed; for no man in his sober senses ever could have put a thought like this upon paper.

Cobbett's Violence
P.R. LXV., c. 114. *French Grammar—26-1-28*

HOW many well-meaning people have exclaimed, " It is a pity that Cobbett is so *violent*"; such persons never ask themselves whether they would think a man too violent who should knock down and break the limbs of a ruffian, who is coming, knife in hand, to cut his throat, and that too, without the smallest provocation on earth. This has been my state: when I began to write, I had attacked no writer, I fell foul of nobody in the shape of a " literary gentleman." I was as modest as a maid, and dealt in qualifications, and modifications, and mitigations to the best of my poor powers in the line of palavering; but when I discovered that it was envy that was at work in my assailants, I called to mind the saying of Swift; namely, " The moment a man of real talent makes his first appearance before the public, the whole battalion of dunces beat to arms and sally forth against him; and down he falls for ever, if he have not courage as well as talent." These are nearly his words; and I am infinitely indebted to him for having enabled me to read these words. They occurred to me, and I instantly resolved to proceed in the very way in which I have always proceeded, giving three, four, or ten blows for one; and never, in any case, ceased to pursue the assailant, in some way or other, until he was completely down. It is a maxim with me, and which I wish to implant in the breast of all that I love, to forgive, and very easily to forgive, wrongs of every kind, but those which proceed from envy, which is the vilest passion which ever accursed the human breast; seeing that it hates, because, and *only* because, it sees something in the hated object, which reason or even nature finds to love and admire. I always detested envious people, for doing which, I have had a practical as well as theoretical reason; and I have always found them insensible to every species of correction except that of the scorpion lash, laid on without ceremony, and laid on as publicly as possible,

Why Not Be Amiable?

P.R. LXV., c. 498.   *Curious Letter*—19-4-28.

MY Correspondent asks, "Why not *be amiable*?" Now, I have no reason to think that I am not, and that I have not been as amiable as most other men. Very pretty girls in two different countries used, when I was young, to be reasonably fond of me. I have never had a servant that did not like his or her master; and, as to my family and friends, I leave them to say, whether there is, the company of any person on earth, in which they delight more than they do in mine. I do not believe, that I have experienced the breaking off of friendship with ten persons in the whole course of my life. Why should he therefore suppose, that I am unamiable: I am not over-bearing in personal intercourse; I am not churlish or niggardly; I am not a gabbler; I am never melancholy or sulky; all that know me, know my readiness to forgive; I have never brought but one action in my life, and that was in the execution of my duty towards other parties. Why the devil then, am I to suppose myself unamiable? No: it is not this that my Correspondent means; by being *amiable* he means, being soft, being mild towards offenders of a heinous character; being only partly just; and trying to wheedle people to do that which is criminal in them not to do; in short, to abandon my duty, to creep to those that Truth and Justice bid me set at defiance, and that ought to be trampled under my feet, if I had the power to do it.

Besides, on the score of *mere policy*, does not my Correspondent perceive, that, if I have that great power which he is so polite as to suppose that I have, that I have acquired this power in spite of all that *bitterness* which he considers as an impediment to my obtaining that rank and power, for which, as he is pleased to think, my abilities mark me out. Does he not perceive this; and perceiving it, does he not see that there would be danger in losing the weight I at present possess, were I to alter the course of my proceeding? I have at present, a good large part of the sensible men of the nation with me; and particularly of the *young* men of that description. I know this from evidence, much better than newspaper paragraphs and

" *reporths* "; and does not my Correspondent perceive that these real and cordial friends of mine are bound to me, because I am *bitter;* because I am *unforgiving;* because I am *uncompromising* with what they deem would be hostile to them as well as myself.

Cobbett's Coarseness
P.R. LXV., c. 670.   *To Sir Henry Parnell*—24-5-28.

"COARSE! " the sons and daughters of Corruption will exclaim. " *Coarse*! " will echo back the scoundrel *seat-sellers*, each of whom ought to swing on one of the trees that he has acquired by the wages of Corruption. " Coarse, coarse! " will cry the reptiles who are the seat-seller's understrappers, and who ought to swing from their heels. " Vary coarse, ma'awm! " will some grinning Scotch sycophant observe to some she sinecurist or pensioner. " *Coarse as neck beef*! " will growl out some Englishman, who has filled his bags by oppressions of the poor; or, some other one, who, feeling in his very bones and marrow an instinctive horror *of work*, is desperately bent on getting *a share of the taxes.*

Yes, it is *coarse* indeed, and coarse it ought to be in a case like this. SWIFT has told us not to chop *blocks* with *razors.* Any *edge*-tool is too fine for work like this : a pick-axe, that perforates with one end and drags about with the other, is the tool for this sort of business. It is, perhaps, seldom that men profit from reading poetry; but I have. When I was about 21 years of age, an old volume of the then " EUROPEAN MAGAZINE " fell into my hands, at Fredericton in New Brunswick; and in it I stumbled upon the following lines, which I have several times repeated in the Register, and which, for the benefit of the young men of the present day, I will now repeat once more.

> Tender-handed press a nettle,
> And it stings you for your pains;
> Press it like a man of mettle,
> And it soft as silk remains.

'Tis the same with vulgar natures;
Treat them kindly, they rebel;
But, be rough as nutmeg-graters,
And the rogues obey you well.

These lines took my fancy; they confirmed me in the conclusions which, young as I was, observation had caused me to draw; they have been fresh in my memory from that day to this; the precept they convey has been to me a rule of conduct; I have found success attend an observance of the rule; and I recommend it to the use of every young man of talent, who is too virtuous to be a slave of those who *call one another* " Noble Lords " and " Honourable Gentlemen," and who are aped in this respect, by that " Honourable " Body, the Common Council of London, one of whose " Honourable " committees spent, in one year, at the public expense, seven hundred pounds in eating and drinking and the like, and took, from the same source, a hundred and fifty pounds for " a *summer excursion!* "

Coarse! aye, to be sure, towards one, who has the audacity to put himself before the people as an " *author*," and as an author, too, fit to instruct merchants and traders in the principles of their calling, and fit to point out to the nation the way to supersede the use of the king's coin! I shall, next week, show how fit you are to meddle with such matters, and shall make you, if you have one grain of prudence left, take care, for the future, how you venture, " *out of doors*," into *print*. " *In doors*," you are, doubtless, fit to put our finances to rights, and to do all other things; at any rate, *there* you are *safely* sheltered by that law, which *banishes us for life*, if we utter any thing " *coarse* " against you.

Cobbett's Plagues

P.R. LXVI., c. 354. *To the Duke of Wellington. On Mr. THOMAS ATWOOD'S Opinions relative to the Remedies, to be applied to the National Disease—20-9-28.*

TALK of " *plagues*," indeed! Where is there a man on earth who has had to endure plagues such as these *nine* Ministers have been to me? Smoky house, scolding wife, squalling children, footmen that cannot eat shoulders of mutton, and even " female domestics " who are too handsome to please their mistress, and who, for the sake of their master, will do any thing in the world, *work* only excepted : all these plagues put together, are not equal to the plagues that my nine Prime Ministers have been to me. When I was a little boy, I made one of four to worry my mother, during more than half the time that our eyes were open, for apples, for nuts, for bread and cheese, or for something or other; and, at times, when we were lugging and tugging at her apron and bothering her in the midst of her work, she, though a very mild and patient and indulgent mother, used to exclaim, " hold your tongues, do, you *plagues of Egypt.*" Little did she dream of *plagues* that her poor son WILLIAM was destined to endure! If she had, it would have made her lament having brought him into the world. PHARAOH'S plagues were mere child's play compared with mine : they were of short duration, and ceased with the conviction that calamity brought with it : mine have never ceased, no experience, no calamity, nothing has been able to procure me a cessation. PHARAOH had TEN, indeed; but, each of my NINE, has been greater than the whole of his ten; and I do, my Lord Duke, most earnestly pray, that I am to be spared the unspeakable anguish of completing his *number*!

On Handwriting

P.R. XLIX., c. 495. *Fatal Effects of Slovenliness*—21-2-24.

IT is an invariable rule with me to fling into the fire at once any blurred or dirty letter that I receive, and every letter that is written *across the writing,* let such letter come from whom it may. People that write in this manner are idle people. What they put upon paper is unworthy of occupying the time of any persons not like themselves. This seems, at first sight, to be a very trifling matter; but if we duly reflect on it we shall find it a matter of considerable importance. At any rate, as I am certain, that I never in my life-time sent a slovenly scrawl to any person whatever, I beseech those who do me the honour to write to me, to write to me in a hand that will not compel me to waste my time, and expose me to the risk of appearing to be guilty of negligence or ill-manners. To young men I would observe, that Slovenliness is no mark of gentility; that amongst their most valuable possessions is their *time;* and I beg them to consider how large a portion of their time is consumed in deciphering even their own bad writing. The hand-writing is, with me, a great thing. I cannot believe that slovenliness of hand-writing can exist without a general slovenliness in the conducting of affairs. Of this, at any rate, I am certain; and that is, that I never should have done a quarter part of what I have done, if to write a plain hand had not been the constant habit of my life. It has cost *many thousands of pounds less* to print from my manuscript, than it would have cost to print from the manuscript of almost any other man. Then, again, as to time: hundreds upon hundreds of articles written by me, could not have been printed *soon enough,* if they had been in manuscript like that of writers in general. Habit has made me write fast, and plain, at the same time; and every man will have the same habit, if he resolutely persevere in *writing plain.* To write plain is the great thing: writing fast comes of itself.

Cobbett's Idea of a Young Man

P.R. LXVI., c. 509. *To Radical Farmers*—18-10-28.

I WANT a young man from 16 to 18 years of age, as a sort of *farming* and *gardening* and *nursery-work* APPRENTICE. The case is this: my farm is taken care of by my only surviving brother, who has been either gardener or farmer all his life time, and who, though he is only thirteen months older than I am, is not able to move about so quickly, from place to place, as is necessary in a concern like mine; nor is it proper that he should be exposed to wet and cold so much as is absolutely necessary to the due looking after of ten or a dozen men. He has, from the fruit of his own labour, raised a family of ten able and good children, who have already brought him about a score of grandchildren. I know that he began to work *hard* more than *fifty* years ago; and verily I believe him to have done more hard work than any man now living in England. While his limbs feel the consequences of this, his experience and skill remain; and I want a young man, or lad, of the age above mentioned, to supply *legs*, which my brother cannot move so nimbly as the case requires. He is not wanted to *work much*; but, if he learn to do every thing on a farm, it will do him no harm. He is wanted to see the orders of myself, or of my brother, obeyed. I do not want a *Bailiff;* for bailiffs do not think that they earn their wages, unless they furnish you with *science,* or, at least, with *advice,* as well as with care; and I want neither science nor advice. I want *legs* that will move nimbly and willingly, and a young head capable of *learning.* The lad ought to be *stout,* and not stunted; he ought to be able to read and write a little; but, two things are indispensable; namely, that his father be *a farmer,* and that his son has lived on a farm in *England,* all his life, and at a distance of not less than forty miles from London; and not less than twenty miles from Portsmouth, Plymouth, Bath, Bristol, Cheltenham, Liverpool, Manchester, Leeds, or Norwich. He is to sit at table with my brother and my niece (who is the house-keeper), and, when I am at the farm, with me also; and is to be treated with every respect as *the young farmer of the house.* He is never to quit the farm; except on my business, and to go to the parish church on the Sunday, and is to be under the control of my brother as completely as if he were his son. He will here learn all about the cultivation of Indian Corn, Mangel Wurzle, and of several things not very common. He will learn to sow and rear trees, and to plant and prune them. He will learn how to raise seeds of various sorts. He will learn how to grind and dress wheat and Indian Corn, and will see how the flour is applied. He will learn how to make beer; to see butter and cheese made before breakfast time; and he will have con-stantly before his eyes examples of early rising, activity, punctual attention to business, *content with plain living,* and *perfect sobriety.*—Now, if any farmer, who is of *my political principles, full up to the mark,* have such a son, nephew, or grandson, to dispose of in this way, I shall be glad to hear from him on the subject. If the lad stay a year out, I will make him a *present* of not less than ten or twelve guineas. It is, I hope, unnecessary to add, that this is a farm-house without a *tea-kettle* or a *coffee-pot,* and without any of the *sweets* that come from the *sweats* of African slaves. Please to observe, that I do not want a "*young gentleman;*" but a good, sturdy lad, whose hands do not instinctively recoil from a frozen chain, or from the dirty heels of an ox or a horse. I hope that the lad, or young man, that I am to have, will never have been at an "*establishment*," vulgarly called a *boarding-school*: if he unfortunately have, and should suit in all other respects, I must sweat the boarding-school nonsense out of him; that is all. If he have a mind to improve himself in study, here are books, and all the other means of well employing his leisure hours.—Letters to me on the subject to be *postage paid*.

Wm. COBBETT.

183, Fleet Street, London.

P.S. The *great qualities* are, a fitness to *give orders,* and *spirit to enforce obedience;* and, above all things, never to *connive* at the misconduct of the men; but invariably to make a true report of their behaviour, whether good or bad. It will be quite useless to engage a soft, milky thing, that has not the courage to make a lazy fellow stir, or to reprove a perverse one. Fathers will know what stuff their sons are made of, and will, of course, not recommend them to me, unless fit for my purpose. *They* know well *what I want,* and I beg them not to offer me what will not suit me.—The lad will, of course, be boarded, lodged, and have his clothes washed in the house.

N.B. I will have no one, who has any near relation that is a *tax-eater* of any sort.

Recipe for Health

P.R. LXVII., c. 181. *A Challenge*—7-2-29.

THE following propositions will be denied by nobody that does not covet a broomstick: that paleness is a sign of feebleness, if not of ill health; that as soon as a body becomes dead, its cheeks are pale; that when a person, from whatever cause, faints, the blood totally leaves the cheeks; and that, in short, a pale face is a sure sign of want of vigorous health. Now, these premises being undeniable, I shall first state a fact, and then throw out my challenge. The fact is this: that during the last three months or thereabouts, no wheat, or any thing proceeding from wheat, and no sort of thing usually obtained from a grocer; or, in other words, no sort of thing which is not the produce of the soil of England; that none of these things have been consumed under the roof of my farm-house. Now, then, my challenge is this: there are twelve of us under this roof, who live in the manner aforesaid, without wheat or any thing proceeding from wheat, and without any thing not produced from the land in England. And I hereby offer to bet any man a hundred pounds, that he does not find, under any one roof, nay, under any six roofs, any twelve persons that have so many square inches of red upon their cheeks as are to be found by due admeasurement upon the cheeks of the twelve who live under this roof, and who feed in the manner above spoken of. I have kept this farm-house for more than a year, without wine, without sugar, tea, coffee, or any sort of grocery; without any of these having made their appearance under this roof, though, observe, I have never been without two women in the house: these things have I done for more than a year, and no doctor or apothecary has ever set *his foot within the doors of this farm-house, during the whole of that time;* though, let it be observed, I am one of the first to apply for medical assistance for any body in my house, in case of even the appearance of illness. But we have had no illness: the accursed tea has not been here to shake our nerves; and the brandied wine, and the vitrioled spirits; and the abominable brewers' poison have been kept away from under this roof, and we have been well, though close upon the border of a marshy meadow, which, I was told, would give us all agues and typhus fevers. Now, if people will not live as we live, let them be ill, say I; I have no pity for them. They are drunkards and gluttons; for drunkenness and gluttony are only things of degree. In short, if people will not restrain themselves from those indulgences which cause sickness, sick they will be, and sick they ought to be.

FABLE

The Wolves, the Zealous Hound, and the Perfidious Hunters

P.R. LXXIII., c. 310. *Fable. The Wolves, the Zealous Hound, and the Perfidious Hunters—30-7-31.*

THERE was a den of wolves, who being as crafty as they were voracious, always took care to keep the hunters off by regularly giving them a share of their plunder, gotten from the flocks and the herds; but, at last, so destructive was their rapacity become, that the whole neighbourhood rose in indignation against the hunters for suffering the murderous spoilers to proceed with impunity, and threatened them with vengeance, unless they, who had all the means at their command, came forth and destroyed this mischievous den of devourers. The hunters, thus pressed with danger to themselves, reluctantly brought out the pack, amongst which there was one particular hound more sagacious, more persevering, more strong, and more swift than the rest. This zealous hound, after trailing the voracious crew to their den, and seeing them dragged forth, took the lead in the full cry after them; and on came the whole pack, followed by the hunters at full speed, hallooing and cheering on the hounds; but the hunters, while they showed all the outward signs of earnestness and eagerness in the chase, took care to place in ambush, in a thicket, one of their *base menials*, with a gun in his hand, to kill or cripple the zealous hound as he was passing by, which the menial endeavoured to do, but *he missed his mark,* and the greedy and ferocious wolves were finally destroyed in spite of the perfidious pursuers, who anxiously wished to preserve them. A MAGPIE who, from her nest, which was near to that of a CROW (who was also a spectator) saw the ambush and heard the shot, said, " Well, neighbour, what do you *think of that?* " " Think of it," answered the crow, " why, to be sure, that the hunters do not want to kill the wolves, and that they mortally hate the zealous hound for leading the pack on so swiftly in pursuit of them."

Cobbett the Cat

P.R. LII., c. 271. *To the British Catholic Association.* 30-10-24.

IT was proposed to present Dr. LINGARD'S History to me, in order to *assist* me in writing my intended " *Tract,*" on the *Reformation.* Mr. BUTLER asked, " How do we know what *sort* of Tract that may be? " Very true; and I have in me much more of the character of the *Cat* than of the *Dog,* in this respect. The servile Dog will fly at *any thing* that his master *sets him on upon.* The Cat, though all vigilance and courage and perseverance in watching and pursuing and destroying of mischievous animals, will not wag an inch, if you attempt *him upon them.* Put him down at a rat-hole and he goes away from it directly. *Carry him to a rat,* and *toss him down at it,* and he goes off, leaving you to kill the rat yourself.

Thus it is with me : I am not to be *hallooed on* upon anybody : I must be left to pursue my own course : I must do what I do from a taste for doing it, and not for the sake of pleasing anybody : in short, I must act from the *dictates of my own mind* : I always have done this, and to it is to be ascribed that strength and originality which have, in so many cases, distinguished my writings.

Normandy Farm

P.R. LXXVIII., c. 514. *Westminster Election.* 1-12-32.

HERE I am in NORMANDY; not, however, that NORMANDY from which the GRENVILLES and the GRINDSTONES (now called VERULAMS), and the BAS-SETS (now called DUNSTAN VILLES), and the rest of those people, who, in their pedigrees, published in the PEERAGE, insultingly tell us, " THAT THEY CAME IN WITH THE CONQUEROR," and who may very reasonably be asked, why they did not *go out* with the CONQUEROR; not *that* NORMANDY, my friends, but the *tithing* of NORMANDY, in the parish of ASH, in the county of Surrey, the church of which parish is just about four miles and a half from the sand-hill, rolling down which constituted a considerable portion of my education; the rolling, however, being associated with the very edifying pursuits of whipping efts about amongst the heath, and finding out rabbit's nests and taking the young ones; I having the misfortune to begin my life before the " schoolmaster got abroad," to teach us to write in the sand, and to sing in heavenly tune the *"Magdalen Hymn," "God save the King," "The Apostles' Creed,"* and the *"Pence Table,"* all of which I heard the little *"antalluctal"* beings bawling out in *Boltcourt* last Saturday. Half maddened by the sound; irritated at the chattering, gabbling, senseless sounds of the WEN, I started up and exclaimed : " Go and get me a place in the coach; for I am resolved not to endure this any longer." " It is too late, sir : the coach is gone." " Go and get me hack, cab, cart, dray, wheelbarrow, get me something to convey me away from these maddening sounds! " After coming from the sensible people in the North, to be compelled to endure the botheration, the senseless gabble, by which I was half stunned, seemed to me to be a punishment, not only too great to be endured in case of necessity, but too great to be described. It was towards evening, and, therefore, I took a place in the coach for the next morning, and off I came, with a resolution to have a few days' *respite,* at any rate. And here I am, looking out of the window of a farmhouse, upon a green common, inhabited by sensible cows, sheep and geese; and, with the satisfaction to reflect, that I am five-and-thirty miles distant from the sound, the pious sound, of *"God save the King,"* and the *"Pence Table,"* by no means excepting that of the *"Magdalen Hymn,"* which, however, really haunts me; and, about four o'clock this morning, waked up by a sort of monotonous sounds, I suddenly started up in my bed; and, from having changed beds so frequently of late, and it being dark, scarcely knowing where I was, I thought that it had been " God save the King " that had saluted my ear. But sitting a little while preparing myself for resignation to my fate, the sounds from half a dozen voices (responsive to each other) were renewed. " Oh! God be praised, it is the crowing of cocks! " Down I lay again, relieved from all my alarm; and here I am thus removed from the scene of noise and of nonsense, to address you upon the important subject of the WESTMINSTER ELECTION.

To my True Disciples

P.R. LVI., c. 641. *To my True Disciples. The Smashings in the City. Thieves Falling out. Peter Macculloch's Cheap Currency. Plymouth Affair. Future Prospects.* 10.12.25.

READER, did you ever pass a winter near the sand-hills of Surrey; did you ever, after a long and dreary season, the ground half the time covered with snow, and the other half drenched with wet; did you ever, at the end of such a winter's last-frost, followed by a gentle thaw, find yourself, just after sun-rise, upon a hillock, scores of linnets singing in an oak tree on your left, the plough-boy's whistle keeping time to the jingle of the traces to your right, the hounds at unequal intervals giving tongue in the thicket in the vale below, and, then, all at once, bursting out in full cry, come rattling up towards the spot where you stood : did you ever feel *this joy*? Did you ever, after being weeks and weeks longer at sea than you expected to be, sit moping in the cabin, hating the look of victuals, hating the sight of books, looking at your half-washed hands; thinking of your dirty face, execrating the ship, the sea, the crew, the captain, and hardly thinking life worth preserving for another day? Did you ever, thus being and thus feeling, hear from the deck (no matter if in the devil's voice) the cry of, *land*? Did you ever, having married a beautiful young woman, the very touch of whose garments once made the blood dance through your veins from the sole of your foot to the crown of your head, see her in a fair way of producing her, or your, like? Did you ever, with unceasing anxiety, watch her every look for six or seven months, your hope and fear both going on increasing all the while, and, at last, after fear alone had got possession of your heart and was on the point of producing distraction : did you ever, at that moment, creep softly, and with your shoes off, to the bed-side, and there, the clothes being slowly turned down, see the little creature, and see the mother's smile upon it, and feel its almost boneless hand : Did you ever feel *this joy*? Were you ever snatched, in dead of night, from your wife and children, hoisted away, and crammed into a dungeon, in consequence of the Bills brought in by Sidmouth and Castlereagh? Did you ever hear, or read, the speeches made on that occasion; and did you, Oh! did you, ever hear of that same Castlereagh cutting his own throat at North Cray in Kent? Did you ever feel *this* joy?

Have you felt these joys? If you have not felt all of them : not one, two, or three of them, but the *whole four,* you can have but a faint idea of the joy which I, at this moment feel at the alarm, the dreadful forebodings, the tormenting embarrassments, and all the other evils present and expected, real, imaginary, contingent and even possible, that now assail or stare in the face the Merchants and Bankers of London, together with all their relations, friends, dependants, abettors and well-wishers in every part and corner of the kingdom. God is *just;* and as man is said to be made in the image of God, man should be just too; and to forget or not to punish as far as we are able, and legally can punish, moral offences, is a neglect of a sacred duty.

Cobbett's Maiden Speech in Parliament

P.R. LXXIX., c. 287. *Proceedings in the House of Commons.* 2-2-33.

IT appears to me that since I have been sitting here I have heard a great deal of unprofitable discussion.

TWO

COBBETT THE TORY

Receipt for effecting the Ruin of a Great and Independent Country

P.R. I., c. 179. *Receipt for effecting the Ruin of a Great and Independent Country.* 27-2-02.

IN order to prepare the body politic, and put it into the best order for taking the following dose—it must be kept for some time previous to the administering of it in considerable heat and agitation.—This will be greatly promoted by keeping the spirits in a ferment by exciting opposite and contending passions. The different sentiments and views of different friends, some strongly urging one line of conduct, others proposing one diametrically opposite;—one party preaching patience and submission, the other rouzing the spirits and exciting to revenge—and all urging their opinions with zeal, with vehemence and with obstinacy—these circumstances will greatly contribute to put the patient into the desired state. Hence will ensue a certain restlessness and disquietude, yet accompanied by indolence and love of ease, an inclination to change, in hopes that some favourable circumstance may thence ensue, yet an aversion to personal exertion in our own behalf, an expectation and reliance that fate will do for us, that, which we are unwilling to do for ourselves. If all these circumstances could be superinduced on the same patient at an age and season when riches abound, and luxury and effeminacy pervade all ranks of life, when all complain of poverty, yet all are enjoying every comfort and every gratification that refinement of arts, extended commerce, exquisite taste, and consumate love of pleasure, can require and supply, so much the better. If all this happens; the receipt will be administered under the most favourable circumstances. No knight of the lancet, nor of the pestle and mortar, need ever hope to find a patient more prepared for his operations, than our patient is now for complete and entire ruin.

The Receipt

Take 6 oz. 5 penny wt. 19 gr. of self-sufficiency. 8 oz. 10 penny wt. 23 gr. of ignorance or inexperience.

N.B. These two drugs, though of different appearance and taste, produce so precisely the same effect, that they may always be used indiscriminately.

3 oz. 16 penny wt. 9 gr. of doubt.

N.B. This medicine made up of diffidence, integrity, and love of good fame on the one hand, of procrastination, fear of censure and overscrupulous prudence, on the other, is to be found in the greatest perfection at a certain apothecary's, not a hundred miles from Bedford-square.

Mix these three ingredients carefully together till they are completely amalgamated and incorporated with each other. Then pour them into a quart of a mixture, one part milk and three parts water, and let it boil well on a slow fire for eight hours. In the mean time you must carefully fling into the liquor, every half hour, one quarter of an ounce of a powder made up of the following ingredients all in equal quantity, viz. Pomp, flippancy, slovenliness, passion.—After this mixture has boiled some time it will be reduced to a thin poor jelly of weak substance.—Let it be well sweetened by a proportionate quantity of places, pensions, and reversions of places, and ornamented *on the surface* with painted emblems of candour, flattery, and smiles—openness of conduct, and gentle manners.

This jelly, though thus sweetened and decorated, will suit but few palates; it must therefore be forced down the throats of unwilling patients by great and high-sounding professions and assurances. Even then it will not always be quietly taken. In that case it must be reduced to the shape of pills, and covered with a double coat of leaf gold.

The dose, when administered at a proper season (such as the one above directed), is sure to take effect; at least several eminent physicians have assured me, they never knew it fail. It operates first gently and kindly, it spreads itself over the whole frame, soothing its cares and assuaging its pains. But at the same time it weakens and enervates prodigiously. Soon, however, its effects grow quick, painful, and terrible.—Colics and gripings ensue, and the strength of the frame being already impaired, the constitution is unable to make any effectual resistance; till at last a violent dysentery succeeds, which soon brings our patient to the grave.

Decline of Great Britain

P.R VI., c. 617-619. *Letter III, to the Rt. Hon. William Pitt. On the Causes of the Decline of Great Britain.—Marks of National Decline.*
27-10-04.

IT would be tedious to dwell upon every striking mark of national decline : some, however, will press themselves forward to particular notice; and amongst them are : that Italian-like effeminacy, which has, at last, descended to the yeomanry of the country, who are now found turning up their silly eyes in ecstacy at a music-meeting, while they should be cheering the hounds, or measuring their strength at the ring; the discouragement of all the athletic sports and modes of strife amongst the common people, and the consequent and fearful increase of those cuttings and stabbings, those assassin-like ways of taking vengeance, formerly heard of in England only as the vices of the most base and cowardly foreigners, but now become so frequent amongst ourselves as to render necessary *a law to punish such practices with death;* the prevalence and encouragement of a hypocritical religion, a canting morality, and an affected humanity; the daily increasing poverty of the national church, and the daily increasing disposition still to fleece the more than half-shorne clergy, who are compelled to be, in various ways, the mere dependents of the upstarts of trade; the almost entire extinction of the ancient country gentry, whose estates are swallowed up by loan-jobbers, contractors, and nabobs, who, for the far greater part not Englishmen themselves, exercise in England that sort of insolent sway, which, by the means of taxes raised from English labour, they have been enabled to exercise over the slaves of India or elsewhere; the bestowing of honours upon the mere possessors of wealth, without any regard to birth, character, or talents, or to the manner in which that wealth has been acquired; the familiar intercourse of but too many of the ancient nobility with persons of low birth and servile occupations, with exchange and insurance-brokers, loan and lottery contractors, agents and usurers, in short, with all the Jew-like race of money-changers; the loss of the spirit of independence, which is perceivable in the almost universal willingness and even eagerness, with which the higher classes seek to lean upon the Treasury, and with which the lower classes throw themselves upon the higher in the character of parish poor, thus forming the whole nation into a string of political mendicants, cringing to the minister of the day for a portion of that which he has drained from them in taxes.—Upon these and many other infallible marks of national decline it would be useless to dwell; for, indeed, why need we look for any other mark than that which is exhibited in our situation considered relatively to France? When I am shown the numerous turnpike roads and canals, the amazing manufactories of Manchester and Birmingham, the immense extent and riches of London, I see indubitable proofs of enormous individual wealth; but no proof at all, of national *wealth*, which, properly understood, is only another word for national *power*. Of what use are all these riches, unless the nation is more powerful in consequence of them? And in estimating her power, we must not, like those profound statesmen Lords Castlereagh and Hawkesbury, count the number of her ships, seamen and boys, and also of her soldiers, militia, and volunteers, compared with the numbers of her own forces of former times and former wars, and conclude, that, because we find the present numbers greater, the nation must now be more powerful than she was in those times. Power is a relative endowment: nor, in speaking of the power of a nation, must we consider it relatively to the nations of the world promiscuously, or in general; but to that of her neighbours, and especially of that particular nation, who has long been known as her rival and antagonist. I may easily beat a child or an old man; I may mow down whole crowds of cripples; but, am I yet able to encounter the man who is my equal in age, health, and size, and with whom I fought in all the stages of life, from infancy up to manhood? This is the question which every man will put to himself, in order to satisfy his own mind as to the fact, whether, in point of bodily strength, he has, or has not, declined. And, as to his neighbours, if they see him suing for a cessation of the combat under the pretext of a necessity of " taking breath," and of gathering strength " against another day of trial; " if they see him submitting to the grossest of insults rather than make that trial; and, when at last compelled to it, if they see his utmost hope, his " glory ", confined merely to the preservation of his existence, must they not conclude that he is a fallen and still falling man?

THREE

THE ENGLISH CHARACTER

The English Character

P.R. XXX., c. 361. *To the People of Southampton. Letter I.* 23-3-16.

AN Englishman, while he eats and drinks no more than another man, labours three times as many hours in the course of a year as any other man. His life is three common lives. People of other countries have some *leisure hours*. An Englishman has none. He always walks or rides as fast as he can. You may know him from all the rest of the world by his head going before his feet; by his pushing along as if going for a wager, and by his stoop and his round shoulders. An American gentleman observed, that, when he first came to London, all the people in streets " seemed as if they were going on an *errand,* and had been charged to *make haste back.*" Never was there a better description. If we see a man walking at a *leisurely* pace, in the country, we suspect him to be a thief, or, at least, a vagrant. Sunday seems to be the only day in the week when an Englishman does not enjoy himself. He lolls about, and looks out of spirits. The old saying, that " when the Devil finds any one with nothing to do, he is sure *to set him to work,*" certainly had its origin in England. I wonder such a people should ever have had a Sunday or Churches. The Pope has left us some *Saint's Days;* but they have been disregarded by the nation at large; and, though retained for a long while in the public offices, they have all been abolished, at last, by Act of Parliament, the nation being *too busy* to indulge the whims of the Holy Father any longer. To have an idea of the everlasting industry of this nation, you have only to look at the garden of a labouring man. This is the scene of his *leisure* hours; that is to say, the *twilight* and the *Sunday,* when he will cultivate flowers or shrubs rather than submit to a minute's rest.

This propensity to incessant labour is common to all ranks of life. The lawyers, doctors, parsons, merchants; all are alike; and, as to the shop-keepers and tradesmen, they know not what leisure or pleasure means. The Gentlemen are as busy as the rest. They are half their lives on horse-back. Hunting and shooting are their labour, and hard labour too. Every man, also aims at *perfection* in his way. He is not content unless he has *something* or *another,* in which he does, or thinks he does, surpass all other men. Hence our fine horses, dogs, sheep, cattle, the herds of which are attended to with such inflexible perseverence. A score or two of gentlemen riding full speed down a hill nearly as steep as the roof of a house, where one false step must inevitably send horse and rider to certain death, is an object to be seen no where but in England. Nor are these sports and that of boxing and other perilous exercises to be left out in an enumeration of the causes of national power, though shallow philosophers affect to despise them. They tend to produce great energy in individuals, and it is of the union of individual energy that national power principally consists. To what does America owe the achievement and the preservation of her independence, but to the arms of a race of men, brave because they are hardy, and hardy because, from their infancy, they have been bred to labour and perilous pursuits?

In England every man tries to excel all others, not so much in rising above them in the scale of life, but in the particular line of life, in which he is placed. He would rather not do a thing at all than not do it *well*. To this unconquerable spirit of perseverence it is that we owe that astonishing perfection, to which we have arrived in most of the mechanic arts, and in whatever appertains to agriculture, though, as to the last, we have, in many respects, to contend against nature itself. In every thing where *horses* are the chief instruments (and horses are second only to men) the English so far surpass all the rest of the world, that there is no room for comparison. The man who has a mind to know something of England in this respect, should walk from the Tower of London to Charing Cross a little after day-light in the morning, while the streets are clear of people. He would then see the teams of immense horses, drawing up from the bank of the Thames, coals, timber, stone, and other heavy materials. One morning last summer I counted, in various places, more than a hundred of these teams, worth *each of them,* harness, waggon, load and all, little less than a thousand pounds. The horses, upon an average, weigh more than *a ton.* But, next after a *fox-hunt,* the finest sight in England is a stage-coach just ready to start. A great sheep or cattle fair is a beautiful sight; but, in the stage-coach you see more of what man is capable of performing. The vehicle itself, the harness, all so complete and so neatly arranged; so strong and clean and good. The beautiful horses impatient to be off. The inside full and the outside covered, in every part, with men, women, children, boxes, bags, bundles. The coachman, taking his reins in one hand and his whip in the other, gives a signal with his foot, and away go, at the rate of seven miles an hour, the population and the property of a hamlet. One of these coaches coming in, after a long journey is a sight not less interesting. The horses are now all sweat and foam, the reek from their bodies ascending like a cloud. The whole equipage is covered, perhaps, with dust or dirt. But still, on it comes as steady as the hand of a clock. As a proof of the perfection, to which this mode of travelling has been brought, there is one coach, which goes between Exeter and London, the proprietors of which agree to forfeit *eight-pence* for every *minute* that the coach is behind its time at any of its stages; and this coach, I believe, travels eight miles an hour, and that, too, upon a very hilly, and, at some seasons, very deep road.

There may be persons to say, " these descriptions may be very amusing to your readers in America, but what use can they be of *to us* in England? " Why, I wish you to see, in these instances of your energy and your creative industry, specimens of the *real causes* of that national strength, which you foolishly attribute to the cleverness of a financier; to a sinking fund; or to any other of the numerous humbugs, with which you have been so long amused.

The *population* of a country is no standard of its strength, or, at least, the population alone is no such standard; if it were, it would be difficult to conceive how it has happened, that a handful of Englishmen have become the masters of India, and have been able to tax the people of that country as completely as we are taxed here, or very nearly so. *A man is a man,* to be sure; but, as Sterne said to the monk, " there is some *difference* in men, my friend." It is very clear, that, if there be one man who does, in the same line of business, as much as two other men, and if he travels twice as fast as either of them, he is better than both of them to his employer, because he eats no more than one of them, and requires no more clothes, lodging, &c. than one of them. It is just the same with a nation of such men. And, therefore, in-estimating the strength of England, or any other country, we must look more at the character and performances of the people than at their numbers. In England every thing moves in a quick pace. The stirring disposition of the people shorten distances. More is done in the same space of time than in other countries. The tradesman in London almost holds a conversation with the tradesman at York or Exeter.

But the great thing of all is the *incessant labour,* which is continually *creating* things, which give strength to a country. I do not know, that we excel some other nations in ingenuity in the useful arts. Workmen are very adroit in America. They build as well, and more neatly, than we do. They work as nimbly. But they do not work *so much.* They take some leisure, which we never do. I must, however, always insist, that we derive infinite advantage from our sports. To these we owe, almost entirely, our second selves, our *horses* of speed, and even these we should not have without our *dogs.* It is very well in the way of joke, to ridicule fox-hunting 'Squires and Parsons; but, if the matter be well considered, we shall find that these gentlemen are as usefully employed in this way as they would be in any other. By following this sport, they set an example of adventurous riding to those beneath them; and, if there had been no fox-hunting in England, I much question if we should have seen five thousand yeomanry cavalry instead of the *hundred thousand,* who, at one time, were actually mounted on their own horses and in their own uniforms. No matter for the *cause,* in which they came forth. The cause might have been different. A regiment of soldiers all of whom can *ride* and *box* and *shoot* must be much more formidable than a regiment of men who only know how to dance and sing and act plays. It must be the same with a nation. The "walking *mania*," as it has been called, is, in my opinion, a thing highly to be prized; and especially that wonderful exploit of Capt. BARCLAY, which, however, has now been surpassed by the man, who has walked *eleven hundred miles in eleven hundred hours,* and whose name I am sorry I have forgotten. What is this but a great instance of the bodily powers of man? What man will now not be ashamed to say, that he wants a horse or a coach to carry him twenty or thirty miles in a day? The standard of the capacity of man has been raised by these performances; and there can be no question that the nation has really been made stronger by them.

The philosophers of the "humanity" school condemn all these things as vulgar, brutal and barbarous. They look upon them as the contrary of *refinement.* They represent it to be an act of cruelty, for a crowd of horsemen to hollow after a pack of dogs in pursuit of a poor animal, who they say has done them no harm, and, in whose torments they feel delight. I notice this more particularly as I perceive the sickly sentimental taste to have made great way in America. But, what is there more cruel in a fox-chase than in those sports with the gun, in which the Americans are so famous, and to their early pursuit of which they, probably, owe their liberties?

FOUR

THE LANDLORDS, THE FARMERS, THE NEW RICH AND THE WEN

The Monied Interest

P.R. VI., c. 370. *Summary of Politics*. 8-9-04.

PAPER-ARISTOCRACY.—Amongst the great and numerous dangers to which this country, and particularly the monarchy, is exposed in consequence of the enormous public debt, the influence, the powerful and widely-extended influence, of the monied interest is, perhaps, the most to be dreaded, because it necessarily aims at measures which directly tend to the subversion of the present order of things. In speaking of this monied interest, I do not mean to apply the phrase, as it was applied formerly, that is to say, to distinguish the possessors of personal property, more especially property in the funds, from persons possessing lands : the division of the proprietors into a monied interest, and a landed interest, is not applicable to the present times, all the people, who have any thing, having now become, in a greater or less degree, stock-holders. From this latter circumstance it is artfully insinuated, that they are all deeply and equally interested in supporting the system; and, such is the blindness of avarice, or rather of self-interest, that men in general really act as if they preferred a hundred pounds' worth of stock to an estate in land of fifty times the value. But, it is not of this mass of stock-holders; it is not of that description of persons who leave their children's fortunes to *accumulate* in those funds, where, even according to the ratio of depreciation already experienced, a pound of to day will not be worth much above a shilling twenty years hence; it is not of these simpletons of whom I speak, when I talk of the monied interest of the present day : I mean an interest hostile alike to the land-holder and to the stock-holder, to the colonist, to the real merchant, and to the manufacturer, to the clergy, to the nobility and to the throne; I mean the numerous and powerful body of loan-jobbers, directors, brokers, contractors and farmers-general, which has been engendered by the excessive amount of the public debt, and the almost boundless extension of the issues of paper-money.

*   *   *   *   *   *

Our paper-aristocracy, who arose with the schemes of Mr. Pitt, have proceeded with very bold strides : theirs was the proposition for commuting the tythes; theirs the law for the redemption of the land tax; theirs the numerous laws and regulations which have been made of late years in favour of jobbing and speculation, till at last they obtained a law compelling men to take their paper in payment of just debts, while they themselves were exempted, by the same law, from paying any part of the enormous debts which they had contracted, though they had given promissory notes for the amount!

*   *   *   *   *   *

The country people wonder how it is that all the old gentlemen's families are dropping off, one by one, and that those which remain are completely out-shone by the new gentlemen, from whose gilded footmen they learn that their masters were, but a few years ago, butchers, bakers, bottle-corkers, or old-cloaths-men, and that, in fact, they are not, as to *visible* profession, much better now. At this the country people stand gaping with a mixture of amazement and curiosity; whereat some footman more profound and eloquent than his fellows, informs them, with sonorous voice and solemn accent, that the circumstance, at which they seem so much surprised, arises from the astonishing prosperity of the country. Upon which the country people gape still wider, not being, for their very souls, able to discover how that prosperity, which elevates bottle-corkers to country-gentlemen, should reduce country-gentlemen to bottle-corkers! But, the talkative footman, who, perhaps, begins, by this time, to grow impatient at their stupidity, flatly tells them, that, as he wants no dispute about the matter, those who differ from him in opinion may walk out of the hall; and, as country people love good things as well as town's people, it is most likely that the far greater part of them will stay. This mode, however, of arguing with the belly instead of the brain I do not approve of; and, therefore, if the country people will listen to me only for a minute, I will endeavour to explain to them the cause of this phenomenon. The prosperity, of which they hear so much, does not extend its influence to *all* the people in the country. Its sphere is, indeed, rather confined, and it would be, I fancy, difficult to find many of its beneficial effects beyond the circle of the paper-aristocracy. The country-gentleman, who wishes and endeavours to live independently upon his estate, is obliged to pay to the government, for the support of the funding system, so great a portion of the revenue of that estate, that he has not enough left to live upon in the style in which his ancestors lived; and, in order to support that style, he sells part of his patrimony; once broken into, it goes piece by piece; his sons become merchants clerks or East India cadets; his daughters become companions or lady's women to the wives of those in whose service the sons are embarked; the father, seeing his end approach, secures a life annuity for his widow; some speculator purchases the tottering old mansion; and thus the funding system swallows up the family.

The Corn Laws

P.R. VI., c. 235. *Summary of Politics: Price of Bread.* 18-8-04.

THE code of corn-laws and regulations presents a mass of absurdities hardly to be equalled; and, what makes the matter worse, they are absurdities which are characteristic of a shallow brain. One would think they had resulted from the deliberations of an assembly of shop-keepers and handicraftsmen. The nation has already paid for these laws, to which no small portion of its present disgrace and danger may be fairly attributed, but it is very likely, that we shall soon experience effects more fatal than have ever heretofore been experienced.

CORN BILL

To the Lords Spiritual and Temporal of the Kingdom of Great Britain and Ireland in Parliament assembled

P.R. XXVII., c. 353.   *Corn Bill.*   25-3-15.

THE Petition of WILLIAM COBBETT, of Botley, in Hampshire, dated on the 17th day of March, 1815.

HUMBLY SHEWETH.

That your Petitioner, on the 10th instant, delivered to the High Sheriff of Hampshire, signed by your Petitioner himself, and by five hundred and eighty one other Inhabitants of the County, many of whom are freeholders, land-owners, and land-cultivators, a Requisition in the following words:—to wit:—

"Sir, We, the undersigned Freeholders and other Land-holders, Tradesmen and Manufacturers of the County of Southampton, perceiving, that, in various parts of the Kingdom, evil-disposed, or misguided, persons are endeavouring to prevail on the Legislature to impose duties on the Importation of Corn, and being convinced, that such a measure would grievously oppress the labouring classes, would be ruinous to Tradesmen and Manufacturers, would, in the end, be injurious to the Growers of Corn and the Owners of Land themselves, and might possibly disturb the peace of his Majesty's Dominions, request that you will be pleased to convene a Meeting of the County on a day as little distant as may be convenient, in order to take into consideration and to discuss the propriety of presenting a petition to the two Houses of Parliament, earnestly praying, That no such Measure may be adopted, and also praying for a repeal of laws, hostile to our rights and liberties, passed during the late wars, and for a constitutional Reform in the Commons' House of Parliament."

That the said High Sheriff has refused to call such Meeting of the County, and that, therefore, your Petitioner, deeply impressed with the injurious tendency of any law to prohibit, or restrain, the importation of Corn, has thus humbly presumed to make his individual appeal to the Wisdom, the Justice, the Humanity of your Lordships.

That your Petitioner does not presume to be competent to judge of the precise degree in which the Merchants, Traders, and Manufacturers of this kingdom may be affected by the proposed law; but while common sense tells him, that it must seriously injure these classes of the community, that it must so enhance and uphold the price of shipping, freight, and manufactured goods, as to transfer the building of ships, the employment of ships, the making of goods, together with vast numbers of our best artizans to countries, where the necessaries of life are at a much lower price : while common sense tells him, that to uphold the price of food is to drive from their native country great numbers of persons in search of better living on their incomes, leaving their share of the taxes to be paid by those who remain, and that, too, out of diminished means arising from a diminished demand for their produce, their manufactures, and their professional labours; while common sense says this to your Petitioner, his own experience, as an owner and cultivator of land, enables him to state, with more precision, to your Lordships, the grounds of his conviction, that any law tending to raise, or keep up, the price of Corn, will prove, in the end, to be no benefit, but an injury to the owner and the cultivator of the land.

That your Petitioner has seen, with great surprise, that, in certain Petitions obtained privately and sent from this County, it has been asserted, that the *Expences* of a farm remain nearly the same as when corn was at the late high price. Your Petitioner's observation and experience enables him most positively to contradict this very material fact. When Wheat was sold at an average of 100 shillings a quarter, the weekly wages of a labourer, in this neighbourhood, were from 15 to 18 shillings, and that now, when the average price of Wheat is about 60 shillings a quarter, the weekly wages of a labourer are from 10 to 12 shillings. The price of Brickwork, which was 50 shillings a Rod, or Perch, is now 40 shillings. The price of Smith's and Wheelwright's work is experiencing a proportionate fall; and the price of plough and cart-horses has fallen a full third.

But, there is another great head of expense, to which your Petitioner is particularly anxious humbly to solicit the attention of your Lordships, as it is intimately connected, not only with the comfort of the great mass of the people, but with their political, civil, and moral conduct; namely, *The Poor's Rates,* which, in the Parish of Bishop's Waltham, where the land of your Petitioner principally lies, have been reduced in such a degree, that your Petitioner has had to pay, in the said parish, during the year just now expiring, one fifth less than he had to pay during the last year,* with the pleasing prospect of a progressive diminution in this head of expense and in the vast numbers of those persons, who are now included under the degrading appellation of paupers; who, in entering the pale of pauperism, have, in general, left behind them all those sentiments of independence, of patriotism, of love of liberty, of hatred of oppression, for which the very lowest classes of Englishmen were, in former times, so highly distinguished, and have, along with the name and garb of paupers, assumed the tone and the manners of slaves.

For the practical, the undeniable proof, that high prices have an immediate tendency towards the creating of paupers; your Petitioner humbly begs leave to refer your Lordships to the official documents amongst the records of your Right Honourable House, where it clearly appears, that pauperism, kept in check for a long series of years by the native spirit of the people, was let loose like a torrent over the land by the enormous prices during the late wars, which, in depriving men of their food, deprived them, and even their children of that shame, which had before kept them from the Poor-List; and, therefore, your Petitioner cannot but view with profound sorrow, that a legislative act should be in contemplation, having, as he firmly believes, a tendency to prevent for ever the restoration of the labouring classes to their former state of comfort, of independence of mind, and of frankness and boldness of manners.

Your Petitioner is well aware, that, unless prices be raised and upheld, it will be impossible for the owners and the cultivators of the land to pay the taxes that will exist after the Property Tax shall have ceased; he is well aware, that to ensure them a high

* In the parish of BOTLEY a still greater reduction has taken place.

price for their corn is the only means of enabling them to pay these taxes; but, then, he is clearly convinced, that a very large part of those taxes might be dispensed with; that the army and navy, which swallows up so considerable a portion of them, might be reduced to the state in which they were previous to the late war, and that the whole of the public expenses (exclusive of those attendant on the National Debt) might be reduced to what they then were, namely, six millions a year; and thus without raising the price of corn, the credit, the safety, the honour of the nation, might all be amply provided for and secured.

For these reasons your Petitioner humbly prays, that your Lordships *will not pass any law to prohibit, or restrain, the importation of Corn;* and, as the nation, once more, happily, sees the days of peace, he also prays for the repeal of all the laws, *laying new restrictions on the Press,* passed during the late wars; and, further, he most humbly but most earnestly prays and implores your Lordships to take into your early consideration that subject, which, in point of real importance, swallows up all others : namely, the state of the Representation of the people in the Commons' House of Parliament.

And your Petitioner shall ever pray.

W. COBBETT.

Squire Jolterhead

P.R. XXX., c. 262. *To the People of the United States of America.*
Letter II. 2-3-16.

SUPPOSE Giles Jolterhead, Esqr. to have 20 farms, each of which yield him a gross rent of 200 pounds a year; and that he pays out of his rent of 4,000*l.* in taxes towards the expences of the government Debt. In consequence of an alteration in the value of the currency, wheat falls from 14*s.* to 7*s.* a bushel. It is clear that his rents must fall from 4,000*l. to* 2,000*l.* a year; and, if he continue to pay 1,000*l.* a year towards the Debt, it is clear, that his spending income is, in fact, reduced to 1,000*l,* instead of 3,000*l.* a year. Thus far this is the real state of the landlords in England. But, while they are thus reduced, by the very same means, the fund-holder's income is *raised,* and that, too, in the same proportion. Well, the situation of 'Squire Jolterhead is truly distressing. He lays down his *hounds* and three out of four of his hunters, and packs off a couple or three servants to begin with. People ask him *why*. He " likes *coursing* better." But, the *Greyhounds* are still expensive. The Taxgatherer comes thundering at the door; talks so loud (with his *hat on* all the while) that the servants hear his voice quite into the Hall. Away go the beautiful Greyhounds dancing and capering to the pippin-tree. Four or five more visits from the man with the ink-bottle at his button-hole send off a brace out of three gardeners, turn the close-shaven lawn into a rough bit of pasture, " Madam *liking to see* sheep and cows grazing close to the " windows." Shooting is now become the 'Squire's sole delight. The Taxgatherer still returns as regularly as old Time himself, and as Time pertinacious and irresistible in his course. What is now to be done? Are the dappled Pointers, with noses keener than the air itself and staunch as a rock; are they, and are the little true-bred Spaniels with ears and dewlaps sweeping the ground, and with sport-anticipating tongues that would almost " create a soul under the ribs of death; " are all these too; are all the family favourites of a century, all to be destroyed " at one fell swoop? " Is their death-warrant signed in the book of taxes? Is their doom irrevocable? Is there no respite? " Parliament will *surely do something for us*! "

Thus exclaims 'Squire Jolterhead, sitting by his parlour-fire, with poor old *Don* resting his chin on one knee while *Bustle* is pawing the other, and both soliciting the applauding pat on the head, which solicitation, in former times, would have been so graciously and gaily answered; but, instead of which their caresses awaken in the master's mind no feelings but those of sorrow, shame, and melancholy. He sees 'Squire Crack-Louse, the army Taylor, and 'Squire Turpentine, the Spirit Contractor, and 'Squire Garbage, the Meat Contractor, and 'Squire Bean-meal, the Biscuit and Bread Contractor, and 'Squire Glanders, the Horse Contractor, and an infinite number of others all sallying out around him with gay equipages or numerous troops of hunters and followers; and, while he is thus musing on his altered state, Madam awakens him with a proposition to apply to his friends in London to get places for his sons. " Don't tell me," says she, " why, who has so good a right as you to ask for places for your sons? Was you not the first man to sign your name to the resolutions for the support of the Bank when it stopped payment? and was it not you who called out the yeomanry cavalry to keep down Paine's Rights of Man and the Jacobins? Did you not fall out with one of your best friends because he blamed the sending the Scotch Reformers to Botany Bay? Did you not carry up an address to his Majesty when Peg Nicholson attempted his sacred life; aye, and you might have been made a Knight, too, and have made me a Lady, that you might, if you had had any regard for me."—(*Weeping*) " Come, come, my dear, never mind that now : let us think how we can save the poor Spaniels."—" Spaniels, indeed! Think how you can save your family. Zounds! go at once and get places for your sons. What have you been voting and bawling for, if you are to get nothing? Did you not go, at the risk of your life, to disperse the Parliamentary Reformers, and when they laughed at you and called you a chuckle-headed fool, did you not charge them with high treason? Did you not keep us up all night and remain booted and spurred ready to set off with your tenants to help put Burdett into the tower? Did you not go into mourning when Tooke and Hardy were acquitted? Did you not get drunk as a beast, and make all the neighbourhood drunk and cram them with sheep and oxen roasted whole, at the Jubilee and when Bonaparte was sent off to St. Helena? Have you not always stuck to your loyalty; would you ever let us have any but a loyal news-paper, and did you not turn out your best tenant because he would continue to take in Cobbett's Register? " —" Yes, yes, my dear, I know I did; I know very well that I did. But, pray for God's sake, say no more about it : say no more about it."—" I will say more about it; and I say that your sons ought to have places under government; for, I do not see why Mr. Crack-Louse and Mr. Garbage and the rest of them are to get so rich and buy all the land up, while we are compelled to lay down our carriage, and " * * * * *

A loud knock at the door puts an end to her harangue. The 'Squire is all in a sweat for fear. It is not the Taxgatherer however, this time. It is the Post-boy with the COURIER, containing an account of the Chancellor's *remedy.* "A *remedy,* my dear! Here it is. Fourteen millions a year to be *thrown into* the country to *relieve* the landed interest."—"Fourteen millions, my dear : bless me! How much do you think *we* shall have?"—"I don't know. . . I don't know. . . Let me see. . . Fourteen millions to be *thrown into the country*. But, then, here is something about taxes to the amount of the same fourteen millions.—These, I suppose, are to be taken from the army taylors and their contractors. . . No. . . Let me see. . . I can't make it out for my life." At last in comes the Apothecary, who has just been reading the Register, and the difficult passage being submitted to him, he says : "Why, Sir, this is the Chancellor's meaning. Your 20 farms that used to leave you 3,000 pounds a year after paying your annual share of the Debt, now leave you only 1,000 pounds. This plunges you into great distress; it makes you want money to live decently and to keep your pointers and spaniels. Therefore the minister means to make *no more loans,* and to lay out 14 millions a year in purchasing stock of the Fundholders, who, when they have sold their stock, will have the money which you have paid in taxes to lend to you upon mortgage, or to give you in exchange for some of your farms; and, as your farms are now worth about 3,000 pounds each in the fee simple, and as you will want, to pay interest and all together, about 3,000 pounds a year, you may live as well as you have done for many years past in consequence of this financial operation."

"Thank you, Mr. Lancet; thank you," says Madam, "I always told my sons, who listen, I am sorry to say it, to that Jacobin Cobbett, that the government would never desert us who had been its best friends. I always told them that things would be brought about, and that they would have as good an estate as their papa has had before them."—"Oh! no, madam," replies Mr. Lancet; "I did not say so. Your *sons,* Madam, will have *no estate at all*. The fundholders will have the estate in exchange for the money which they will give you, and which money you will have first given them in the shape of taxes."—"What! My sons no estate! My sons no estate!". . .

. . . . . Here a terrible knocking at the door announces the approach of the Taxgatherer, and the parties sneak into their chairs as quiet as mice.

Sir Pompous Jolterhead : A Dialogue

P.R. XXXVIII., c. 866. *To Lord Viscount Folkestone. On the Grand Battle between Land and Funds.* 31-3-21.

SIR POMPOUS JOLTERHEAD.—Farmer GRUB, why don't you pay your rent?

GRUB.—I can't, Zir, I have got no money.

JOLTERHEAD.—Got no money! What have you done with the proceeds of your crop?

GRUB.—Done wee't, Zir! why, the Poor took away a deal, and the taxing man took the last penny away this very morning, dame's egg-money and all.

JOLTERHEAD.—But, you know, that the land is *mine,* and you ought to pay me *first.*

GRUB.—I thought the crop was *mine;* but the Overseers and the Taxers threatened to *seize,* if I did not give them the money that I sold it for; and so, I found out that the crop was *not mine;* and began to think, then, that the land did not belong *to you.*

MONEYLENDER.—There is a good deal of reason, Sir Pompous, in what the farmer says.

JOLTERHEAD.—A good deal of *reason*! Why, G— d— (*Aside,* but, the rascal will enter up his mortgage if I don't hold my tongue.)

MONEYLENDER.—Yes, Sir, I say a good deal of reason, Sir!

JOLTERHEAD.—Well, Mr. DISCOUNT, there may be; but, with great submission, I *thought* the land was *mine.*

DISCOUNT.—Yours, and so it is yours in some respects. The *title* is in you; (*Here Jolterhead whispers to himself, sighing,* "but *you* have got the *deeds*") you are *seized in fee;* you are the "*lord of the soil;*" you can bequeath it, or sell it (*saving reprises,* you know!); you can ride over it, hunt over it, and *call it yours;* but, the poor must have support, *and the King his taxes.*

GRUB.—Just the very words that Mr. SHARP, the collector told me. I talked about my *rent,* and said Sir Pompous would be *angry.* " Poh," said he, " angry! Who cares for his anger! What is *he,* I wonder? Would he rob the King, and be a rebel? "

DISCOUNT.—Very just.

JOLTERHEAD.—But, ought they to take *all* away, and leave nothing for the landlord?

DISCOUNT.—Really, Sir Pompous, begging your pardon, I must say, that you are very unreasonable, and that you do not talk like a *loyal* man.

GRUB.—Nay, now, Mr. DISCOUNT, I do think that you do his honour wrong; for, did not his honour raise a troop of Cavalry at his own expense, and march at the head of us in the face of volleys of brickbats and rotten eggs?

JOLTERHEAD.—Grub knows, that I have always been ready to fight for our Glorious Constitution in Church and State, and that I roasted an ox and half a score of sheep, at the deliverance of Europe.

DISCOUNT.—Very good, very good, Sir Pompous; that was very good; but, you must *persevere* : loyalty, like faith, is nothing worth, unless you go on to *the end* : backsliding is more criminal than being in darkness; and I have no hesitation in saying, that for a loyal man to become disloyal is worse than downright " radicalism."

JOLTERHEAD.—But, Mr. DISCOUNT, is it to be disloyal to wish to have *something* out of one's land?

DISCOUNT.—Yes, it is, if the necessities of the state require *all*.

GRUB.—Just the very words of Mr. SHARP, the tax-collector. " Not a farthing is *yours,*" said he, " till the king have got his taxes."

JOLTERHEAD.—But, if the *necessities* of the state do not require all?

DISCOUNT.—*If?* No *ifs,* Sir Pompous! No *ifs* upon this subject, if you regard *my* friendship. No *doubts,* no *reasonings,* as to such matters. These are very serious things, and I appeal to his Reverence there, whether it be not criminal to oppose your-self to the powers that be, whether in deed or in word.

SLEEK.—Certainly; for all power is from above; and, therefore, he who resisteth the power, resisteth the giver of the power.

JOLTERHEAD.—But, is it criminal in me to wish to have *some little matter* of rent?

DISCOUNT.—Yes, I say it is, if the State need the whole. And, of that need, the State itself is the judge, and the only judge. Nothing can be taken by the tax-gatherer but in virtue of *acts of parliament;* and, do you call the *justice* or the *wisdom* of these acts in question? Shall I see my friend, Sir Pompous Jolterhead, pretending, like the audacious Radical, to call in question the justice and wisdom of *" the Great Council of the Nation"* with His sacred Majesty at its head! O, fye, fye, Sir Pompous!

SLEEK.—Fye, Sir Pompous; fye upon you! That I should live to see the day, when the heir of the ancient and loyal family of Jolterhead, for ages such firm friends of Church and State, is calling in question the justice and wisdom of the " Great Council of the Nation." O fye, Sir Pompous!

GRUB.—(*Aside.*) How sheepish his honour looks!

JOLTERHEAD.—But. . .

DISCOUNT.—*But,* what? I really have not patience to hear you, Sir Pompous; and must take my leave, if you persevere.

JOLTERHEAD.—Why, good Mr. Discount, I hope no offence. We may *differ in opinion,* without. . .

DISCOUNT.—Not upon a subject *like this.* We may differ as to many points : as to *religion,* for instance, as I differ from Mr. SLEEK there, he being a Minister of the Church and I not believing a word of what he teaches. (*Exit SLEEK, giving DISCOUNT a furious look.*) But, in a case like *this,* there can be no difference of opinion. Besides, how it is *possible* for the state to take from you less than it takes? Let us see : would you refuse to support the poor, and set them to *help themselves,* and to plunder your pantries and cellars?

JOLTERHEAD.—No : the poor must, at any rate, have their mouths stopped.

GRUB.—That they must; and I can tell you it takes something to stop them!

DISCOUNT.—Would you disband the army, and leave your throat for the Radicals to cut?

JOLTERHEAD.—No : God forbid!

GRUB.—(*aside*) I don't see *why* they should cut *mine*!

DISCOUNT.—Very well, Sir; and would you leave the royal family, the officers of state, the accomplished ambassadors, the "venerable judges of the land," without ample provision for the "support of their dignity," and for the "commanding of respect?"

JOLTERHEAD.—No, no, Mr. Discount, I would not.

DISCOUNT.—What would you have, then? What do you want? If *all* be wanted for these purposes, how can you expect any for your own private purposes?

JOLTERHEAD.—You understand these matters better than I do, Mr. Discount; but, I thought, that a good deal of the taxes went to pay what is called the *interest of the debt*.

DISCOUNT.—(*hastily*). Well, and if they do; what then? You don't *mean*, I hope, to. . .

JOLTERHEAD.—No, upon my sacred honour I do not! God forbid I should think of wishing for "a breach of public faith."

DISCOUNT.—Why, then, *talk at all,* about the *interest of the Debt*? Why *talk* about it? Why *name* it? Why *allude* to it? You have been reading that villain COBBETT; and, to be frank with you, Sir Pompous, if you read COBBETT's papers, all that I have to say is, I'll read *no more of yours*!

JOLTERHEAD.—I read his papers! I read COBBETT's papers! D—— the rascal, I hate the very sound of his name; and, I have told all my tenants that I'd turn them out of their farms, if they read the fellow's paper. I told them so years back, didn't I, GRUB?

GRUB.—Yes, Zir, that your honour did (*aside,* and I have read them ever since, and I have to thank Cobbett for a stocking full of guineas that neither taxer nor landlord nor overseer nor bum-bailiff will ever get out of my Dame's clutches.)

DISCOUNT.—Well, Sir Pompous, I am glad to hear this. No man is more *sincerely your friend* than I am. If the times are hard, we must assist one another. In this "sudden transition from war to peace," we must have a little patience; and you may rely upon *my friendship* for every *accommodation* in my power.

JOLTERHEAD.—That's kind. Give me your hand. (*They*

shake hands.) Good morning, GRUB. Be sure to keep off the d—— poachers, and keep the game for Mr. Discount and his friends.

GRUB.—Good morning to your honour and to you Mr. Discount. (*Aside.* But as for the game, that goes into my pot, instead of the guts of this grinding rascal and of his hook-nose and round-eye race from London.) *Exit* Grub.

JOLTERHEAD.—Here is your coach, Mr. DISCOUNT. Pray do us the favour of bringing Mrs. Discount and the Young Ladies the next time you come.

DISCOUNT.—Thank you. (*Exit* Jolterhead.) Mrs. Discount and " the Young Ladies " will, I believe, *bring themselves* very soon, without any invitation from you!

The New Farmers

P.R. XXXIX., c. 513. *To Mr. Coke. On the question of Large Farms and Small Farms, and on the fall of the System out of which they have arisen.* 26-5-21.

BUT, besides this, a *new race* of farmers sprang up. Attorneys, Bankers, Merchants, Big-manufacturers became *farmers,* and not a few of the *Lords* and *Gentlemen,* owners of lands, who had, certainly, *a legal right to do what they pleased with their estates;* but, who will find, in the end, that they did not pursue the wise course. Even *fashion* helped the accursed paper-money system in this its pernicious work. The *cattle-shows,* the *sheep-shearings,* had *good motive;* but were unwise. Those lords and gentlemen did not recollect, that the sheep-shearing, at which they assisted, was *instead* of a *thousand sheep-shearings* that formerly took place! Their sheep-shearing was a *brilliant* thing. It *dazzled.* It was *magnificent,* and, in *itself munificent;* but, if the hospitable host, in retiring from the festive board, had been met, in his bed chamber, by the ghosts of only a hundred thousandth part of those who formerly held sheep-shearings, and who had been brought to the death of paupers by the system which created the *grand sheep-shearing,* he would, unless his heart were as hard as a stone, never have tasted joy again. I assure you, Sir, that I say this without any desire to aim a blow at you. You have been deceived by the *false glare.* You saw assembled around what you thought the effect of *improvement in agriculture,* when it really was the effect of a false, fraudulent, amassing paper-money; that brought before your eyes the prosperous *tens,* and that kept the starving *hundreds* carefully hidden from your sight.

* * *

So long ago as 1804, I went round a little common, in Hampshire, called *Horton Heath.* "The better day the better deed," and, on a Sunday I found the husbands at home. It was when the madness for *enclosures* raged most furiously. The Common contained about 150 acres; and I found round the skirts of it, and near to the skirts, about 30 cottages and gardens, the latter chiefly encroachments on the Common, which was *waste* (as it is called) in a manor of which the Bishop was the lord. I took down the names of all the cottagers, the number and ages of their children, the number of their cows, heifers, calves, sows, pigs, geese, ducks, fowl, and stalls of bees; the extent of their little bits of grounds, the worth of what was growing (it was at, or near Michaelmas), the number of apple-trees, and of their black cherry-trees, called by them *merries,* which is a great article in that part of Hampshire. I have lost my paper, a copy of which I gave to Mr. WINDHAM; and, therefore, I cannot speak positively as to any one point; but, I remember *one hundred and twenty-five,* or *thirty-five stalls of bees,* worth at that time *ten shillings* a stall *at least.* Cows there were about *fifteen,* besides heifers and calves; about *sixty pigs* great and small; and not less than *five hundred head of poultry!* The cattle and sheep of the neighbouring farmers *grazed the Common all the while* besides. *The bees alone* were worth more annually than the Common, if it had been enclosed, would have let for, deducting the expense of the *fences.* The farmers used the Common for their purposes; and my calculation was, that the cottages produced from their little bits, in food, for themselves, and in things to be sold at market, *more than any neighbouring farm of* 200 *acres!* The cottages consisted, fathers, mothers, and children, and grand fathers, grand mothers and grand children, of *more than two hundred persons.*

Why, Sir, what a system must that have been that could lead *English* gentlemen to disregard matters like these! That could induce them to tear up *"wastes"* and sweep away occupiers like those that I have described! *"Wastes"* indeed! Give a dog an ill name. Was Horton Heath a waste? Was it a "waste" when a hundred, perhaps, of healthy boys and girls were playing there of a Sunday, instead of creeping about covered with filth in the alleys of a town, or, at least, listening to the ravings of some weekly-penny hunting hypocrite? Was it a "*waste?*" No: but, *it would have been a waste,* if it had been "*improved.*"

Enclosures

P.R. XXXIX., c. 329. *To Mr. Attwood. The Manifold Blessings of a Large Loaf.* 5-5-21.

YOU, indeed, hear of *no more new enclosures,* and, I hope, most anxiously, that we shall hear of many of the late new enclosures being thrown again to common. They were, for the most part, useless in point of quantity of *production*; and, to the labourers, they were malignantly mischievous. They drove them from the skirts of commons, downs and forests. They took away their cows, pigs, geese, fowls, bees, and gardens. They crowded them into miserable outskirts of towns and villages, for their children to become ricketty and diseased, confined amongst filth and vermin. They took from them their best inheritance : sweet air, health, and the little liberty they had left. Downs, most beautiful and valuable too, have been broken up by the paper-system; and, after three or four crops to beggar them, have been left to be planted with *docks* and *thistles,* and never again to present that perpetual verdure, which formerly covered their surface, and which, while it fed innumerable flocks, enriched the neighbouring fields. LORD LIVERPOOL, in a speech made last spring, observed, that some *persons* thought, that the enclosure-system had been *carried too far.* Who were they, my Lord? I never heard of any body but myself who in a *public manner,* expressed any such opinion. I, indeed, when Old Rose used to be boasting of the number of enclosure Bills, as a proof of "*prosperity,*" used, now-and-then, to show how beastly the idea was; and I proved, over and over again, that (taking in a space of eight or ten years) it was *impossible* to augment the *quantity of produce* by new enclosures; to say nothing about the mischievous effects as to the labourers.

However, the breaking up of the Commons and Downs was a natural effect of the forced increase of money; and, in this way, amongst the rest, that increase worked detriment to the labourer. It was out of his bones that the means came. It was the *deduction made from him by the rise of prices* and by the *not-rise of his wages*: it was the means thus raised that enclosed the Commons and Downs; and that put pianos into the farm-houses and set the farmer up upon a cavalry horse. And these, and such as these, have been the effects of that accursed paper-money, that seven vials of wrath, which you wish to be poured out upon us again!

The New Rich

P.R. XXXII., c. 40. *An Address to the Men of Bristol.* 11.1.27.

IT seems to me, therefore, very wonderful, that those who *have property,* and who do not *share in the taxes,* should not be eager to promote meetings to petition; but the conduct of some of *your* rich neighbours has more than folly in it; it is deeply tinged with tyranny. I allude to the *threats* which they published against all those of their workmen, who should attend the meeting on Brandon Hill, and which threats ought never to be forgotten by *you.* But this hatred to the cause of public liberty is, I am sorry to say it, but too common amongst merchants, great manufacturers, and great farmers; especially those who have *risen suddenly* from the dunghill to a chariot. If we look a little more closely into the influence of riches, in such a state of things as this, we shall be less surprised at this apparently unnatural feeling in men who were, but the other day, merely journeymen and labourers themselves.—As soon as a foolish and unfeeling man gets rich, he becomes desirous of making the world believe, that *he never was poor.* He knows that he has neither *birth* nor *education* to recommend him to the respect of those who have been less fortunate than himself,

Though they pull their hats off to him, he always suspects that they are looking back to his mean origin; and instead of adopting that kindness towards them, and that affability which would make them cheerfully acknowledge his superiority, he endeavours, by a distant and rigid deportment, to extort from their fears that which he wants the sense to obtain from their love. So that, at last, he verifies the old maxim: " *Set a beggar on horse-back, and he'll ride to the Devil.*"

This is the very worst species of aristocracy. It has all the *pride* and none of the *liberal sentiments* of the nobility and great gentry; and, the *farming* and *manufacturing* aristocracy is worse, a great deal, than the *mercantile,* because the latter must have more knowledge of the world, which is a great corrector of insolent and stupid pride. As to the *farmers,* who have grown into riches all of a sudden, they are the most cruel and hardened of all mankind. There are many of them, who really look upon their labourers as so many brutes; and, though they can scarcely spell their own names or pronounce the commonest words in an intelligible manner, they give themselves airs, which no gentleman ever thought of. I have heard sentiments from men of this description, which would not have disgraced the lips of negro-drivers, of a Dey of Algiers. Such men are always seeking to cause their origin to be forgotten. They would with their hands pull down their superiors and with their feet trample down their inferiors; but, as they are frequently *tenants,* and as their meanness is equal to their upstart pride; as they are afflicted with

" Meanness that soars, and pride that licks the dust,"

their chief aim is to trample into the very ground all who are beneath them in point of pecuniary circumstances, in order that they may have as few equals as possible, and that there may be *as wide a distance as possible between them and their labourers.*

Such men are naturally enemies to any Reform that would restore the great mass of the people to liberty and happiness; and so blinded are they by these their base passions, that they almost prefer being *ruined themselves,* to seeing their labourers enjoy their rights. Of the same materials a great part of the *Master Manufacturers* appear to be composed; for, in almost every instance, they have declined to condescend to co-operate with the people at large. They will, however, soon see, that their hopes of maintaining their monopoly of happiness and plenty are delusive. They and the Upstart Farmers have only *begun* to taste the fruit of the system, which they have so long assisted to support. The axe is, indeed, *laid* to the *root* of their riches; but, as yet, the trunk and branches hardly feel the effects of its blows. They will find, when, perhaps, it may be too late, that prosperous farmers and master manufacturers cannot exist without happy journeymen and labourers; and, they will also find, that the measures, which are necessary to preserve their property, are those and those only which will insure to the people at large the enjoyment of all their constitutional rights.

The Wen

P.R. XLV., c. 480. *The Leader of the Blind. To Mr. Canning.* 22-2-23.

LET me, Sir, beg of you just to take a ride out round this WEN. When you come back you will tell me that you see the foundations and part structure of about *three thousand new houses*. I shall then ask you, whence this can arise? You will hardly have the face to tell me, that it is a proof of increasing *national prosperity;* and I have the vanity to think, that, after getting you to sit down, to forget, for a quarter of an hour, all the allurements of Whitehall, and all the botheration of its neighbourhood; I am really of opinion, that I should make you confess, that there is something radically wrong; and that, at last, some dreadful scenes must arise, unless measures of prevention be adopted. In short, it is to suppose a man an idiot, to suppose him not to perceive, that this monstrous WEN is now sucking up the vitals of the country.

And by what means does it suck up those vitals, but by the means of that enormous taxation, which takes away the capital of the farmer, the rent of the landlord, and the wages of the labourer? Having taken a ride round London, you then ought to take a ride round the country; go into the country towns, see the wasting tradesmen and their families; but, above all things, go to the *villages,* and see the misery of the labourers; see their misery, compared to the happy state in which they lived before the swellings out of this corrupt and all-devouring WEN. When I tell you that the villages, the homesteads, the cottages, are growing daily more and more out of repair, you will say it is *not true*; therefore, let that tell for nothing. But you will not deny the wretchedness of the *labourers*! The landlords and the farmers can tell their own tale. They tell their own tale in remonstrances and prayers, addressed to the House. Nobody tells the tale of the labourer. Nobody compares his half belly-full of bread with the living of the fat soldiers, clerks and all the long troop of the dead-weight. Nobody compares his skin and bone with the fat cheeks of the pampered purveyors to the pleasures of the placemen and the pensioners. But, enough has come to your knowledge, for you to be well assured that his situation is a thousand times harder than that of those negroes about whom so much is said in the speech from the throne. How happens it, that he is become so miserable; how happens it that he is ready to prefer transportation for poaching to his present state; how happens it that, upon an average, three quarters of a bushel of wheat is now his weekly pay, instead of the two bushels and a half of wheat, that he formerly received; how does this happen, while this immense number of houses are rising up about London? Can any one but an idiot fail to perceive, that he is robbed of his food, his raiment, his fuel, and that the worth of all these is *transferred,* along with the rent of the landlord and the capital of the farmer, to fatten those who live in these new houses?

The Wen

P.R. XLVII., c. 91. *Bourbon War, And state of France, compared with that of England and Ireland.* 12-7-23.

OUR pretty fellows and their "Collective Wisdom" appear to act upon a precisely opposite principle. They favour the growth of our *Wen* in all sorts of ways. Not content with placing all the *Public Offices* in the Wen; not content with surrounding it with barracks; they build places to imprison the *debtors* and *thieves* of the *country* as well as those of the Wen itself. They swell out the Wen with *hospitals* and *mad-houses*.

They *tax the country at large,* and draw up its wealth for these purposes. The tax-eaters, being encouraged by every means to live in and round the *Wen,* the Government taxes the country at large to *build churches,* rendered necessary by tax-eating piety. Thus is the whole country impoverished for the purpose of favouring this monstrous assemblage. Ours is essentially a stockjobbing government. All its favours are reserved for the crew who deal in money. The French government is a government of the *country.* On our *Wen,* for the purpose, as it would seem, of swelling our *Wen,* more than *ten millions* have been drawn from the country, during a very few years. The "*improvements,*" as they are called, at Westminster, have drawn an immense sum from the country, and have caused thousands of labouring people to be half-starved. In short, this Government seems to have done all that it had power to do, in order to render the catastrophe as dreadful as possible. For, *dispersed* this *Wen* must be, mind, by *some means or other!* This must happen at last. Houses equal to those of ten market-towns cannot be *added yearly* without a dreadful dispersion at last. Of the million and a half of people who are drawn together here, more than a million have *no business here.* They have been drawn here by unnatural causes. They must and they will be *scattered.* A considerable reduction of the interest of the Debt would scatter many of them at once. A sudden blowing up of the Debt would scatter them as a whirlwind scatters a hay-cock.

FIVE

THE ROYAL FAMILY

The Royal Family of England

P.R. XXX., c. 161. *The Royal Family of England.* 8-6-16.

AFTER the account of the Borough-mongers, which I have given in the last number, the reader will naturally have anticipated, that this is a very inferior set of persons in point of real importance. This is called a *"limited monarchy,"* and it really is very *limited* indeed, the person who fills the office of king having no more power of his own than has the bauble put upon his head, or the seat that he sits on. We usually call this branch of authority the *Crown,* or the *Throne,* and with great propriety, for the poor creature who wears the one, and sits on the other, is neither more nor less than a passive tool in the hands of those who own the seats in Parliament, and who, in fact, appoint all the Ministers, Ambassadors, Judges, and Commanders, and who, if they were to meet with a refractory king, or one who, from excessive folly, was troublesome to them, would very soon dispose of him, by shutting him up for life, or by some other contrivance, so as never to be pestered by him again.

Of all the objects which the Borough-mongers would most dread, next after free elections, would certainly be a king of sound understanding, good talents, aptness for business, and really desirous to promote the honour and happiness of the country. And, it must be confessed, that, in this view of the matter, they could hardly have been more fortunate than they are in the Guelphs, not one of whom, since their being pitched upon to fill the throne of England, has ever discovered symptoms of a mind much more than sufficient to qualify the possessor for the post of exciseman.

It appears, at first sight, very strange that England should have for its sovereigns a race of *foreigners,* and that the marriages should be so made up as that no king should, supposing nothing illicit go on, ever have a single drop of English blood in his veins. But, if we consider these apparent sovereigns, as we ought, nothing more than mere puppets in the hands of the Borough-mongers, we shall find a very substantial reason for this seemingly strange taste. It is the interest of this body of men, to have upon the throne a person for whom the people have no regard. The English nation have a rooted hatred, or, at best, contempt, for all foreigners : yet, be they who or what they may, these foreign princes and princesses always surround themselves with Hanoverians, Brunswickers, and other Germans, and care is taken that the race shall never mix with any English race; so that this contempt, on the part of the people, is constantly kept alive.

The language that is made use of in conversation, with regard to this family, would astonish any stranger. All sorts of names, expressions of contempt, are constantly used by all ranks of people towards them.

The " d——d Germans " they are called in a lump by the common people; and when the nobility and gentry reject vulgar epithets and terms, it is only to choose others more severe. This abuse is made use of by *all* parties; by all men in, as well as out of, office. When the war was declared against France, at the rupture of the peace of Amiens, the princes went to the House of Lords to support the address to the Throne. The Duke of Clarence made a speech upon this occasion, and I was standing with a crowd of others below the Bar (as it is called) at the time. The House, which was exceedingly full, were very merry at his expense; and two Peers, who sat close to the bar, at the side of the House on which I stood, indulged themselves in this sort : " What a Jack-ass! " said one : " What a great fool! " said the other : " did you ever hear such a beast? " And, towards the close of the speech, the Royal Duke having declared, that he spoke the sentiments *of his whole family,* a third Peer exclaimed : " *his* family! who the d——l cares about his family! " All this was said loud enough for twenty or thirty persons to hear, who stood or sat nearest to them. Other Peers were smothering a laugh; some affected to be blowing their noses; and the Lord Chancellor, ELDON, sat and looked at the Duke with one of those smiles which contain the double expression of pity and contempt. To be sure the speech was a foolish rant; but, if it came from a Duke of Newcastle or an Earl of Lonsdale, or any other great Borough-monger, it would have been listened to with the greatest attention and apparent respect.

Strangers to the workings of this system wonder how it comes to pass, that we *obey* a family, whom we so abuse. The fact is, we do not obey them; and, the very lowest man in the country knows that we do not. The Borough-mongers, 23 of whom have from 140 to 200 votes, are our real rulers; and, it suits them to have the forms of monarchy, while they possess all the substance of its powers. If the family on the throne were really *English*, the people would have a regard for them, exclusive of the powerful connexions which an English Royal Family would have in the country, in consequence of marriage alliances. Such a family would be a formidable rival of the Borough-mongers; and might, like the Plantagenets, side with the people against those who have usurped their rights. In such a struggle the people might, perhaps, get some share of the power into their hands. Therefore, the Borough-mongers prefer this race of foreigners; and the lower and more paltry its origin, and the more despicable the character and conduct of the individuals belonging to it, the better it suits their purpose.

I have, since I have been acquainted with the real situation of the Royal family, often laughed at the old story about "an *influence behind the throne* greater than the throne itself." This is one of the numerous cheats that have been practised upon the world. *What influence* could there be of any practical consequence? *Charles Jenkinson*, who was afterwards Lord Hawkesbury and Earl of Liverpool, and whose son is Earl of Liverpool now, was looked upon as one of the *influencing* persons. As if this man, who was once a *Page* to the king's father, could have any weight in dictating measures, to which the Borough-mongers had been opposed! as if he and Lord Bute, and three or four other contemptible people, could have supported the king against old Lord Chatham, if the men who had three votes out of every four had not been on the same side?

The rejection of " Catholic Emancipation " was attributed to

the " *conscientious* scruples " of the king; and by others to his
" *obstinacy.*" The poor old man had no more to do with it than
had any one of the little land turtles in the American woods. It
has always been foreseen, that, if the Catholics are " indulged,"
as it is impudently called, any further, they will next demand an
" abolition of tithes," and the Church demesnes would follow of
course. This is property, altogether, worth more annually than
a fourth part of the *rent* of all the Land and Houses in Ireland.
And to whom does this property belong? Why, to the nobility
and a few commoners who own the seats in parliament. Three
fourths of the Church Livings are their own *private* property.
The rest, and the Bishopricks and other Dignities, they, in fact
cause to be filled with their own relations, or by those who serve
them, or whom they choose to have appointed. If, then, we find
them in real possession of a quarter part of the rental of the
kingdom of Ireland, by the means of the existence of a protestant
Church, is it wonderful that they do such abominable acts as they
notoriously do, in order to support the Church? Did it need any
" conscientious scruples " on the part of an unfortunate old man,
who had no interest in the rejection, to prevent the " *emancipation* " taking place? Besides, the Emancipation would have
opened the place of Judge, Chancellor, Attorney, and Solicitor
Generals, Master of the Rolls, Privy Councillor, Field and
General Officer, Captain and Admiral, and of Parliament men,
and Sixty Peers, to *Catholics*. Was it likely, that those who had,
as we have seen in the last number, all these in their own hands,
should call in more persons to share in the rich spoils? Is it usual
for men to act thus? Did Cochrane and Cockburn, when they
had packed up the plunder of Alexandria, call in the crews at
Halifax or Jamaica to partake with them? Ireland is one of the
estates of the Borough-mongers; and do men ever call in other
men to participate in their rents?

Mr. Fox and his party, who brought forward this measure in
1807, stood *pledged,* however, to the Catholics. They had given
the pledge when they were out of place, and, most likely, when
they never expected to get in. But, still, it is surprising that they
should have attempted the fulfilment; knowing, as they did, the
all-ruling power that was naturally opposed to it. The truth is,

they were deceived. Some seat-owners *appeared to acquiesce;* and the ministers, who were, in the *arts* of the trade, not half so deep as their opponents, thought that, if they carried their measure, they should have the Catholic Peers and Commoners with them; and should, thus, acquire permanent strength. The Borough-mongers took the alarm. Lords Eldon, and Hawkesbury, (now Liverpool,) and Perceval, were despatched to the king, who was told that he was about to act "in violation of his *Coronation Oath,*" and that he *must turn out the ministers.*

The Foxites finding themselves undermined, endeavoured to keep their places by *withdrawing the Emancipation Bill* from the Table of the House of Commons, on which it was laid, and in which House it had been read a first time. But, it was now too late. The Borough-mongers could not trust them; and out they were driven. That *the king* was a mere instrument on this occasion is certain; else how came he *to approve of the Bill* before it was introduced? How came he first to do this, and then, all of a sudden, to turn out his ministers for having proposed the measure? Nay, how came he to put them out, even after they had withdrawn the Bill? If I am asked why the Borough-mongers did not *vote* out the Bill and the Ministers. I answer, that that would have been to expose themselves to great odium, especially in Ireland, every impartial man being for the measure. It was, therefore, much better to throw the failure of it upon the "*tender conscience* of the king." And to set up all through England, a tremendous cry of, "God bless the king, and *No Popery,*" which the new minister did, and with such success, that when Mr. ROSCOE offered himself to be re-elected, the people of his own town, where his talents and his virtues were so well known, almost buried him with dirt and stones, amidst shouts of "Down with the *Pope*;" and that, too, as the event has proved, while they were paying loads of taxes to restore the Pope and the Inquisition.

But, if those who really *knew* any thing of the matter could have had any doubt upon this subject in 1807, the events of 1811 and 1812 would have completely removed such doubt; for the king was then shut up; he was put aside; his son was, in fact, put in his place. The king's *conscience,* therefore, was no longer an obstacle. The Prince Regent stood pledged to the Catholics both verbally and in *writing*. Yet he did not attempt to redeem the pledge. Suppose him, if you like, a *faithless* man; but faithless men do not, any more than others, *voluntarily* and gratuitously expose themselves to the hatred and contempt of mankind. At first, he had only *limited powers*. The Borough-mongers actually openly kept a part of the very exterior of royalty in their own hands, lest a man, on whom they could not depend, should be guilty of some thing that would rouse the people against them. But, at the end of a certain time, they enlarged his powers. To this time his old friends and companions looked with eagerness. The Catholics thought, to be sure, that they should *now* get their long-sought emancipation.

All London heard the execrations that were, upon this occasion, poured out upon the Prince. He was called every thing descriptive of baseness and perfidy; when he really had no more power with respect to Catholic Emancipation than I had. He might be perfectly sincere, when he pledged himself to the Catholics; nor is there any good reason to suppose that he was not sincere. As Duke of Cornwall he owns *two seats* in that County. His two Members voted *for* the Emancipation. Even Castlereagh, to make good *his* pledge, was suffered to vote for it, in 1812. But when there appeared so large a majority against it, was it not then become clear, that the *conscience* of the king had been a mere pretext? Could any man, however stupid, still be deluded by so stale a trick? What miserable nonsense is it, then, to talk of " an influence *behind the throne* greater than the throne itself! " Will any body believe, that any *favourites* of the Prince could have persuaded him thus to falsify his word? Why should they? His favourites had been Lord Holland, Mr. Tierney, Mr. Sheridan, and generally, the friends of Catholic Emancipation. He had supposed that some *real power* would come into his hands, when he should be king; but, he soon found his mistake; he found himself to be a mere tool in the hands of the owners of the seats in parliament; namely, about 120 Borough-mongers, who have, at all times, a dead majority; and who, though they very willingly would permit the Prince to do such odious things as the creating of Bate Dudley a Baronet, and are glad to see him disgrace himself and disgust the people by his amours, his excesses, and his squanderings, take special care that he shall do nothing that shall trench upon their real and solid dominion.

Of the real nothingness of the king and the people called *his* ministers there were ample proofs in the history of PITT. It is very well known, that Pitt, who had formed to himself a hope of immortal fame from his financial schemes, went with extreme reluctance into the war with France in 1793. The account of the conversation between him and Mr. MARET, which was published in the Annual Register, from a translation of Mr. MARET's notes, proves, that the minister, who was thought to *rule* in England, was in *great fear,* lest the French Convention should, by their violence, give a handle to the Aristocracy here to force him into the war. His chief *reliance* was upon the *Opposition,* which was then formidable. He hoped that the great seat-owners, who belonged to that Body, and who had so long affected to *follow* Mr. Fox, would *continue firmly united against his ministry;* in which case, he could have resisted the warlike commands of his own masters, that is to say, the Borough-mongers on his side. But, his hopes were disappointed. It has been a thousand times stated, that the *Court Influence* drove him into the war. That the *king* told him " war, or *turn out.*" This was, indeed, the alternative; but, the *source* of the command was different; and, upon this occasion, it was *openly seen to be* so.

A great body of Borough-mongers, who had, until now, been in the opposition, finding that the example of France might produce reform in England, the necessity of which reform, by the by, was most ably urged by men of great talent and weight, resolved to have for minister some man that should go to war with France. They found that Mr. Fox would not; and, after due preparations, over they came to Pitt, who would rather have had the company of Satan himself. Amongst the leaders of the seceders from Mr. Fox were the Duke of Portland, Lord Fitz-william, and Lord Spencer, each of whom having ten times the influence of Pitt himself. BURKE, who had been the trumpeter of the war, and who had been for two years labouring to work people's minds up to it, was a mere tool in the hands of Earl FITZWILLIAM, in one of whose seats he sat. He belied his conscience through the whole of his work; but, he received, not only his seat, but his very *bread,* at the hands of this opulent nobleman, who was bent upon preserving his borough powers and his titles, or, at least, to take the chances of war for that preservation. Earl SPENCER was, at the time of his leaving Mr. Fox, asked by a gentleman, who had long voted with that party, and who was opposed to the war, what were the *motives* that could have induced a man so worthy as his Lordship to join in such an enterprise. " I will be very frank with you," said Lord Spencer, " and save you the trouble of *discovering* my motives. My lot is cast amongst the nobility. It is not my fault that I was thus born, and that I thus inherit. I wish to remain what I am, and to hand my father's titles and estates down to my heirs. I do not know that I thus seek my own gratification at the expense of my country, which has been very great, free, and happy, under this order of things. I am satisfied, that if we do not go to war with the French this order of things will be destroyed. We *may* fall by the war; but we *must* fall without it. The thing is worth fighting for, and to fight for it we are resolved." The *substance* of this has been stated in print by Mr. MILES, in his letter to the Prince of Wales; but, I have here put down the words as I heard them from the gentleman who had the conversation with Lord Spencer, having made, in 1812, a memorandum of them in a few minutes after I had heard them.

When one gets thus behind the curtain, how amusing it is to hear the world disputing and wrangling about the motives, and principles, and opinions of *Burke*! He had no notions, no principles, no opinions of his own when he wrote his famous work, which tended so much to kindle the flames of that bloody war, which, in its ramifications, have reached even to the Canadian Lakes and the Mexican Gulf. He was a poor, needy dependant of a Borough-monger, to serve whom, and please whom, he wrote; and for no other purpose whatever. His defence of " our own Glorious Revolution," under the " deliverer *William,*" and his high eulogium of that king for introducing and ennobling a *Dutch* family or two, seem to be quite unaccountable to most readers, as they are disgusting to all; but, no longer wonder then, when we reflect, that Earl *Fitzwilliam* is the descendant of a natural son of *William the Third;* and that the ancestors of *Bentinck,* Duke of Portland, were Dutchmen, who came to England, and were here ennobled, in the same king's reign. And yet, how many people read this man's writings as if they had flowed from his *own mind;* and who seem to regard even the pension, which Lord Fitzwilliam soon after the change procured for him and for his widow after him, as no more than the proper and natural reward for his great and *disinterested* literary exertions in the cause of " *social order!* "

From this account of the real *cause* of the war of 1793, it is clear how the world, in general, have been deceived as to the *king's* commands upon that occasion. He, I dare say, *wished* for war. It was the cause of *kings* and *electors* as well as of Borough-mongers. But, his mere wishes were unsupported by any power of his own. And, as to PITT, if he had taken his place with Fox on the Opposition benches, he would have found, as he afterwards did, when he opposed his own understrapper, Addington, that out of his majority of four hundred and thirty votes, not more than thirty-seven would have gone over with him.

In 1801 Pitt resigned, because Catholic Emancipation was not permitted to be brought forward. But, when the Borough-mongers, in 1804, found, upon the renewal of the war, that Addington was insufficient for the purpose, they recalled Pitt, who, however, in spite of all his *pledges,* never dared to talk of Catholic Emancipation again, to the day of his death. Upon the occasion of this last change, it is notorious, that the king discovered his reluctance in all possible ways; and when it actually took place, it drove him into one of his fits of insanity. He personally liked Addington, who is a smooth supple creature, though very artful, and can be, when he chooses, very malignant. His father was a mad-doctor, had treated the king with great tenderness, while others used harsh, not to say cruel, remedies. Addington, who had always been an underling, behaved in that humble manner which the king and queen and royal family liked very much; and, besides, he did all their little *jobs* in the way of pensions and places for their personal friends. So that the life they led with him was perfect elysium, compared with what they were obliged to endure from the neglect and insolence of Pitt, who was domineering towards every living creature, the Borough-mongers excepted. But, the war was again begun. Addington was thought by the seat-owners unfit for their purpose; both sides of the House joined to put him out; and, a very little after he had left Pitt in a minority of thirty-seven, Pitt saw him (the Members being all the same persons) in a minority of about the same number! Where was *now* that " *influence behind* the throne greater than the throne itself?" What was become of it upon this memorable occasion? The truth was, that Pitt was thought, by those who had the real power in their hands, the fittest man to carry on the complicated machine; and, no sooner had they made up their minds, than they put out the poor thing who had filled his place for a couple of years, *keeping in almost all the rest of the ministry.*

Is it possible for any thing to show, more clearly than these facts do, the *nothingness* of the Royal Family and the Ministers, if considered in any other light than that of puppets and tools? When the present cabinet was formed, the Earl of Lonsdale, who owns *nine* seats, had made it a point that Lord *Mulgrave* should be Master General of the Ordnance. It being found difficult to comply with this request without clashing in another quarter, the Earl of Lonsdale was informed, that His Royal Highness the Prince Regent had *been graciously pleased to make an arrangement* by which Lord Mulgrave would have a very lucrative post *out* of the cabinet, sensible men, most likely, not wishing to have such an empty coxcomical gabbler *in* the cabinet. Upon seeing this information by letter, at one of his country seats, it is said that Lord Lonsdale exclaimed : " *His Royal Highness* has been *pleased,* has he! Bring me my *boots* !" Whether this be true or not, it is very certain that he undid the arrangement, and that he put Lord Mulgrave into the Ordnance and the Cabinet. In fact, it is notorious, that the Prince has no power at all of any public consequence; that he cannot procure the appointment to any office of considerable trust or emolument; that it is not *he* that chooses Ministers, Ambassadors, Judges,

Commanders, or Governors; that it is not *he* who grants pensions, or bestows sinecures; that it is not *he* who gives to the Dean and Chapters *leave* to elect Bishops any more than it is the " Holy Ghost " that inspires the said Deans and Chapters upon the occasions when these at once impious and farcical scenes are exhibited. Of all the *elections,* that ever the world hear of, *these* are the most curious.

When a Bishop dies, another must be put in his place. The Bishop is elected by the Dean and Prebends of the Cathedral Church of the Diocess. The king, who is called the *head* of the Church, sends these gentlemen, who are called the Dean and Chapter, a *congé d'élire,* or a *leave to elect;* but he sends them, at the same time, the *name of the man,* whom, and whom only, they are to elect. With this name in their possession, away they go into the Cathedral, chant psalms and anthems, and then, in a set form of words, *invoke the Holy Ghost to assist them in their choice.* After these invocations, they, by a series of good luck wholly without parallel, always find that the dictates of the Holy Ghost agree with the *recommendation* of the king. And, now, if any man can, in the annals of the whole world, find me a match for this mockery, let him produce it. But even this shockingly impious farce loses part of its qualities, unless we bear in mind, that it is not the *king,* but some Borough-monger, in virtue of some bargain for votes, who has really nominated the Bishop; and, that the King, the Minister, the Dean and Chapter, and the Holy Ghost proceeding, are neither more nor less than so many tools in the hands of the said Borough-monger. Good and pious people wondered amazingly that the Holy Ghost, or even the king, should have pitched upon the present gentleman to fill the Archbishop's Chair of Canterbury; but, these good and pious Church people did not know, that the Duke of *Rutland* had, as he still has, *seven* or *eight* votes of his own in the two Houses, besides, perhaps, twenty more that he could, upon a hard pinch, make shift to borrow.

It makes me, and hundreds besides me, laugh to read, in American and French publications, remarks on the men engaged in carrying on this curious government of ours. We laugh at the idea of the *influence of the Crown;* of the *party of Pitt;* of the *party of Fox;* of the intrigues of this Minister, of the *power-ful eloquence* of that Minister; of those great men, the Wellesleys, and Liverpools, and Castlereaghs, and Cannings, on the one side; and the Tierneys, and Horners, and Broughams, and God knows who, on the other side; and the Thorntons, and Wilberforces, and Banks's, and Romillys, and the rest of that canting crew in the middle. We know them all; yea, *one and all,* to be the mere tools of the Borough-mongers; and, that, as to the *deciding of any question,* affecting the honour, liberty, or happiness of the country, the Duke of Newcastle, who was, only a few years ago, a baby in his cradle, had, even while he was living upon pap, more power than this whole rabble of great senators all put together; and, I dare say, now that he is grown up to be a young man, he pays much more attention to the voice of his fox-hounds than to the harangues of these bawlers, and that he has more respect for the persons and motives of the former than for those of the latter. One thing I can state as a certainty; and that is, that, if I were in his place, I should flee to the dog-kennel as a relief from that filthy den, the House of Commons.

" *The king's friends* " is an expression frequently used. Poor man! He has no friends, unless it be in his own family, and amongst his and their menial servants, the greater part of whom are Hanoverians and Brunswickers. The common people do not *hate* the Royal Family; they despise them too much to hate them. They listen greedily to all the dirty stories about the Queen and her Daughters, of which I have, for my part, never heard any thing bordering upon the nature of *proof.* Every body speaks ill of all the sons; they *blackguard* them in all manner of ways. In *print,* indeed, the Attorney General takes care that a little decorum should be observed; but, even he suffers the assailants to go pretty good lengths. The story at this moment (10th Feb.) is, that the Prince Regent is *mad.* In vain is there no *proof* of this; in vain do the physicians report, that his ailment is merely the *gout.* People will not believe this. They laugh at you if you affect to believe it. The life that the Prince has led may be easily guessed at from the following fact, for the truth of which I refer to publications in London notorious to every body. One Walter, now dead, the proprietor of a newspaper called the *Times*, which is now carried on by his son, published, during the first agitation of the Regency question, previous to the French war, some outrageously gross libels, very *false* as well as foul, against the Duke of York and the Prince of Wales. Walter, who was a very base and infamous fellow, was prosecuted by the Attorney General, sentenced to be imprisoned two years for each libel, and to pay a fine for each. The *Treasury* itself (Pitt at the head of it) were the *authors* of the libels. Walter threatened *to give up the authors*. The Treasury gave him a sum of money to keep silence; and, after he had suffered the two years imprisonment for the libel on the *Duke*, the Prince obtained the scoundrel's pardon for the libel on himself, which WALTER repaid by every species of malevolence towards the Prince to the day of his death, the Prince's enemies being better able to *pay* the ruffian than he was!

Now, let any one suppose what the situation of this family must be, when the Treasury itself could unite, and cause to be published, infamous libels against two of the King's sons! And the truth is, that the whole family, the Prince Regent not excepted, are compelled to subsidize the newspapers, in order to blunt or repel, the shafts aimed, or launched forth, against them. If any one could paint this part of our press in its true colours, it would shock every man of common justice. The fears of the whole family are constantly kept alive. They know very well what is said about them. However false the story, they dare not attempt to contradict it; for the bare attempt alone would be produced as *proof* of their guilt. The sons and daughters cannot marry without *leave of the Borough-mongers*, as was recently shown in the case of the Duke of Cumberland. He *did*, indeed, marry, and by his brother's consent, which was precisely what the *law* required; but, because the Prince had not asked *their* leave, they would not give him a farthing of *money*, though such grants have always been customary in like cases. And, what is more, they prevented the Queen from receiving his wife at court. It is true, that very bad whispers had been long afloat about the Duke, and I do not say, because I do not know, that they were without foundation; but, I believe, his great sin, a sin for which most certainly there is no forgiveness for him in this world, was his very foolish attempt to uphold Addington against the Borough-mongers, and which attempt, nevertheless did not succeed for one single day. With what truth the story is told of the poor old king's expressing his resolution, upon one occasion, to *go off to Hanover,* I do not know; but really one can easily believe, that a man would go almost any where, and live almost any how, or with almost any body, to get out of such a state of mock-majesty and of real slavery.

The "Royal Dukes," as they are called, in order to gain a little popular favour, run about to Bible Societies, Lancaster schools, sometimes to societies for assisting *lying-in women,* and to the most popular Methodist Meeting Houses, when any Thundering Preacher holds forth on a popular occasion. Their names are in all great subscription Lists; and they make speeches on many of these occasions; and always give away some of their money. All this exposes them to ridicule. The Borough-mongers never expose themselves in this way. They are at their great country seats with their packs of hounds and troops of hunters, and with their good cheer for their numerous guests. Not a single country seat has the Royal Family; not an acre of land; not a pack of hounds, except the Stag-hounds kept up *for the use of the old king*! The kings of England had, formerly, *immense landed estates.* They lived upon these estates. They wanted no *public money,* except for purposes of war, and sometimes they carried on war out of their own purses.

The Borough-mongers took all these estates away from the Guelphs, in the early part of this king's reign; they have divided the greater part of them amongst themselves, and settled a pension, or, what they call a *Civil List,* on the king in lieu of them, thus exposing him and his family to all the odium that the annual exhibition of a great *charge upon the public* naturally excites and keeps alive.

After this view of the situation of this family how we must laugh at De Lolmes' pretty account of the *English Constitution.* After seeing that about three or four hundred Borough-mongers actually possess all the legislative power, divide the ecclesiastical, judicial, military, and naval departments amongst their own dependants, what a fine picture we find of that wise system of *checks* and *balances,* of which so much has been said by so many great writers! What name to give such a government it is difficult to say. It is like nothing that ever was heard of before. It is neither a monarchy, an aristocracy, nor a democracy; it is a band of great nobles, who, by sham elections, and by the means of all sorts of bribery and corruption, have obtained an absolute sway in the country, having under them, for the purposes of *show* and of execution, a thing they call a *king,* sharp and unprincipled fellows whom they call *Ministers,* a mummery which they call a *Church,* experienced and well-tried and steel-hearted men whom they call *Judges,* a company of false money makers, whom they call a *Bank,* numerous bands of brave and needy persons whom they call *soldiers and sailors;* and a talking, corrupt, and impudent set, whom they call a *House of Commons.* Such is the government of England; such is the thing, which has been able to bribe one half of Europe to oppress the other half; such is the famous "Bulwark of *religion* and *social order,"* which is now about, as will be soon seen, to surround itself with a *permanent standing army* of, at least, a hundred thousand men, and very wisely, for, without such an army, the Bulwark would not exist a month.

SIX

THE FRENCH REVOLUTION AND THE NAPOLEONIC WARS

Letter to Windham

P.R. X., c. 844. *Letter to the Rt. Hon. William Windham*—29-11-06.

ONE of the worst features in the aspect of our affairs is, that we have *no plan,* whether for domestic or foreign operations. Every one sees the danger; every one agrees that something great must be done; but no one, that I hear of, attempts to tell us *what.* In my view of the matter a great change is necessary in our financial and fiscal affairs; for, after all, it is *here* that the feeling of the people is most alive; and, I imagine, it will not now be contended, that it is even *possible* to defend a country, where the people are indifferent as to its fate. Never could the French in so few days, have arrived at Berlin, if the people's hearts had been made of the right sort of stuff. A province, or a kingdom may be invaded and over-run, indeed, in certain cases, though the whole of the people may be bent upon resistance; but, for an enemy to advance with post horse celerity, driving over regularly constituted armies as if it were over so many flint stones, and to take possession of cities and fortresses with as little difficulty as if they were sheepfolds, argues a total rottenness in the conquered state; a rottenness, from the fatal effects of which God preserve our country!

Napoleon's Conquests

P.R. XIII., c. 65. *Summary of Politics*: 16-1-08.

THIS state of things is described in very few words : Napoleon has conquered the continent of Europe. The three states, Russia, Austria, and Prussia, who retain their former names and sovereigns, and who are not actually governed by his generals and his troops, are, nevertheless, not independent; but are, and must be, compelled to do whatsoever it may please him to command them to do, and, of course, to injure, as far as they have the power of injuring, this country; while all the maritime states, from the Baltic to the Hellespont, are under his absolute and immediate controul; England alone, (for the fate of Sweden is hardly known) of all Europe, remaining truly independent of his power.—Such is the state of things; and, in order to form a judgment as to what ought to be our terms of peace, if now made, we must first consider, what are the probable views of Napoleon respecting us. He has conquered all Europe, England excepted; and, it is in the nature of ambition, never to rest, until it can go no further. The nearer, too, that it approaches its utmost limits, the more eager it becomes. Thus have we constantly seen it, in the case before us. Long ago was Napoleon so firmly seated, his power so decidedly greater than that of any other prince in Europe, that, if security and superiority would have satisfied him, perfectly satisfied he must have been. But, we have seen, that his eagerness for conquest has increased with his success; and we now see him grasping, in every direction, to add to that power, which seems almost incapable of receiving an addition. Upon what ground, then, can any man pretend to hope, that he does not wish to conquer England; and that he has not resolved upon the conquest? England, without the conquest of whom many of his other conquests are insecure; England, whose example, if left independent, might and would, be so troublesome to him; England, of whom, for so many reasons, he bears a deadly hatred; England, who has, in all times, been the rival of France; England, between whom and France, it is now, in the presence of all nations, a contest, which shall hereafter be looked upon as the first nation in the world? Upon what ground, then, I ask, is it, that any one can pretend to hope, that he does not seriously meditate the conquest of England: and that, while he lives, there is any thing but an exertion of our power that will give us a chance of escaping the fate of Holland and Portugal?

Deliverance of Europe

P.R. XIX., c. 1354.   *Deliverance of Europe.*   1-6-11.

IN the year 1792, and from that year to the year 1800, or there-abouts, the *Deliverance of Europe* aimed principally at the Jacobins; enemies to *Social Order* and *Regular Government*, to the *Altar* and the *Throne*. These were the catch-words for many years. The Loyalty Loan and the Voluntary Contributions and the Habeas Corpus Suspension and many other memorable things took place while these words were in vogue. Well, what have we now to find fault of, then? There is Social Order and Regular Government in plenty in France at this time; and as to the Altar and the Throne, we hear of nothing else but their Imperial Majesties, the King of Rome and of Bishops and Masses. Here is Altar and Throne and enough of them if we wanted Altar and Throne. What, then, displeases us now? Will nothing suit us? Will neither *republicans* nor *emperors* do for us?—Ah! we may *pretend* what we will, but nothing that we can say, or that we can now do, will deceive the people of France or of any of the countries of Europe. They all saw us at the very head of the league against the people of France, long before Buonaparté was heard of; and, they are not now to be persuaded, that we hate Buonaparté merely because he oppresses, or is said to oppress, the people of France, or any other people. No : they will never believe, that those who approved of the Duke of Brunswick's Proclamations, are hostile to Napoleon on account of his hostility to freedom. The PITT CLUB may, therefore, another time, keep their breath to cool their porridge, as far as relates to the *Deliverance of Europe*. Not only did the people of France and of Europe see England at the head of a league against the French before the name of Napoleon was known to us; but they saw us, after he became known, and after he became chief of the nation, make peace with him, make a treaty of *friendship* with him, and heard us say, that we liked *him better than we did the republican government*. After this the people of France and of Europe are not such brutes as to believe, that our hatred of Napoleon arises in any degree, from his being an oppressor of the people.

Invasion

P.R. XX.,, c. 435. *Invasion.* 5-10-11.

THIS, in all probability, will soon become a copious subject. In another part of this Number the reader will find some documents relating to a threatened, or talked of, or surmised intended invasion of *Jersey* and *Guernsey*. I have no time to make any remark upon these at present, and shall content myself with a decided expression of my opinion, that, *if we have a timely reform of the Commons' House of Parliament,* we may *laugh* at all Napoleon's threats of invasion; but, *if we have not that reform* . . . what then? Why, then we may LAUGH AT THEM TOO!

The Last Ten Years

P.R. XXI., c. 1. *The Last Ten Years.* 4-1-12.

THIS day ten years ago (the 1st of January) I sat down to write the first number of the Register. When I look back to that time, and consider how the country then stood, what a contrast presents itself to my mind! The preliminaries of peace had just then been concluded; the price of provisions had just then been lowered; the people were on tiptoe for commerce and manufactures; every print-shop window presented something demonstrative of friendship with Buonaparté, and the Attorney General, (now the prime minister) stood ready to prosecute, by information ex-officio, any one who dared to write what was called a libel upon that new friend of England.—Now, what is the picture? A war with that same Buonaparté, for the possession of the island of Malta, has led to the overthrow of every state formerly in alliance with us. A war for the island of Malta has put into the hands of that same Buonaparté the whole of Italy from the confines of France down to the shores of Calabria. It has united the Seven United Provinces to France. It has raised a new kingdom in the heart of Germany under a brother of Napoleon, in which kingdom are included the ancient dominions of the House of Brunswick. It has driven from their thrones the sovereigns of Spain and Portugal, and has gone pretty far towards putting those countries also into the hands of

Buonaparté. It has made a naval arsenal at Antwerp, whence have already issued many ships of the line. It has paved the way for France becoming a great naval power. It has added five hundred millions to the national Debt of England. It has banished gold from circulation. It has ruined commerce and manufactures in England. It has, in this respect, produced a new order of things both in Europe and America, both of which can now dispense with English goods.—What inroads have been made upon English liberty during this period, I shall not, and need not, attempt to describe; and, as to the weight of taxes, who need be told of that?—Our state is now such as it never was before; and, that man must be blind indeed, who does not see that it is daily becoming more and more perilous.—Ask any man, be he of what party he may, what he thinks of the present state of things, and you will find, that he expects, that a *great change,* of some sort or other, will take place ere long. He cannot tell what it will be; he cannot even guess; he is full of fears, and that is all. The very hirelings of the press, whose trade it is to buoy up the spirits of the people, have no longer any plausible grounds of hope to hold out. They have uttered false-hoods so long, they have played off so many tricks, that their budget seems, at last, to be quite empty.—What will the state of the country be, then, at *the end of the next* ten years? What shall I have to record, before I come to the end of the *next twenty volumes* of this work?—I will hazard no speculation; nor, indeed, is it in the power of any man to form any idea of what is likely to happen. But, I think, one may venture to say, that the conduct of this government will not change; that, let which party will be in power, the system will, as long as it can, go on: and that it will continue to produce effects similar to those which it has already produced. How long the system will last no man can tell; but we may, by observing what it has done in *the last ten years*, judge of what it will do in each succeeding year; and, if we suppose its existence for another ten, we may form some idea of what our state will then be.—At any rate, come what will, the people will not have to blame the " *Jacobins* and *Levellers.*" They were against the war, which has produced all the evil effects we witness. They were for letting the French republicans alone. They have had no hand in any of the measures that have been pursued; they have had no power, and are liable to no responsibility and no blame. They have been an object of incessant attack and abuse. The next ten years will shew whether they have merited this, or any part of it. If the country shall be preserved by the present system; if it shall find itself secure from without and happy within at the end of the next ten years, why, then, I shall be ready to allow, that the " Jacobins and Levellers " have been in error; but, if the contrary should prove to be the case, surely we shall then hear them acquitted; surely we shall no longer see them the object of attack and abuse.—It is the common practice of men, to judge from *experience*. If a farmer finds that the managing of his land in a certain way produces loss instead of gain, he loses no time in changing his course; and so it is with all other men who act according to the dictates of reason. But, it would really seem, that governments act upon no such principle; that they are wholly deaf to the voice of experience; that they either do not see, or that they heed not, the consequences of their measures. Were not this the case, how could it possibly be, that no change should have taken place in the measures of any of the old governments that we have seen annihilated? In no instance have we seen them attempt to make any change; nay, they seem to have grown more and more attached to their several systems in proportion as the evil consequences of them became manifest to all the world. It can be accounted for only in this way : that the persons in the enjoyment of power and of the emoluments belonging to power have thought, that they would lose both by a *reformation* as effectually as by a *destruction* of the government; and, therefore, that, as they could lose no more by the latter than by the former, they have, in every case, endeavoured to uphold corruptions and abuses to the last possible moment, though they clearly saw the destructive consequences that must finally ensue. Destruction being, *to them*, the same thing as reformation in its effects, they have preferred the former to the latter, because the latter must, of course, be *earlier* in its operation. To tell a man in the enjoyment of the fruits of such a system, that the government would be finally destroyed unless it was speedily reformed, was not likely to weigh with him in favour of reformation; because he saw, at the same time, that, *to him,* reformation of the government was, in fact, destruction; and, therefore, the later it came the less grievous it was to him.

Here we have the real cause of what has been called the *blindness* of the old governments, but which was nothing more than the natural desire of those, who lived by corruptions and abuses, to live as long as they could.—We here see, also, the cause of that *persecution of opinions,* which has invariably increased as the old governments felt their danger increase. Those, who enjoyed the wealth sucked from the veins of the people, by the means of corruptions and abuses, would naturally make use of their *power* to prevent the propagation of opinions tending to undermine and destroy those abuses; and, as the danger of destruction became more imminent, the endeavours to prevent it would, of course, become more active. The persecution has, therefore, in all these cases, been the effect of fear; and, it is well known, that cruelty is never so great as when it has such a foundation. Look at the murders that are committed, and you will find nine-tenths of them arising from the same cause. It is the fear of detection that draws the murderer's knife and steels his heart. The tyrants of Africa are bloody from fear : they kill others, lest those others should kill them. The persecutions of the propagation of opinions, which we have witnessed in the old governments now no more, have proceeded from the same cause as the horrible murders at Marr's and Williamson's : the *fear of exposure,* and the consequent infamy and punishment.—When men have expressed their surprize at seeing those old governments grow more and more tyrannical and cruel in proportion as their situation became perilous; when they have exclaimed : " how blind! how mad! thus to excite additional hatred against themselves *at such a time,* when they ought to see that they stand so much in need of the good will of the people! " When men have thus exclaimed, they have not duly considered the *motive* of those governments; if they had, they would have felt no surprize.

Dethronement of Napoleon

P.R. XXV., c. 481.   *Dethronement of Napoleon.*   16-4-14.

"IT is ended," says the COURIER newspaper. "*The Drama is closed,*" says the CHRONICLE; "Mine eyes have seen thy salvation," says the half-canting and half-blasphemous TIMES.—Indeed, the grand contest is now come to an end, and we shall have leisure to look back and to contrast our situation at the commencement of it, with what it is now.—At present, I shall confine myself to some few observations (for thousands offer themselves) upon the *causes* and the *effects* of the dethronement of Napoleon.—The *immediate* causes of this event were, evidently, the loss of his army in Russia, the subsequent abandonment of him, in the midst of battle, by his German Allies, and the overwhelming force of the combined armies. But, the more distant cause, and the only cause, was his *vanity;* that vanity, which led him to seek family alliances with the ancient sovereigns of Europe. He lost the hearts of all the best men of France; that is to say, of the enlightened friends of freedom, by abolishing the Republic, by assuming the title of Emperor, and by acting the despot; but, he lost his crown by his vanity; and, by a species of vanity, too, the most contemptible of all.—He must needs be, not only a *Royal* personage, but he must be related to the *old* Royal race; he must marry amongst them; and, which was most abominable, after all that the people of France had done to get rid of the family influence of the House of Austria, he must needs bring a daughter of that house and must bring the niece of that same Marie Antoinette, whom the French people, in the excess of their resentment against her, had dragged to the scaffold.—This was an unpardonable offence in the eyes of the friends of freedom; and would have been atoned for by nothing short of his employing his power to the general benefit of mankind. But, to himself, the consequence of this vanity of his has been ruin. For, if he had been possessed with no such vanity; if he had even been resolved to be an *Emperor,* or a *King,* without this alliance, he would, as he was able, have *destroyed all the old dynasties;* ALL the sovereigns of Europe would have been of his creation; their right to reign would, everywhere, have rested upon the same basis; and, of course, whatever *wars* might have arisen amongst them, the *dethronement* of no one would have been in contemplation. If he had, when he had it in his power, furnished Austria and Prussia with kings, he would not now have lived to accept of his life at the hands of the sovereigns of these countries. But, this would not have suited the purposes of his vanity; his contemptible vanity, which urged him on to seek family alliances with the old Royal race. He spared the father in order to obtain the daughter: He supported the old Royal race, because he wanted to secure a dynasty of his own: He made common cause, in fact, with the old Royal race, as towards the people, hoping thereby to have their aid and countenance in support of his title and that of his descendants: He joined the old Royal race, in the hope of their being reconciled to his power; he discouraged and forbade every act in France tending to expose to hatred or contempt, any of the old Royal race in any country of Europe; and, as in the instance of FONTANES's speech, he sought to curry favour with sovereigns in general, by speaking contemptuously of the *people*. For *these things* he deserves his fate, and a fate a great deal worse than that which appears to have befallen him. *These* are his sins in my eyes. He had the power of doing great good; he had the power to give freedom to all Europe; he did much good to France; he established, or rather, he did not destroy, the good laws which the Republicans had made; he did not bring back and replant the curses, which the Republicans had rooted out: France, under him, was much happier than France was before the revolution. But, the lovers of freedom put great means into his hands; he had a mind calculated to give effect to those means; he did, for a while, employ them well; but, being seized with the vanity of being a king, and with that most abominable itch of being a *papa* and leaving a son, descended from a mother of the old Royal race, he, from that moment, wholly abandoned the good cause, and laid the foundation of what has now come to pass.

Jacobin Principles

P.R. XXVII., c. 518. *To the Merchants of England, on the projected war against France, and on the subject of Parliamentary Reform.* 29-4-15.

IT has long been a fashion amongst you, which you have had the complaisance to adopt at the instigation of a corrupt press, to call every friend of reform, every friend of freedom, a *Jacobin,* and to accuse him of *French principles.* For my part, though I wish the French people great prosperity and happiness, and wish to see them receive all the praise due to their matchless deeds in arms and to their progress in the sciences and arts, I am Englishman enough to deny them any share in the honour of having a claim to the Principles, to which I allude, and which you so incessantly censure. What are these principles?—That governments were made for the people, and not the people for governments.—That sovereigns reign legally only by virtue of the people's choice.—That birth without merit ought not to command merit without birth.—That all men ought to be equal in the eye of the law.—That no man ought to be taxed or punished by any law to which he has not given his assent by himself or by his representative.—That taxation and representation ought to go hand in hand.—That every man ought to be judged by his peers, or equals.—That the press ought to be free.

Now, I should be glad to know, how these came to be *French* principles. It is sometimes said, that the French learnt them, or, as the expression is, *"imbibed"* them in *America.* The Americans, to be sure, have most wisely and virtuously acted upon these principles; but, the principles are the *growth of England.* Ten thousand times as much has been written on the subject in England as in all the rest of the world put together. Our books are full of these principles. You can read nothing: law, history, poetry, divinity, romance; nothing, without meeting with these principles. There is not a single political principle which you denominate *French,* which has not been sanctioned by the struggles of ten generations of Englishmen, the names of many of whom you repeat with veneration, because, apparently, you forget the grounds of their fame. To Tooke, Burdett, Cartwright, and a whole host of patriots of England, Scotland and

Ireland, imprisoned or banished, during the administration of Pitt, you can give the name of Jacobins, and accuse them of French principles. Yet, not one principle have they ever attempted to maintain that Hampden and Sydney did not seal with their blood.

"The Play is Over"

P.R. XXVIII., c. 97. *Letter VIII. To Lord Castlereagh. Surrender of Napoleon.* 29-7-15.

MY Lord—At last, then, you have Napoleon in your power. That is to say, you have a composition of bones, skin, flesh and blood, warmed and kept alive by the vital principle; but this is all; and, whether this vital principle be now to be speedily extinguished, or the whole body be to remain a few years longer above ground, you have not the power, and you never will have the power, either to efface the memory of his deeds, or to destroy, or even to lessen, the effects of those deeds. A man is no more to be blamed for yielding to force, such as that which has come against Napoleon, than he is to be blamed for yielding to a thunderbolt or a hurricane. You are, by some of our journalists, recommended to surrender Napoleon to Louis. By others, to imprison him for life. Do what you will, in this way; if you were to thumb-screw him, flog him, and, at last, cut him to mince-meat, you could do away not one jot of his military renown; his battles, his victories, his conquests, his mastership of all the old families of the continent, are recorded in a way never to be forgotten; they form a portion of the knowledge of mankind; they occupy a seat in all men's minds; and, as to his *fall*, why, we all fall at last; only the far greater part of us fall with little more noise than is occasioned by the fall of a bullock, whereas his fall is the subject of conversation amongst, and excites *strong feeling* of some sort or other in the breasts of *all the people of the civilized world*. If the fame of all the other famous men that ever lived could be embodied into one mass, it would not equal his individual fame. He has excited more hatred, and more love, than all the other great men that have figured on the stage of the world. The Prussians, with " *the* HONEST *old*

Marshal," as our newspapers call him, at their head, may blow up the *bridge of Jena;* the Austrians may pull down the *column of Austerlitz;* and so on; but, they will do nothing to efface the memory of his valiant deeds, unless they can take out the *brains* of every human creature in the world; for all have heard of these deeds; all have felt their effects.

The baseness of those writers, who have the impudence to recommend you to treat Napoleon as a *criminal,* deserves some notice. They say, but they speak without authority indeed, that he is to be *imprisoned for life.* And, under *what law,* I should be glad to know? If brought hither, or, if remaining in our ships, he can be considered only in the light of a *prisoner of war.* I defy any man to shew that he can be considered in any other light : and, therefore, to treat him other than as a *prisoner of war* would be an act of injustice.

However, there may be opportunities to discuss this point hereafter. At present I have to speak to your Lordship upon the subject of the expectations, excited here by this event. The COURIER says : " *The play is over; let us go to supper.*" And this is the general opinion. When men have long been intent upon one single object; when they have long bent their minds to one sole wish, they are always disappointed in their expectations, because they have not given themselves time to think of the consequences to be produced by the means which they make use of to obtain the accomplishment of that wish. Thus will it be with *John Bull,* who has been made to believe, that, if Napoleon could but be gotten rid of, England would be freed from all the calamities which she feels; that she would once more come back to her former state; and that the visits of the taxing people would cease to be as frequent as those of the apothecary. Napoleon is actually our prisoner, but still the taxing people come.

" *The play*" may be over; but, oh! no! we cannot " *go to supper.*" We have something to do. We have *forty-five millions a year for ever to pay for the play.* This is no pleasant thing. But, indeed, the play is *not* over. The *first act* is, perhaps, closed. But, that grand revolution, that bright star, which first burst forth in the year 1789, is still sending forth its light over the world. In that year, feudal and ecclesiastical tyranny, ignorance, superstition, received the first heavy blow; they have since received others; and in spite of all that can be now done in their favour, they are destined to perish.

This 22 years of war, has it been *to put down one man?* Have we sent hundreds of thousands to shed their blood, and have we loaded ourselves with endless burdens, to put down *one little Frenchman?* Have we all been paying the greater part of our incomes, for many years, for *this purpose?* No: we are *now beginning to be told,* it was not for this; it was for the purpose of putting down *French principles.* And, what were they? Why, those very principles, which are at this moment more firmly than ever rooted in the minds of Frenchmen, and more generally imbibed throughout Europe. The bridge of Jena, the column of Austerlitz, all the memorials of French triumph, brought from Amsterdam, Naples, Vienna, Rome, Turin, Madrid, Munich, Berlin, Moscow, and dearest *Hanover:* all these may be destroyed; but, never will the whole world, combined in arms, be able to destroy the effects of those principles which sent the conquerors forth, which first warmed their hearts with enthusiasm, and which are now become part of the settled possessions of their minds.

Dialogue on the American War

P.R. XXVI., c. 681. *LETTER I. To the Earl of Liverpool, on the American War.* 24-11-14.

MRS. FRIEND. Well, Mr. Cobbett, we shall soon get rid of the Income Tax (for so it is always called in the country) *now.*

Mr. Cobbett. Shall we, Madam? I am very glad to hear it. It will enable me to get a better horse for my gig.—(*She had just been laughing at my scurvy equipage.*)—But, why *now,* Madam? What has happened to excite such a cheering hope?

Mrs. Friend. Why, have you not heard the *news?*

Mr. Cobbett. No.

Mr. Friend. We have taken the *Capital* of America.

Mrs. Friend. And the cowardly dogs, to the amount of 9,000, ran away before 1,500 of our soldiers.

Mr. Friend. President and all ran away! Nobody knows where they went to, and the people were ready to submit to us all over the country.

Mrs. Friend. Cowardly dogs! Not stand to fight a moment for their Capital. They are a pretty nation to go to war with England!

Mr. Friend. They ran away like a great flock of South Down sheep before a pack of hounds.

Mrs. Friend. The cowardly creatures will never dare shew their faces again. What can you say for these Americans *now*?

Mr. Cobbett. Why, I say, that you appear to know no more about them than about the people said to be in the moon. Let me look at the paper. (*It lay before her on the table.*)

Mrs. Friend. No: we must tell it you. It is too long for you to sit and read to yourself.

Mr. Cobbett. Well; now, mind, I tell you, that, instead of putting *an end* to the war, this event will tend to prolong it; and, mind, I tell you, that, unless we *give up* what we contend for, the war will be of many years' duration, and will be as expensive and more bloody than the war in Europe has been.

Mrs. Friend. WE *give up* to such cowards as the Americans!

Mr. Cobbett. I do not mean to give up either *territory* or *honour*. I mean give up the point in dispute; or, rather, our *present apparent object*. The Americans, like other people, cannot meet disciplined armies, until they have had time to organise and discipline themselves. But, the Americans are not *cowards,* Madam. Their seamen have proved that; and, what I fear is, that a continuation of the war will make the proof clearer and clearer every day, by land as well as by sea; and, I am *now* more than ever afraid of a long continuation of the war; because, if such people as *you* seriously think that we are able to conquer America, I can have no reason to hope that any part of the nation remains undeceived.

Mr. Friend. But, do you think that the *States will divide*?

Mr. Cobbett. Certainly not.

Mr. Friend. No!

Mr. Cobbett. No. And, I should be glad to know what are your *reasons* for believing that they will divide. If you will give me any *reasons* for your belief, I will give you mine for a contrary belief. Do *you* think, Madam, that the people of America are weary of living for thirty years without an Income Tax?

Mr. Friend. I have no reasons of my own about the matter. We see, in all our *papers,* that the Americans are a very divided people. They say that they cannot long hold together.

Mr. Cobbett. And do you really believe what these corrupted vagabonds put into their columns? You believe, then, of course, that "the American navy would be swept from the face of the ocean in a month;" for so they told you. Yet, how different has been the event! No, no: the Americans are not *cowards,* Madam.

Mrs. Friend. Have you had such heaps of melons this year as you used to have?

French Revolution of 1830

T.T., p. 49. *To the Working People of England and Scotland.* 1-9-30.

NEVER since the world existed was there, to man in civil life, a time more important and critical than this; and never was it so manifest, that the condition of mankind depends wholly on their own conduct, and especially on that of the *working people*. It is, therefore, of the greatest importance that you be perfectly well informed of the causes which have produced the recent glorious event at Paris. The great deed was there performed by the working people; and by the working people here, must finally be produced those salutary effects which every good man wishes to see produced. There are some men who happen to be so fortunate as to be able to keep their bones from labour, who consider the working people merely as being made to toil for others. Others, again, who have their motives, doubtless, choose to assert, that the working people of England are poor things compared to those in France. My friends, your conduct, when you have had a fair opportunity, has always given the lie to this assertion; and, I am sure, it will always give it the lie.

SEVEN

THE STATE OF THE LABOURERS

Appeal to the New Ministry

P.R. IX., c. 133. *Summary of Politics. New Ministry.* 8-2-06.

WE must, too, remember the state of the *poor*. Upwards of *six millions* a year are now raised upon the parishes to be dealt out in aid of those means by which the labourer obtains his bread; and of persons receiving this aid there are upwards of a million. *All,* all, the labourers, having families, are now *paupers*! This is a new state of things; a state of things which has been produced by the funding and taxing system, pushed to an extreme. Let us not be answered, by the observations, that there must be poor, that there always have been and that there always will be, in every state of society in every country in the world. We know there must be poor; we know that some must be very poor; we know that some must be maintained, or assisted, at least, either by the parish or by voluntary alms; but, is there any one who will deny, that this is a new and most deplorable state of things, which has rendered all the labourers, having families, paupers? The plain fact is, that a man with a wife, and with four children that are unable to work, cannot now, out of his labour, possibly provide them and himself with the means of living. I do not mean, that he cannot live *comfortably,* for, to comfort, such men have long ago bid farewell; but, I assert, and am ready to prove, that he cannot provide them, without parish aid, with a sufficiency of food, not to *satisfy* their cravings, but to *sustain life*. And, will any one say that this state of things is such as England ought to witness? Will even Old Rose, wallowing in the luxury of eighteen thousand a year drawn from the public purse, say that nothing ought to be attempted to alleviate these sufferings? There are hundreds of thousands of the people of England who never taste any food but bread and vegetables, and who scarcely even know what it is to have a full meal even of these. This is *new* : it was not so in former times : it was not so even till of *late* years : the causes are obvious, and they ought to be removed. I know, that, to remove them is not the work of a day. There must be time, and even a long time, allowed for it; but, the new ministry should lose no time in convincing the people, that they perceive, and that they wish to alleviate their sufferings; that they sincerely wish to restore the labourer to something like life; for, in his present pining famishing state, it may, almost without a figure, be said, that, "in the midst of life he is in death." That this is not an exaggerated picture : that it does not proceed from thoughtless feeling or from a base desire of currying favour with the rabble, will, I think, be readily believed by anyone who will but bestow a single minute in contemplating the situation of the agricultural labourer. His weekly wage (for I shall suppose him *never to lose a day's work,* either from recreation or *sickness*) is, upon an average 12 shillings, putting it at the very highest. The average price of the quartern loaf is eleven pence. Upon an average it is, indeed, much more; but, let us take the very lowest. Here, then are the means of purchasing 58½ pounds of bread in a week; which is a little more than 8½ pounds a day for a *working* man, his wife, and 4 children! Absolutely not enough to support life. *Nothing* for drink; nothing for clothing; nothing for bedding, for household goods, for fuel, or for house rent! The evident conclusion is, that some of them must die, unless they are supported in existence by the parish, or by voluntary alms. " Well," some overgorged upstart will say, "and what matter is it, so that they are supported, whence the support comes? " The matter is this, that the labourers are humbled, debased, and enslaved. The tendency of the funding and taxing system is, carried to its extreme, to draw the produce of the labour into unnatural channels, into the hands of upstart cormorants, and to deal it back again in driblets, under the name of relief or of charity, just to support the life of those from whose pores it has been drained. And thus is the nation debased; thus, without any direct abolition of the liberties of the common people, have these liberties been destroyed, or, at least, suspended. I repeat, that this terrible evil cannot be, all at once removed; but, I also repeat, that, in order to convince the people, that their situation is known to and felt by their rulers, the new ministry should make some specific declaration upon the subject; and that, with all convenient speed, they should adopt measures for relief. In the mean while (and this is the point which I have at present, principally in view), I conjure the new Chancellor of the Exchequer not to imitate his predecessor in making an annual boast about the *prosperity*, the *flourishing* state, of the country. From him we should hope for, and, indeed, from him I do confidently expect, a *true* picture of our financial concerns; an unvarnished statement of our internal affairs; and I as confidently expect, from the wisdom of the ministry and the public-spirit of parliament, an adequate remedy.

The Poor

P.R. XIV., c. 73. *Summary of Politics.* 16-7-08.

UNTIL of late years, there was, amongst the poor, a horror of becoming chargeable to the parish. To become chargeable was a reproach; and never to have been chargeable was a subject of proud exultation. This feeling, which was almost universal, was the parent of industry, of care, of economy, of frugality, and of *early* habits of labour amongst children. But, this feeling is now extinguished; the barrier, shame, has been broken down, and in have rushed for parish aid all those, whether young or old, who are not of a turn of mind which must always be rarely met with.——The parishes, instead of endeavouring to check the evil by a vigilant attention to the different earnings and means and manners of the poor, have, in general, adopted the easy course of giving *wages* in the shape of relief. For instance, the week's wages is, in some places, ten shillings, and, in order to put the labourer with a family upon a par with the labourer without a family, the former receives, in the shape of relief, a certain allowance for each child above two. So that, as *a matter of course*, every labourer, who has more than two children, becomes, with all his family, paupers; they sink quietly and contentedly into that state, from which their grandfathers, and even their fathers, shrunk with horror. Nay, when a labourer, in such a state of things, marries, he counts the pauper chest among his ways and means; and even his hours of courtship are partly spent in anticipating the receipts from that never failing source. That men should possess *spirit,* that there should be any independence of mind, that there should be frankness, amongst persons so situated, is impossible. Accordingly, whoever has had experience in such matters, must have observed, with deep regret, that instead of priding himself upon his little possessions, instead of decking out his children to the best advantage, instead of laying up in store the trifling surplus produce of the harvest month, the labourer now, in but too many instances, takes care to spend all as fast as he gets it, makes himself as poor as he can, and uses all the art that he is master of to cause it to be believed, that he is still more miserable than he really is. What an example for the children! And what must the rising generation be? It used to be the boast of the labourer, that he could mow or reap or hough so much money by his labour; but, now, if he does earn great wages, his first and greatest care is to disguise the fact; and, it frequently happens, that he will change from master to master, and from one sort of work to another, for the express purpose of preventing the parish from being able to ascertain the amount of his earnings. When part of his children become able to assist in maintaining the family, he takes care that the amount of their earnings shall never be known; and, as he still gains by counting them amongst the number to be maintained, he keeps them at home, in preference to sending them to annual service, where they would, under the command of others, contract those habits of industry, regularity, and obedience, which, in very few cases, in any rank of life, children contract at home. So that this system operates in producing a twofold mischief, 1st, in encouraging the labourer to rear his children paupers, and 2ndly, in preventing them from ever shaking-off their pauper-like habits. When children, thus reared, do become servants, they are generally the very worst of servants. Bred up in dissimulation, no word that they utter can be believed; they are totally unworthy of confidence; and, as is universally the case with slaves, they are sure to be insolent when they can be so with impunity.

Dialogue on Nutrition

P.R. XXIX., c. 164.   *To the Chancellor of the Exchequer.   Letter III.*
Real Remedies.   11-11-15.

A DIALOGUE between me and one of my labourers will give you as correct a notion of the state of the country, in this respect, as you will be able to obtain from the Board of Agriculture, though that Board of wise men costs us some thousands a year.

L.—600 rod of water-furrowing at 9d. a score rod £1.2s.6d.

Mr. C.—But 9d. a score is too much, Emery.

L.—*Too much,* Sir!   Why it always used to be *a shilling*!

Mr. C.—Yes, but flour *used* to be 20s. a bushel, and now it is 10s. at the same mill.

L.—*Flour* is cheaper, to be sure, Sir, but *every thing else* is as dear as ever.

Mr. C.—Will you give me 18s. a score for a nice fat hog?

L.—No, Sir, (*with a smile and twist of the neck.*)

Mr. C.—But, you know, that, one year, since I have lived at Botley, hogs did sell for 18s. a score; and that, for years, they sold at 16s. or 17s.

L.—Yes, Sir, but a man wants something else besides *bread* and *bacon.*

Mr. C.—I know he does.   He wants some good, fresh, hearty *beer.*

L.—Beer, Sir!   How is a poor man to buy beer at 6d. a pot?

Mr. C.—Why should he buy it at 6d. a pot, when he can have a bushel of malt for 9s. and hops for 1s. enough to make 21 gallons of as good beer as any man need wish to drink. Beer that will make him feel bold when he has drunk a pot of it.

L.—I *never brew,* Sir.

Mr. C.—Pray then, what do you drink?   You must drink *something* with your victuals.   What is it?

L.—Tea, Sir!

Mr. C.—Tea!   And how much a week, and how much sugar? And what do they cost you?

L.—Why, Sir, we have 1½oz. of tea, and 3lb. of sugar.   The tea cost 1s. 6d. and the sugar 3s.

Mr. C.—So, here is 4s. 6d. a week, laid out by my servant with the nabobs and the West Indians, when you might have four times as much nourishment out of *half* a bushel of malt. *Two* weeks, at this rate, would cost you 9s. while, for 10s. you might have four full pots of good beer a-day for *three* weeks. But, this is not all; during three weeks you lay out 13s. 6d. to obtain whatever nourishment 9 lbs. of sugar yields; while, if this 13s. 6d. was laid out in 1½ bushel of malt, you would obtain for it the nourishment which 37½ lbs. of sugar yields; because it is a well known fact, that every bushel of good malt contains, at the least, 25 lbs. of sugar.

L.—(*With a laugh like that of Cymon when he first discovered Ephigenia sleeping by the fountain*.) Ah, Sir! But how is a poor man to get it out?

Mr. C.—Why, as you do the bitter taste of the stuff that you call tea; and which, for the greater part, is, perhaps, composed of the leaves of the *ash* or the *black thorn*: that is by brewing; only, instead of brewing *three times every day*, you need brew only *one time in three weeks*; or, if you prefer it, only one time in six, nine, or twelve weeks.— No wonder that you go so late in the morning to your work. No wonder that you are shuffling home a mile or two to dinner, instead of bolting out (as I did when I was a boy) with your meat and bread in your satchel, and your beer in a wooden bottle, slung over your shoulder. No wonder that you are all as thin as owlettes, and that that son of yours there, who is 19 years old, and is five feet nine inches high, is, as you told me last summer, " too weakly to do man's work." No wonder that his knees bend under him, and that he has a voice like that of a girl, instead of being able to carry a sack of wheat and to jump over a five-barred gate.

L.—Aye, Sir, it is easy to talk; but how am I to brew without barrels, or any thing to brew with?

Mr. C.—All these would not cost you as much as you lose by tea-drinking in one single quarter of a year. But, besides, does the tea-kettle, with its everlasting cookings, summer as well as winter, cost you nothing? Do the tea-pots, spoons, cups and saucers cost you nothing? Do you pay nothing, in the course of a year, to those vagabond pedlars, whom I frequently see in the village with their moveable houses and their crockery-ware, whose licence to traffic they seem to interpret into a commission to plunder, the tax upon whose licences do not amount to a thousandth part of the injury they do in their tramping through the country, and who, indeed, you may look upon as your friends, because they tear and burn the hedges that you are employed to make and to mend. Do you give none of your money to these wretches, instead of giving it to the cooper and the brazier?

L.—(*Having had time to bethink him.*) Why, now, there, Sir; there are *potatoes* as dear as ever. A poor man cannot get a bushel under 3s.

Mr. C.—And what business has he with potatoes, then? This trash is *always* dearer than flour. Ten pounds of potatoes are equal to one pound of flour in point of nourishment, and no more. And yet you buy potatoes for *cheapness*. This is your *economy*. You give 30s. for the same quantity of nourishment that you can get for 10s. And this, too, in a smaller bulk, more cheaply prepared for the stomach, liable to no waste, convenient to carry to your work, at any moment ready to be eaten. This is your *economy;* but, I must say, that I do not so much blame you for this, when I consider how many great writers on food, and how many wise law-givers have lent their hand in the misleading of you. This potatoe diet constitutes, however, a component part of the tea-drinking system. Neither will permit you to sally out in the morning as soon as your eyes are open. Both demand candle-light and an hour for cookery. Both send you forth with something wet, warm, and weak in your belly, to face the cold winds and soaking rains, or the melting sun. Both bring you home at noon, through all sorts of weather and from all distances. Both leave you, if thirsty in the interval, to drink at the pump or the brook. Both tend to make you poor, weak, ill, and unhappy. Both tend to multiply your cares, to give you a brood of puny children, to lower your spirit, to impoverish your blood, and to shorten your days of labour and of life. But, I see the people are going to the Methodist Meeting, and, as I suppose you want to go too, let us come to a settlement.

L.—Your son did, indeed, Sir, make the bargain for 9d. a rod.

Mr. C.—Very well, a bargain is a bargain. But, as it was an error, which, if it had made against you, I should have corrected in your favour, so ought you to correct it in my favour; and, you will perceive, that though the prices of our produce have fallen *one-half*, I have reduced your price but *one-third*.

L.—I do not know, I'm sure, Sir, how that is; I'm no scholar, worse luck's mine.

Mr. C.—Very true; but that bread and bacon and malt are only half the price that they used to be when you had a shilling a rod? You are scholar enough for that?

L.—Your son did, indeed, Sir, say 9d. a rod.

Mr. C.—Very well, then; here, take the £1 2s. 6d. I say it *ought* to be but one pound. You, therefore, in conscience, owe me 2s. 6d. and when you pay it me, I will employ you again, and not before.

L.—Good morning to you, Sir.

Mr. C.—Good morning to you.

John Bull's Great Lottery

P.R. XXX., c. 611. *To the People of the United States of America. Letter XIII. John Bull's Great Lottery.* 18-5-16.

YOU have *Lotteries* in your country, and, I think, it would be a great deal better for your morals if you had none. Qualify the thing how we please, be the object of it what it may, still it is *gaming*; it is, at the very best, a game at hazard. It is an endeavour to get money out of the pockets of others, by exciting in those others, a hope, which, *upon the whole*, must of necessity be *false;* and, where is there any man of character, who would not be ashamed to acknowledge, that he had wilfully and deliberately excited a false hope in another for the purpose of getting money from him? But, I am now about to talk to you of a lottery of a very different description indeed. It is John Bull's great annual Lottery. You have blanks as well as prizes in all your lotteries; and so have we in some of ours. Those who put into your lotteries purchase tickets, or shares of tickets. So it is in some of ours. But, in John Bull's great National annual Lottery, there are *no blanks;* and the parties give nothing for their tickets.

Not to keep you longer in suspense, this is the nature of the thing. Just after Easter Tuesday, the officers of the several Parishes hold a meeting, at which, by the way of Lottery, they distribute amongst the most able parishioners, *young paupers,* to be kept by the said parishioners and *brought up by* them in their own houses, or, at any rate, maintained by them, clothed, fed, lodged, and doctored, at their own particular expense, until they grow up to be men, or women. Luckily I have just had a prize drawn for me in this lottery : *a girl,* about 10 or 12 years of age. So that, besides about *six hundred dollars* a year that I pay towards the keep of the paupers *in money,* I shall if I live so long, have this girl upon my hands for *seven years!* This is Big John Bull's Great Lottery. If I had all my share of paupers quartered upon me as this girl is, I should have about *twenty-eight,* of all ages. This number I maintain, and have maintained for years, while, upon an average, I have not employed more than *twelve* labourers, or *thirteen* at most, including garden and every thing. In my own house we are *twelve* all-together. So that I have more than one pauper to every other human being moving within the sphere of my support.

These facts, which I state in the face of the country and of my own neighbours, cannot be denied; and, it is from facts like these that we are enabled to judge of the real state of a nation. The coaches and chariots and landaus that rattle through the squares and streets of London; the forests of masts that rise in the sea-ports; the loads of pearls and diamonds that shine at the Court; even the beautiful mansions and pleasure grounds that are seen all around the metropolis : these; no one; no, nor all of these put together, are a proof of the prosperity of a *nation* : all these may exist, and the nation be plunged in the deepest of misery and degradation.

Let any sensible man apply his mind to this subject for a moment, and (for it is worth his while) trace this poor girl to her probable fate; and then he will see the effects of a taxing and pauperising system. What am I to do with this child, whom the law compels me to take and maintain? I know not whether she be bastard, or orphan, or one of a family whose father and mother are alive. She is forced upon me to be kept and reared up by me. Were I so disposed, it would be impossible for me to pay any attention to her morals or any part of her conduct. I must of necessity leave her to the care of some other person. My intention is to place her in a farm-house, under the authority of a woman, who may teach her, perhaps, to feed pigs and poultry, to milk, and make butter and cheese; but, can I expect *any one* to have due care of the moral behaviour of this girl? Yet, what is to become of her? Can I point out any thing *better*? I cannot; for, in the poor-house her chance would be infinitely worse. My wife? Faith she has the rearing of *her own* children to attend to. Her time is as precious as mine; for no children of ours will have to reproach us with having committed their education to hirelings.

I do not complain of the expense imposed upon me in this instance. I do not complain of any unfairness in the drawing of the Lottery. My neighbours would scorn an act so mean. But, I complain of a state of things, that imposes upon me a duty, which it is out of my power to perform. All I can possibly do is to see that this girl has plenty of food and clothing, and that she is properly lodged, and duly attended in sickness. But, do I not do all this for my horses and my cows? What I complain of, is, a state of things, which takes so large a part of the children from their natural guardians, their fathers, mothers, relations and friends, and throws them upon the mercy of those who are utter strangers to them, and who, instead of natural feeling *for* them, must, unless they bring great consideration to their aid, naturally have a feeling *against* them; and, especially in cases, where the support of a pauper is a serious pecuniary burthen to the party on whom it is imposed.

Now, my Old English Friends in America, who used to join me (for I took the lead) in singing the praises of the English government and Pitt, what do *you* think of this? Perhaps you think, by this time, as I do; that we were a set of very ignorant though honest fellows, who confounded admiration of men in power with love of country, and whose violent prejudices, though bottomed in the best of principles, led us into a thousand follies, and really made us, perhaps, instrumental, in some small degree, in producing the enormous evils, under which our country now groans. I remember a book that we used to look at a good deal, entitled "*A Picture of England.*" It contained views of *Country Seats* and of fine hills and valleys. This book and *Grose's Antiquities* were enough for me. Alas! This was no picture of *England,* if by England, we mean any thing more than a certain portions of the Houses, Trees, and Herbage. If, by England, we mean the English *nation;* and, if, by the nation, we mean the great *body of the people,* I now give you the means of judging of the real state of England; I give you the true "Picture of England." Here am I, with twelve persons in family, including servants, and with thirteen labourers, on an average, constantly employed; and the maintenance of *twenty-eight paupers* falls fairly to my share! This, my old Friends; this, my worthy countrymen, is the real Picture of England; and should I not be a very despicable man, if the false shame of acknowledging past erroneous opinions were to prevent me from laying this picture before you?

Now, in a state of things like this, what a farce it is to talk about "*enlightening*. the lower orders!" How are my twenty-eight poor wretches of paupers, and my thirteen labourers and their families, but one step above paupers; *how*, I ask, are they to be *enlightened*? And, if this were *possible,* which it is not; what would be the *use* of it? What could it do more than add mental to bodily suffering? Away, then, with all the talk; all the palaver; all the cant; all that cunning can suggest to hypocrisy for the purpose of deluding the well-meaning, thoughtless, but liberal men, who subscribe their money to support this shew of regard for the minds and souls of the poor! Were not a system of eleemosynary education *necessarily* calculated to debase the objects of it, in a state of things like this it is pure folly to attempt it. It is bread, and not books, that the poor creatures stand in need of. The government takes from me so much, that I am unable to give more than I give to my labourers. I have only enough left to give them the means of barely keeping life in their bodies. They, therefore, successively become paupers. If, as in America, the labourer took the share, or the far greater part of it, which the government takes here, there would be no paupers : Labourers would save money against a day of sickness. This, however, has all been so clearly shown, in No. 2 of this Volume, that I will here take it as an established fact, that it is the increasing, and now enormous weight of our taxes, and that only, which has caused the fearful increase in pauperism, crimes, and capital punishments.

Away, then I say again, with all the projects for *enlightening* the people by the means of *schools,* and of *enriching* them by the means of *saving banks.* What! Put by the " *savings* " of my twenty-eight paupers and thirteen labourers, few of the latter of whom *taste meat once a week*! What! a project for putting out the *savings* of such people to interest! Yet I should not wonder if this project were to *reach you;* there being none of our projects, of the humanity kind, that you do not adopt, as it were in the way of *rivalship.* Would you not do well to make haste and *rival* us in number of paupers? I hope to be able to give a check to this ape-like disposition, which leads you to look for example to follow, where you ought to look for example to shun. As to the *professed* object of the Saving Bank project, nothing would be easier, if it were worth while, than to show the *impossibility* of its doing any good in *any country;* but, as to the *real* object, a word or two may be said. With regard to the labouring people in *country* places, they will never hear of the thing. But, in large towns, where there are numerous journeymen, who may save now and then a shilling, and who are sturdy chaps that read news-papers and that *talk politics,* it is thought to be of importance to get sums of money thus collected, and to place them in the *funds,* and thereby *attach* these swarms of sturdy, talking, and active men *to the System.* Not another word need be said, only that the project will *fail.* The *Friendly Societies* were great favourites. GEORGE ROSE, their patron, brought in many acts of parliament to encourage their increase. Their money was put into the *funds* too. But, these Societies are now found not to be good. They *drew men together;* and, when assembled together, they TALKED! Wicked rogues!

The saving bank project, which has originated in that seat of all that is, at once, conceited, impudent and servile, Edinborough, whence, too, is coming a project for changing our *weights* and *measures,* and for throwing into utter confusion the trade and transactions of England, the Colonies, and the United States, as connected in trade with England; this saving bank project has in view to avoid the *congregating* evil of the Friendly Societies. It is intended to *collect* the money, *without collecting the people.* But, the projectors do not seem to reflect, that, in getting rid of the gregarious quality, they throw aside the strongest lures of all such schemes; to wit : the pot, the pipe, the song, and the chat. For the sake of these, journeymen will yield up a little of their wages to go into a fund; but, when there are no lures of this sort, they will not so easily discover any solid reason for their giving up the means of present gratification with a view to spare the purse of the parish in their old age.

Back, then, we still return to the old point; the taxes, the taxes, the taxes! while we are loaded with them as we now are, nothing can retard the progress of pauperism and of crimes. A trades-man, who works for me, and to whom I was talking, the other day, about the distresses of the times, observed, that he found it very hard to stagger along with four children upon his back. " But," said he, " I could make shift to carry them, if I had not *somebody else* to carry. I have a soldier or two to carry besides; and you, Sir, have a general, I dare say, upon your back." The idea put me in mind of HANNAH MORE'S religious tract, entitled, *" Bear ye one another's burdens,"* which was intended to reconcile the nation to its sufferings under the calamities of 1796, and, at the head of which she put a wood-cut, representing a parcel of people carrying bags and bales of *sins* and *mis-fortunes;* for HANNAH was, perhaps, as artful, as able, and as useful a scribe as ever drew pen in the cause of the system. But, Mrs. HANNAH, with your leave, it is not exactly *one another's* burthens that we bear. It is, according to the idea of my trades-man, that some of us carry others upon our backs. In the first place; I, for instance, have twenty-eight paupers fastened upon me. Then, I pay taxes direct and indirect, about a thousand pounds a year besides the poor-rates. Perhaps a great deal more. Now, as I am a sort of literary man as well as a farmer, I may suppose myself ridden by WILLIAM GIFFORD, who has two or three sinecures, which amount to about a thousand pounds a year. Here I stagger along, then, with the Political Editor, Poet and Reviewer astride upon my shoulders, and with my twenty-eight paupers hanging upon my arms, and in my skirts. Come, then, my old English friends in America, you who still confound the *System* with *England,* and who bid us be content, and call us *Jacobins* if we complain; come here yourselves, and stick to it as we do. Do not remain there abusing republican government. Do not content yourselves with giving us advice. Come and *share* with us. Come, any one of you, and take a leg of William Gifford, and fourteen of my paupers; and then preach patience and divine right as long as you like.

Gang Labour

P.R. XXXI., c. 258. *To the People of the United States of America. On the conduct of the English Board of Agriculture.* 14-9-16.

HERE you see, in the first place, that the land is rapidly going out of cultivation; that the price of farm produce, not being articles immediately fit to eat, is fallen so low as to produce ruin to the farmer. But, the whole sum total of the misery and degradation of the people is found in the single fact, that the labourers are, for the greater part, become paupers; that they are now under the supervision of the overseers; and that they are put up to auction by name! I would now ask my old English friends in America, whether they any longer wonder that I should have changed my note with regard to the tendency of the English government. Did they imagine, when they and I used to sing the praises of this government, that the time would shortly come when a considerable part of the labourers of England would actually be put up to auction by the overseers of the poor? Amongst the persons thus put up to auction, there are, perhaps, many of the relations of my old English friends in America. Can they endure the reflection, that their brothers, or brothers' children, are thus let out, like slaves in the marts of the West Indies?

*   *   *   *   *   *

It is *not a voluntary act of theirs* to let themselves out to hire. They are let out without any consent of their own. They have made no contract for service. They have not received, nor are they about to receive, any benefit in exchange for their labour. The overseer lets them to whomsoever he pleases; not only without their consent, but, sorely against their will; they are placed in his hands by the compulsion of want; and he disposes of them to the highest bidder, not for any fixed period, at the end of which plenty and ease are to be the reward of their services; but for periods that may be short or long, as accident may determine, and without the smallest prospect of their lot ever being better.

I am not prepared to say, that the letting out of paupers in this way is not justifiable. Indeed, I do not very clearly see how we shall be able to avoid doing it all over the kingdom. The farmers as well as the people in trade are all so much reduced in the amount of their means, that it is impossible that pauperism should not go on increasing. It is impossible that the labourers and their families should be maintained by wages, while the taxes remain what they now are. Therefore, a reduction in quantity of food consumed, and of raiment made use of must take place in every family, not fed out of the taxes; and of course, the labourer's family, who had before little more than the bare means of existence, must now be pared down so closely as to leave them not one single mouthful beyond what is absolutely necessary to keep them alive. Hence it is that the labourers now come in a body to be fed at the hands of the Government.

To William Wilberforce

P.R. XLVII., c. 522. To William Wilberforce. On the state of the Cotton Factory Labourers, and on the Speech of ANDREW RYDING, who cut HORROCKS with a cleaver. 30-8-23.

IT is notorious that great numbers of your "*free* British labourers" have actually *died from starvation;* and that, too, at a time when the Minister declared from his seat in Parliament that there was in the country an over-production of food. This is notorious. This can be denied by no one. The devil himself, if he were to come to the assistance of the hypocrites, could not embolden them to deny this fact. This being the case, then; and it being equally notorious that no Black slave ever suffered for want of food, will not the care, will not the anxiety of a really humane Englishman be directed towards the Whites, instead of towards the Blacks, until at any rate, the situation of the former be made to be as *good* as that of the latter. A very large portion of the agricultural labourers of England. A very large portion of those who raise all the food, who make all the buildings, who prepare all the fuel, who, in short, by their labour, sustain the community. A very large part of these exist in a state of almost incesssant hunger. The *size* of the people is diminishing from this cause. They are becoming a feeble race, they suffer from numerous bodily ailments engendered by the poverty of their food. Their dress is fast becoming nothing but rags; and, in short, every hardship and every suffering that labour and poverty and the starvation can inflict, are becoming their lot. You know this as well as I do; but instead of being, as I am, engaged in constant endeavours to put an end to this degradation and suffering, you are constantly endeavouring to perpetuate them. Never do you utter a syllable against any of the measures by which the suffering of the labouring classes has been produced : never do you propose, second, approve of, or in any way give countenance to, any thing tending to turn the villainous cold potatoes into bread; and you do all the mischief which it is in your power to do, by endeavouring to draw public attention away from the real sufferings of the people at home to the imaginary sufferings of the Blacks. In many respects, your charges against the West India planters and Assemblies are false; and the whole of what

you say about them is a tissue of disfigurings and misrepresent-
ings. But, suppose the *whole to be true*. Still it is manifest
from your own showing, or, at least, upon the supposition that
you have shown all; it is manifest that your *"free* British
labourers "* are worse off than your Black slaves. This fact alone
is sufficient to characterize you and your endeavours. But my
charge against you is this : that you do the labourers of England
great harm, or, at least, all the harm in your power; that you
not only do them no good; that you, the great canter and noise-
maker about humanity, never seem to admit that they have any
thing to complain of; but, on the contrary, that you describe their
situation as desirable, by putting it in contrast with that of the
Blacks, by the use of the words *free* and *freedom,* as applicable to
their situation; and in short, by every trick that the invention of
a crafty political hypocrite can furnish.

State of the Poor

P.R. L., c. 31. *The Poor.* 3-4-24.

IMPUDENT assertions about *joyous country, smiling in
plenty,* a people happy, contented and grateful to the great
House, these are the things that suit the Government. Let them
form a Committee to inquire into the condition of the labouring
classes. And what so easy as to ascertain this condition? What
so easy as to ascertain the average height of wages in the different
counties, the average price of provisions in the different counties :
what so easy as to call up Overseers and Churchwardens from a
parish in the North, one in the South, one in the East, one in the
West, and one in the centre of each county? What so easy as to
bring the surgeons and apothecaries (not being half-pay officers)
of those parishes, to describe the state of health of the labourers,
to declare what portion of the ailments and deaths arises from
the deficiency of food, deficiency of drink of the right sort,
deficiency of clothing, deficiency of fuel; and, in short, deficiency
of the necessaries of life. What so easy as all this? How many
days of the Session would it occupy a Committee, industrious,
zealous, and intelligent as a Committee of law-makers ought
to be?

Aye, aye! but this would show England to be peopled by the most miserable set of beings that ever breathed the breath of life, and would, of course, give the lie direct to the incomparable *braggery* of Mr. FREDERICK ROBINSON. No inquiry is so necessary, and none could be so useful as this. This inquiry would explain a great deal about the imprisonment for killing game. It is the one thing needful at this moment, and, therefore, it is precisely what we shall not have.

The State of Ireland

P.R. L., c. 719. *To the Chancellor of the Exchequer on his " joyous country, smiling in plenty, with a happy contented and grateful people."* 19-6-24.

MUCH has been said, and especially by the notoriously impudent crew, about the evils arising from *priestcraft* and *superstition*. There is, indeed, no priest-*craft* in Ireland. It is quite *frank*. It seeks no disguise. It scorns affectation. The mettle of which brewing-kettles are made is not more free from any thing calculated to make its nature doubtful. But, what I ask is this : Have any set of priests, in any country; have Jesuits, have Franciscans; have popes and cardinals; have the priests of Mahomet; have any priests upon the face of the earth ever exercised authority over, ever existed in the same country with, a set of human beings so miserable as the people of Ireland have become under the laws passed by the Parliament that you so highly praise, and that received your praises with "loud and long-continued cheers"?

Two-and-twenty years did we wage war against the French revolution. And, *for what*? To prevent revolution here. And why were the *people* to wish to prevent it here? Because *revolution would make them miserable*! And here we are, after these twenty-two years of war to *prevent misery,* with the most miserable people that the world ever saw; with *females,* a large part of whom are "*perfectly naked,*" and with a *gentry,* " so *used to see this* as not to be shocked at it." This is the " House's " own description; and, what must be the state of the country; how must all have become, when this could, and that, too, without any seeming horror, be heard in the House! The "*gentry*" of

Ireland are *so used* to the sight of naked female human beings, that they are not shocked at it, and are "*not aware*" that it is not the usual and "*proper way for females to exist.*" And this is said in that House, who have been making laws for these Irish for ages! This is said at the end of a twenty-two years' war, waged to *prevent us from experiencing misery*!

What! could a revolution, then, have brought us misery more complete than this? Could it have done *more* than strip the *females naked*? Could it have done more to dishonour human nature, than to produce "A GENTRY" (pretty gentry!) who are "*not aware*" that *nakedness* is not "the *proper* way for females to exist"? Mind: this is said in your famous House, or the newspapers are liars. This is a statement made without hesitation, and, apparently, exciting no horror. There have been revolutions in America and France. Did misery like this ever exist in either? In the whole world did you ever hear of any thing so degrading to human nature? And yet, mind, this state of things not only exists; but has risen up under *laws made by that House* which you so eulogised. This is the point to stick to: this is the fact to be kept constantly before the people. That, no matter, naked or not naked, hungry or full, shut up from sunset to sunrise or suffered to go at large, Skibbereen or no Skibbereen, "redundant population" or not reduntant population, the people of Ireland have come to their present state *under laws made by your House*!

Holidays and Enclosures

P.R. LII., c. 146. *To Lord John Russell. On the Doctrine of Surplus Population.* 16-10-24.

MAN was not born to be *always at work*. Very shallow, indeed, are those who regard the numerous holidays of the Catholic church as tending to promote *idleness*. Men will do a great deal more work, if days of leisure be interspersed amidst days of toil. These days of leisure are necessary to their pleasure and their happiness; and it is of advantage, if the regulations of the community be such as to make the same a day of leisure for all. In the "*dark ages*" we never heard of any complaints about a surplus population; and be you assured, my

Lord JOHN, that where such complaints can be made, there is something radically wrong in the state of the law.

The truth is, that the system which has been pursued in England from the time of the Revolution; the system of Government Debt, is a system which begins by totally abasing the labouring classes, and that ends by producing its own overthrow, and, generally, that of the State along with it. It draws property into great masses; it gives to cunning the superiority over industry; it makes agriculture a subject of adventure; it puts down all small cultivators; it incloses every inch of that land which God himself seems to have intended for the poor.

*   *   *   *   *

Your Lordship must well know that this consolidation of farms has taken place all over the country. I do not believe that it would be going too far to say, that nine-tenths of the farmhouses of England have been destroyed since the day that the " good old King " came to the throne. As if this were not enough, *large part of the commons have been enclosed*. Nothing that man could devise would be more injurious to the country than this. In all times it has been deemed by the common people a grievous injury. It drives the labouring man from the only spot where he has a chance to alleviate his toil. It has always produced incalculable mischief.

The Rights of the Poor

P.R. LIX., c. 394. *State of the Poor; and Projects of the Scotch and English Landlords.* 12-8-26.

TO me it seems the most astonishing thing in the world, that any man in England can talk about the people *starving*! When we all know, that every inch of land, every brick and tile in a house; that all is pledged by the law, to prevent the people from suffering from want. Every man of common sense knows that the field, for instance, which he calls *his,* is only his upon certain conditions; and that one of those conditions is this; namely, that he shall continue to pay money to the Overseer of the Poor, in order that the said Overseer may take care that no person in the parish may suffer from want. This is a condition attached to every man's tenure and every man's land. What do people mean, then, by saying, that there are *starving* Weavers and *starving* Spinners, and *starving* Labourers? How are there to be any starving people, as long as this law remains, and as long as there are houses and land? and, if there be any starving people in the country as long as this law is in existence, then the laws are set at defiance, and we are living in a state of Tyranny: for Tyranny is that state of things, in which men are, when they are compelled to obey those, who, themselves, set the law at defiance.

Cobbett and Poor Relief

T.T., p. 83. *To the Industrious Classes at Botley in Hampshire. On the conduct of their rich neighbours, and in particular of that one WILLIS (who is now called FLEMING), and who is one of the Members for that unfortunate County.* 1-10-30.

I MADE it a rule, that no man that worked regularly for me, should, during his being employed by me, be a *pauper,* that is, receive *parish relief.* I paid my men, however large their families, enough to maintain them well. Most of them lived in my own cottages, and *rent free,* with plenty of fuel carried to their doors, each having an *oven* to bake in. I paid them, besides this, on an average, two shillings a week more than other farmers paid their men. There was one exception as to parish relief, that of RUBEN PINK, who belonged to Titchfield parish, and whom I allowed to get from the parish what they chose to give him, and that parish behaved very well in this case. He had a very large family of small children, and, in spite of high wages, free house, fuel, and a really humane parish, he was still poor, ragged, and, in the winter of 1815, fell ill. I sent Dr. BLUNDELL to him, and when he came back, and I asked what ailed him, " Why," said the sensible Doctor, " he wants *good victuals* and *warm clothes,* and a *good deal* of both, for he is a *big man."* I made him, as soon as a little better, come with his plough and horses (which he used better than any man that I ever saw in my life), and go to plough near my own house, where he came in every day at dinner-time and took the physic prescribed by the doctor,

I giving him, at the same time, some of my clothes, and particularly a great-coat, which I had worn very little. The doctor's prescription was completely successful; and he remembers how soon his patient recovered. But this was my, I should say *our,* constant practice with all of them, or their wives and families, when they were ill. With this one exception, no man was *a pauper* that worked for me, though, in the three parishes of Botley, Waltham, and Doxford, I paid, in the years that I lived there, not less than about *two thousand pounds in rates*. While other farmers were paying wages out of my rates, my people were receiving none. I saw how unjust this was towards me; but, at any rate, I was resolved, that the man who laboured for me should not be degraded by the *name of pauper*. These facts are notorious; you all know them; and yet the GRASP-ALLS had the baseness to *cheer* and *applaud* the empty-headed Willis Fleming, while he was representing me as an " *oppressor* of my *miserable dependents!* " These wretches, these greedy, grinding, *all-grasping* vagabonds, ought to have been stricken dead upon the spot; and, safe as they think themselves now, heavy as are their bags, fast as is their hold on the property of unfortunate people, they are not beyond the reach of God's judgments on the robbers of the poor; and I, even I, shall yet see them punished for their monstrous extortions, which are really incredible.

I found, living in two cottages, on the farm of Fairthorn, a widow and her daughters, and an old man and his wife. I let the widow remain rent free, and gave her wood to burn, as long as I had the farm. The old man paid me no rent; when he died I had a head-stone put to his grave to record, that he had been an honest, skilful and industrious labouring man; and I gave his widow a shilling a week as long as I was at Botley. And yet the vile extortioners *cheered* and *applauded* Willis while he was representing me as *illiberal* and *oppressive* to dependents!

My people, though *never* hired but by the *week,* lived with me for years; and, indeed, no man that I recollect, ever quitted me by choice. Robinson, you know, was my gardener for years; Bob Hammond, who worked for me occasionally, has come up, three summers, to work for me at Kensington; Mr. DEAN, who became my bailiff, lived in one of my cottages as long as the cottage was mine, has since kept my shop in London, is now a news-man in London, was with me through my tour in the counties last spring, is, *this very day,* managing my affairs at Barn-Elm in Surrey, and is become, as you know, a man of considerable property, which, as I know, is the just reward of his industry and fidelity. These facts are undeniable and notorious; and yet the *all-grasping,* the *extortioning, vagabonds,* sat and *cheered* and *applauded* the stupid and malignant fellow, while he was calling me an *"oppressor of my miserable dependents."*

And, as to the people in the *neighbourhood* of Botley, what have I not done and attempted to do, in order to prevent them from being robbed of the blades of grass for their pigs and their geese? In 1805, the moment I went to Botley, I wrote a memorial to Mr. Windham, on the state of HORTON HEATH, and showed how injurious it would be to enclose that common. He showed my memorial; but, at last, the greedy graspers have prevailed, and that common, the outlet to so many cottages, is enclosed, to the ruin and degradation of the cottagers. In 1827 a more ruinous measure was attempted; I mean the enclosure of WALTHAM CHASE, studded round with cottages, and covered with the cows, pigs, and geese of the cottagers, who also get fuel from the heath, the turf and the dead wood. The graspers fixed their eyes on this spot: the labourers were too well off: they had pigs and geese, and some of them cows, and even asses or little forest horses! This was too much for the graspers to endure. They made a bargain with the Bishop, who was lord of the manor; their attorney was set to work; an enclosure-bill was prepared; and the rights of the poor, of the See of Winchester, and of the Crown, were all to be sacrificed to the greediness of the graspers. Their attorney came up with the bill to get passed; and, in spite of the laudable and able efforts of Mr. RICHARD HINXMAN, the bill actually passed that *precious House of which Willis Fleming is a member.* But, before the bill got to the House of Lords, I, who had heard of this cruel grasping scheme, wrote a memorial on the subject, showing how injurious the measure would be to numerous families of labouring people; this memorial I sent to a ministerial member of parliament, whom I knew to be a humane man; he communicated the information to the Committee of the Lords'; the *bill was thrown out;* the poor people were saved, and the greedy fellows and their attorney had to slink home like sheep-biting dogs that have been met by a shepherd with a gun in his hand. Now, your everlasting gratitude is due to Mr. OVERINGTON and Mr. RICHARD HINXMAN for their exertions on this occasion; and, indeed my memorial might possibly have no effect; *the whole* of the merit might be due to those two spirited and worthy gentlemen; but, I did my best, at any rate; and *this the graspers know*; and for this, amongst other things, they hate me, and, as this was my *last* offence against them, it had, perhaps, the greatest weight. This was a cruel disappointment to them and their attorney; they had subscribed money to pay him, and to carry the job through; they were calculating how *much more land* they should have than they had before; they were counting their gains over and over again. You have heard or read of the man, who sold the lion's skin before he had caught the lion; and some of those greedy fellows had actually *sold their share of the chase* before they came to London to get the law to enclose it! Judge you of their mortification! You have, sometimes, seen a dog when about to seize hold of a piece of meat, or to run his mouth into a luncheon-bag, and, just at that moment, getting a blow across the nose with a broomstick. You have seen the greedy robber shake his ears, and go jogging off with his tail between his legs. You have seen an egg-sucking cur, when an egg-shell filled with hot coals has been crammed into his mouth; and you have seen him twist his jaws about, and stare like mad. Like these curs were the GRASPERS, when the House of Lords refused to give them the power of robbing the poor of Waltham Chase of the last blade of grass. As Christians you are to forgive them for this attempt, *when they have repented, and made atonement,* but, not before; and, even then, you are not to *forget* the attempt; you are to be on your guard against them in future; and, you ought to get *all their names,* and send them to me, and I will *put them in print,* which will, doubtless, delight them; for, as I said before, the fellows, stingy as they are, will squeeze out some few shillings now-and-then to pay dirty printers in the country to print their names. To be sure, this is when they are speech-makers, or presidents, or vice-presidents; and they may not like it, when they appear as robbers of the poor; as *extortioners;* or *graspers* surpassing in greediness the very wolves themselves. But, yet, as enemies of *radicals,* they cannot object to have their names put into print. At any rate, in print they shall be, if I can do it, and you shall have them to stick up over your fire-places; and the name of their attorney too.

In the year 1816, I think it was, when the labouring people of our neighbourhood were suffering very much from want of employment, I proposed to the parish of Bishop's Waltham, that we should petition the Bishop, who was lord of the manor, to grant an acre of waste land to any married labourer who would enclose and cultivate and live on it. I called a vestry of the parish, and to the farmers and land-owners made this proposition. We put the matter to the vote, and every man voted against me, with the single exception of Mr. JENNINGS, the schoolmaster! The three orators against me were, BUDD, of Stakes; CHIDDLE, then with three farms in his hands; and STEEL, of Ashton. BUDD said, that to give the labourers a bit of land would make them "*sacy;*" CHIDDLE said, that it would only make them "*breed more children;*" and STEEL said, that it would make them demand "*higher wages.*" What is the present state of Budd I do not know; Chiddle has *now not so much land,* I hear, as one of the labourers would have had; and, as to Steel, he who used so to swagger, has since *blown his brains out with a pistol!* When I heard of the awful end of this man, and of the great change in the affairs of Chiddle, I could not help calling to mind their conduct on the above occasion, and to call to mind also the denunciations of God against the oppressors of the poor : " Hear this," said I, when I heard the death of STEEL. " Hear *this,* O ye that swallow up the needy, even to make the poor of the land to fail! I will turn your *feasting* into *mourning,*" saith the Lord God, " and your *songs* into *lamentations.*" These words of the prophet AMOS, let the GRASPALLS, *young* and *old,* bear in mind; and, as they are remarkably *pious* people, let them turn to

ISAIAH, chapter V and verse 8, and there read, " WOE unto them who *join house to house,* that *lay field to field,* till there be no place, that *they may be placed alone in the midst of the earth."* Let them think of these words; let them bear in mind the curses which God has laid on the guilty head of the *extortioner*; and let them remember, that, of all extortions, the most detestably wicked is that by which the labourer is *defrauded of his hire,* whether by cunning or by force, whether in the field or in the chandler's shop.

EIGHT

THE INDUSTRIAL REVOLUTION

Public Works

P.R. XII., c. 836. *Summary of Politics.* 28-11-07.

MR. SPENCE'S scheme of employing the ousted manufacturers upon "works of public utility" he has not, I am sure, duly considered; or else he would have perceived, that that was the most effectual way of preventing them from finding out new sources of livelihood. To *make work* for people is to war against nature as well as common sense; and when this is done by a *nation,* and that too with a view of preventing a part of its people from being miserable, it is a mark of downright insanity. Let us try it a moment. "Works of *public utility*" Mr. Spence talks of. Has the nation not already every thing that it *wants*? As fast as it wants, in the way of roads and canals, increase, does it not, in its own natural mode, take care to provide them? And, does not the provision keep an exact pace with the want? Surely it does, and always will. "Aye, but, supposing a canal, for instance, not to be necessary; yet, if the money expended upon it go to support ousted manufacturers, who would otherwise be upon the parish books, it is a good to make such a canal." No more a good than it would be to give the ousted manufacturers money for throwing stones against the wind; and, it would have this mischievous effect, that, while the present cost of maintaining them would be the same, or greater, than if they were upon the parish books, it would be much *more durable;* because, in the latter case there would be much more powerful motives for the finding out of new sorts of employment.

Riots at Nottingham

P.R. XX., c. 652. *Riots at Nottingham*. 23-11-11.

FOR some days past the news-papers have contained accounts of riots in this town and in the country of the same name. Stocking-Weavers going in search of machines, the use of which threw them out of work, appears to have been the original character of these assemblages. Much mischief is stated to have been done; one of the rioters killed in an attack upon a house. It is stated that the price of *bread* became one of the subjects of discontent amongst the rioters; and it is also stated, that a scarcity of work, added to the other causes, first led to the riots. The *military* having been collected together in great force, the riots appear to have been put an end to.—Now, that these riots may be traced to the American non-importation Act, and to Napoleon's continental system, is very clear; because it was the misery arising out of *a scarcity* of work that produced the riots; and, it is well known that the scarcity of work amongst the manufacturers has arisen out of the American and Napoleon system of interdict. It does not follow, that the government are to blame, however; because it was not in their power to prevent the interdict of Napoleon at any rate. What I point out the fact for is, to shew, that his system has produced such effects, that it may produce others of the same kind, especially in a season of scarcity of corn, and that measures ought to be adopted, not so much for the putting an end to riots, as to prevent the misery out of which they arise. It is in vain to hope for the return of such a state of things as would restore the manufacturers to their *former* state. That state of things will *never* return, or, at least, in the life time of any man now twenty years of age. Something else must therefore be thought of. There must be something done to give employment to persons formerly employed in the manufactures. I do not mean, the *work should be made* for them, as we make work for the people in the Highlands of Scotland. But, I mean the adoption of such measures as would give all possible facility to the employment of additional hands in *agriculture,* amongst which measures certainly is that of relieving all enclosure bills from the heavy expence that now attends them, and which operate as a very great discouragement. A wise government would find out many means to adopt in such a case; and though I am sensible, that no government can do much in this way in haste; yet *something* might be done.

Letter to the Luddites

P.R. XXXI., c. 561. *A Letter to the Luddites.* 30-11-16.

FRIENDS AND FELLOW COUNTRYMEN,

At this time, when the cause of freedom is making a progress which is as cheering to the hearts of her friends as it is appalling to those of her enemies, and, when it is become evident that nothing can possibly prevent that progress from terminating in the happiness of our country, which has, for so many years, been a scene of human misery and degradation; when it is become evident that so glorious a termination of our struggles can be now prevented only by our giving way to our passions instead of listening to the voice of reason, only by our committing those acts which admit of no justification either in law or in equity; at such a time, can it be otherwise than painful to reflect, that acts of this description are committed in any part of the kingdom, and particularly in the enlightened, the patriotic, the brave town of Nottingham?

The abuse which has been heaped upon you by those base writers whose object it is to enflame one part of the people against the other; the horrid stories which have been retailed about your injustice and cruelty; the murderous punishments which these writers express their wish to see inflicted on you; the delight which they evidently feel when any of you come to an untimely end; all these produce no feeling in my mind other than that of abhorrence of your calumniators. The atrocious wickedness of charging you with the burning of BELVOIR CASTLE, in support of which charge there has not been produced the slightest proof, in spite of all the endeavours to do it and all the anxiety to fix such a crime upon you; this alone ought to satisfy the nation, that it can rely upon nothing which a corrupt press has related relative to your conduct. But, still it is undeniable, that you have committed acts of violence on the property of your neighbours, and have, in some instances, put themselves and their families in bodily fear. This is not to be denied, and it is deeply to be lamented.

However enlarged our views may be; however impartial we may feel towards our countrymen; still, there will be some particular part of them whose conduct we view with more than ordinary approbation, and for whom we feel more than ordinary good will. It is impossible for me, as a native of these Islands, not to feel proud at beholding the attitude which my countrymen are now taking; at hearing the cause of freedom so ably maintained by men who seem to have sprung up, all at once, out of the earth, from the North of Scotland to the Banks of the Thames. At Glasgow, at Paisley, at Bridgeton, throughout the noble counties of York and Lancaster, and in many other parts besides the Metropolis, we now behold, that which to behold almost compensates us for a life of persecution and misery. But, still, amidst this crowd of objects of admiration, Nottingham always attracts my particular attention. I have before me the history of the conduct of Nottingham in the worst of times. I have traced its conduct down to the present hour. It has been foremost in all that is public-spirited and brave; and, I shall be very nearly returned to the earth when my blood ceases to stir more quickly than usual at the bare sound of the name of Nottingham.

Judge, you, then, my good friends, what pain it must have given me to hear you accused of acts, which I was not only unable to justify, but which, in conscience and in honour, I was bound to condemn! I am not one of those, who have the insolence to presume, that men are *ignorant* because they are *poor*. If I myself have more knowledge and talent than appears to have fallen to the lot of those who have brought us into our present miserable state, it ought to convince me, that there are thousands and thousands, now unknown to the public, possessed of greater talent, my education having been that of the common soldier grafted upon the plough-boy. Therefore, I beg you not to suppose, that I address myself to you as one who pretends to any superiority in point of rank, or of natural endowments. I address you as a friend who feels most sincerely for your sufferings; who is convinced that you are in error as to the cause of those sufferings; who wishes to remove that error; and, I do not recollect any occasion of my whole life when I have had so ardent a desire to produce conviction.

As to the *particular* ground of quarrel between you and your employers, I do not pretend to understand it very clearly. There must have been faults or follies on their side, at some time or other, and there may be still; but, I think, that we shall see, in the sequel, that those circumstances which appear to you to have arisen from their *avarice,* have in fact arisen from their want of the *means,* more than from their want of *inclination,* to afford you a competence in exchange from your labour; and, I think this, because it is their *interest* that you should be happy and contented.

But, as to the use of *machinery in general,* I am quite sure, that there cannot be any solid objection. However, as this is a question of very great importance, let us *reason it together.* Hear me with patience; and, if you still differ with me in opinion, ascribe my opinion to *error,* for it is quite impossible for me to have any *interest* in differing with you. But, before we proceed any further, it may not be amiss to observe, that the writers on the side of Corruption are very anxious to inculcate notions *hostile* to machinery as well as notions hostile to Bakers and Butchers. This fact alone ought to put you on your guard. These men first endeavour to set the labouring class on upon their employers; and then they call aloud for troops to mow them down.

By *machines* mankind are able to do that which their own bodily powers would never effect to the same extent. Machines are the produce of the *mind* of man; and, their existence distinguishes the civilized man from the savage. The savage has no machines, or, at least, nothing that we call machines. But, his life is a very miserable life. He is ignorant; his mind has no powers; and, therefore, he is feeble and contemptible. To shew that machines are not naturally and necessarily an evil, we have only to suppose the existence of a patriarchal race of a hundred men and their families, all living in common, *four men* of which are employed in *making cloth by hand.* Now, suppose some one to discover a machine, by which all the cloth wanted can be made by *one man*. The consequence would be, that the great family would (having enough of every thing else) use *more cloth;* or, if any part of the labour of the three cloth-makers were much wanted in any other department, they would be employed in that other department. Thus, would the *whole* be benefited by the means of this invention; the whole would have more clothes amongst them, or more food would be raised, or the same quantity as before would be raised, leaving the community more leisure for study or for recreation.

See ten miserable mariners cast on shore on a desert island with only a bag of wheat and a little flax-seed. The soil is prolific; they have fish and fruits; the branches or bark of trees would make them houses, and the wild animals afford them meat. Yet, what miserable dogs they are! They can neither sow the wheat, make the flour, nor catch the fish or the animals. But let another wreck toss on the shore a spade, a hand-mill, a trowel, a hatchet, a saw, a pot, a gun, and some fish-hooks and knives, and how soon the scene is changed! Yet, they want clothes, and, in order to make them *shirts,* for instance, six or seven out of the ten are constantly employed in making the linen. This throws a monstrous burden of labour upon the other *three,* who have to provide the food. But, send them a *loom,* and you release six out of the seven from the shirt-making concern; and *ease* as well as plenty immediately succeed.

In these simple cases the question is decided at once in favour of machines. With regard to their effects in a great community like ours, that question is necessarily more complicated; but, at any rate, enough has been said to show, that men cannot live in a civilized state without *machines*; for *every implement* used by man is a *machine,* machine merely meaning *thing* as contra-distinguished from the *hand of man*. Besides, if we indulge ourselves in a cry against machines, *where* are we to stop? Some misguided, poor, suffering men in the county of Suffolk, have destroyed *thrashing* machines? Is not the *flail* a machine? The corn *could* be *rubbed* out in the hand, and winnowed by the *breath;* but, then nine hundred and ninety-nine out of every thousand of us must starve, and the few that remained must become savages.

I will not insult that good sense, of which the men of Nottingham have given so many striking proofs, by pushing further my illustrations of the position, *that machinery in general is not an evil.* But, the great question to be decided, is, whether machinery, *as it at present exists, does not operate to the disadvantage of journeymen and labourers, and is not one cause of the misery they now experience?* This is the great question to be decided. But, before I enter on it, give me leave to shew you, that the *corrupt* press, by which you are so much abused, is actually engaged in the work of sending us back by degrees into the savage state just described!

There is a paper in London, called the COURIER, which is always praising the acts of the government and always abusing the Reformers in the most gross and outrageous manner. The Morning Chronicle asserts that the proprietor of this paper has regular communications with the offices of government. I do not know how this may be; but, certain it is, that through thick and thin, it praises the acts of the government. This paper, on the twenty-first instant, contained the following paragraph:— " Amongst other employments for the poor, it is recommended, that parishes should furnish themselves with *hand corn-mills;* that *parish bake-offices* should be established; and that the *women and girls* should be employed in spinning and carding of wool. In Essex, many hands have been employed to *shell beans in the fields,* which has been done so low as 3*d. per bushel,* a sum *under that usually paid for thrashing.* By this means, the beans are got *quick to market,* first being dried upon the kiln, with the advantage of not being bruised, as they must otherwise have been, if thrashed with the flail."

This is actually a bold step towards the savage state. It is exceedingly foolish, but, as I shall presently show, exceedingly *mischievous* also; or, at least, it would be so, if the people had not too much sense to be misled by it. The mind of man has discovered a mode of preparing corn for making him food by the use of brooks, streams, rivers, and the wind. His mind has subjected the water and wind to his controul, and compelled them to serve him in this essential business. But, these barbarians would fain render his discoveries of no avail. They

would deprive us of the use of the *Wind* and the *Water* in this
respect, and set us to grind our corn *by hand*. Still, hand-mills
are *machines*. Come, then, let us resort to ROBINSON
CRUSOE's *pestle and mortar*. No : those are *machines*. Why,
then, let us, like cattle, grind the corn with our *teeth* !

But, what *good* are these hand-mills to do the *poor* ? Let us
see. There is *one mill* in Hampshire which is capable of
grinding and dressing 200 sacks of wheat in a day. The men
employed in and about this mill are, or would be if in full work,
about *twelve*. Now, there are about 200 parishes in Hampshire
Suppose each has a hand-mill, capable of grinding and dressing
a sack in a day, and that is full as much as can be done by *two
able men*. Here are *four hundred men* and *two hundred
machines* employed to do that which would be a great deal better
done by *twelve men* and one stream of water ! Aye, but this
would find *employment* for 400 men ! Employment ! Why not
employ them " to fling stones against the wind? " What *use*
would their labour be to any body ? May they not as well be
doing *nothing* as doing *no good* ? In short, if the powerful
assistance of the Wind and the Water were thrown aside in this
important business, we should find ourselves making a rapid
progress towards the feebleness of savage life.

" Bake-houses : " parish bake-houses are recommended; and,
for what? People now bake at their own houses, if they choose,
and yet they find, in general, that there is little economy in so
doing. Why, then, this new invention ? It is a gross folly. Why
not recommend us all to make *our own shoes,* our own *hats,* and
so on throughout all the articles of dress and furniture ? Why is
the baker's trade become more unnecessary now than at any
former period ? But, the *folly* is here surpassed by the
mischievousness; because this recommendation has a tendency
to excite *popular discontents against the bakers,* and to cause such
acts of violence as form an excuse for the calling forth of *troops*.
Seeing that this is a matter of great importance, I will lay before
you a statement of the *Bakers' profits,* by which you will see how
unjust are all the attacks which are made upon that description
of persons. The best way, however, to satisfy your minds upon
this subject is to suppose the same man to be both *Miller* and

Baker, and to shew you how much a *Load* of *Wheat* is sold for to
the Miller, and how much it brings back from the public when
paid for by them in the shape of bread.   There is no man in
England better able to speak confidently upon this subject than
I am, having myself caused corn to be ground into flour by a
horse-mill, under my own immediate inspection and super-
intendance, and having verified all the particulars with the
greatest exactness. This very year I have sold wheat at market,
and, at the same time, have ground the same sample of wheat
into flour, for my own use and that of my labourers. Thus I
know to a certainty the profits of the Miller and the Baker both
put together, and my wonder has been, that they find the means
of living upon so small a profit.

I speak of a *Load* of wheat, because my experiments have been
made upon that quantity. A Load is 40 Winchester Bushels. A
load of my wheat, weighing 58½lb. a bushel, and, in the whole,
2349lb. yielded me 1487lb. of flour, fine and seconds; but, I take
it, 1475lb. of fine flour, and 807lb. of Bran, Pollard, and what we
call Blues. The 1475lb. of flour made 1890lb. of *Bread,* according to repeated experiments. The distribution of the Load of
Wheat stood thus :

In flour	. . . .	1487 lbs.
In offal	. . . .	807
Waste	. . . .	55
		————
Weight of Wheat	.	2349

The waste arises partly from what goes off in *dust* about the
mill, but *chiefly* from the *evaporation* which takes place when the
grain comes to be bruised, because, though apparently quite dry
and hard, there is a certain portion of *moisture,* or else there
could be no *vegetation* in the grain, and, it is the small remnant
of this vegetative principle, which causes the flour to *swell.* If
dried upon a kiln, wheat will never produce light bread. Now
as to the *money* part of the concern.

The 1475lb. of flour made 1890lb. of bread, or 438 *quartern*
loaves, at 4lb. 5oz. each. The offal was worth, at the market

price, *a penny a pound weight.* The Bakers in the village sold
bread at the same time, at 1s. 1d. the quartern loaf.

438 loaves amounted to	.	.	.	£23	14	0
807lb. of offal	.	.	.	.	3	17	0
					£27	11	0
Market price of the wheat	.	.	19	0	0
			Balance	£8	11	0

Here, then, is £8 11s. 0d. more than the wheat cost. But,
only think of what is to be done for this sum; The wheat to be
put into the mill; beer for the carters; the grinding and dressing
of the wheat; the sacks to put the flour and offal into; the carrying out of the flour and the offal; a delay in the sale; interest of
the 19*l.* and of all those other outgoings; trust and bad debts;
the taxes on the Miller's horses, on all he uses and consumes.
Then comes the Baker. Fire for his oven; yeast; labour in
making the bread; labour in sending great part of it out; rent of
his house; all his numerous taxes; trust and bad debts; and payment for his time. Is it not wonderful, that a load of wheat can
be manufactured into bread and distributed at so *cheap* a rate?
But, in order to shew you what would be the consequence of
destroying the trade of a Baker, let us suppose the *flour* of this
load of wheat bought by 26 good large families, who require
about a bushel of flour each a week. Here would be 26 ovens to
heat and 26 women employed during the better part of a day.
This would be a cost *double* in amount to the Baker's profit;
and, what then would be the case, if there were 50 or 70 ovens
to heat? My good friends, I know it from very careful observation, that no family can *afford* to bake their own bread, even
where they have ovens, unless they have their *fuel for nothing;*
and I know, too, that labourers, who live in cottages of my own,
who have nice little ovens and *fuel for nothing,* who yet purchase
their bread of the Bakers in the village, if their wives have any
sort of employment in the fields; and, they have convinced me,

that, if the wife loses a day's work in a week for the sake of baking, they *lose* by baking their own bread.

The story of *women and children shelling beans in the field at* 3d. *a bushel* must be false. But, if true, is it possible for any human being to shell in that way a *bushel a day*, while it is well known that a man with a flail will thresh more than *twenty bushels* of beans in a day, and be in the *dry* and be *clean* and warm all the while! But, this is such miserable nonsense, that I will not any longer detain you with further notice of it. Satisfied, that you will be convinced, from what has been said and from the operation of your own good sense, that there is no just ground for anger against Bakers and Butchers, and that the cause of your suffering must be very different from that of any extortions on the part of such tradesmen, I shall now return to the subject of machines, and beg your patient attention, while I discuss the interesting question before stated : that is to say, *Whether Machinery, as it at present exists, does, or does not,* "*operate to the disadvantage of Journeymen and Labourers.*"

The notion of our Labourers in agriculture is, that Thrashing Machines, for instance, *injure* them, because, say they, if it were not for those machines, we should have *more work* to do. This is a great error. For, if, in consequence of using a machine to beat out his corn, the farmer does not expend *so much money* on *that sort* of labour, he has so much *more money* to expend on some *other sort* of labour. If he saves twenty pounds a year in the article of thrashing, he has that twenty pounds a year to expend in draining, fencing, or some other kind of work; for, you will observe, that he does not take the twenty pounds and put it into *a chest* and lock it up, but lays it out in his business; and his business is to improve his land and to add to the quantity and amount of his produce. Thus, in time, he is enabled to feed more mouths in consequence of his machine, and, to buy, and cause others to buy, more clothes than were bought before; and, as in the case of the ten sailors, the skill of the mechanic tends to produce *ease* and *power* and *happiness*.

The thrashing machines employ women and children in a dry and comfortable barn, while the men can be spared to go to work in the fields. Thus the weekly income of the labourer, who has a large family, is, in many cases, greatly augmented, and his life rendered so much the less miserable. But, this is a trifle compared with the great *principle,* upon which I am arguing, and which is applicable to all *manufactories* as well as to farming; for, indeed, what is a farmer other than *a manufacturer of Corn and Cattle?*

That the use of machinery, *generally speaking,* can do the journeyman manufacturer *no harm,* you will be satisfied of in one moment, if you do but reflect, that it is the *quantity of the demand* for goods that must always regulate the *price,* and that the price of the goods must regulate the *wages* for making the goods. I shall show by and by how the *demand,* or *market,* may be affected by an alteration in the currency or money of a country.

The quantity of demand for *Lace,* for instance, must depend upon the quantity of money which the people of the country have to expend. When the means of expending are abundant, then a great quantity of Lace will be bought; but, as those means diminish, so will the purchases of Lace diminish in amount. But, in every state of a country, in this respect, the effect of *machinery* must be the same. There will always be a quantity of money to spare to expend in Lace. Sometimes, as we have seen, the quantity of this money will be greater, and sometimes it will be less; but, in no case do I see, that machinery can possibly do the journeyman lace-maker any harm. Suppose, for instance, that the sum which the whole nation have to expend in Lace, be 100,000 pounds a year; that the number of yards of Lace be 500,000; and that the making of the Lace, at 40*l.* a family, give employment to 2,500 families. The Lace by the means of *machinery* can be made, it is supposed, at 4s. a yard. But, destroy all machinery, and then the Lace cannot be made, perhaps, under 20s. a yard. What would the effect of this be? No advantage to you; because as there is only 100,000*l.* a year to spare to be expended in Lace, there would be a demand for only *one hundred thousand yards* instead of *five hundred thousand yards.* There would still be 2,500 families employed in Lace-making, at 40*l.* a year for each family; but, at any rate, no *advantage* could possibly arise to you from the change, because the whole quantity of money expended in Lace must remain the same.

Precisely the same must it be with regard to the *Stocking* and all other manufactures. But, while the destruction of machinery would produce *no good* to you with regard to the *home* trade, it would produce a great deal of *harm* to you with regard to the foreign trade; because it would make your goods so *high in price,* that other nations, who would very soon have the machinery, would be able to make the same goods at a much *lower price.*

I think, then, that it is quite clear, that the existence of machinery to its present extent cannot possibly do the journeyman manufacturer *any harm;* but, on the contrary, that he must be injured by the destruction of machinery. And, it appears to me equally clear, that if machines could be invented so as to make Lace, Stockings, &c. for half or a quarter the present price, such an improvement could not possibly be injurious to you. Because, as the *same sum of money* would still, if the country continued in the same state, be laid out in Lace, Stockings, &c. there would be a *greater quantity* of those goods sold and used, and the sum total of your wages would be exactly the same as it is now.

But, if machinery were injurious to you now, it must *always* have been injurious to you; and there have been times, when you had no great reason to complain of want of employment at any rate. So that it is evident, that your distress must have arisen from some other *cause* or *causes.* Indeed, I know that this is the case; and, as it is very material that you should have a clear view of these causes, I shall enter into a full explanation of them; because, until we come at the nature of the *disease,* it will be impossible for us to form any opinion as to the *remedy.*

Your distress, that is to say, that which you now more immediately feel, arises from want of employment with wages sufficient for your support. The want of such employment has arisen from the want of a sufficient demand for the goods you make. The want of a sufficient demand for the goods you make has arisen from the want of means in the nation at large to purchase your goods. This want of means to purchase your goods has arisen from the weight of the taxes co-operating with the bubble of paper-money. The enormous burden of taxes and the bubble of paper-money have arisen from the war, the sinecures, the standing army, the loans, and the stoppage of cash payments at the Bank; and, it appears very clearly to me, that these never would have existed, if the Members of the House of Commons had been chosen annually by the people at large.

Now, in order to shew, that taxes produce poverty and misery generally, let us suppose again the case of a great Patriarchal Family. This family we suppose to consist of many men and their wives and children; we suppose them *all to labour* in their different branches; and to enjoy each of them the same degree of wealth and comfort and ease. But, all at once, by some means or other, nine or ten of the most artful men make shift to impose a *tax* upon the rest; and to get from them in this way enough to support themselves and their wives and children *without any work at all.* Is it not clear, that the *taxed part* of the community must *work harder* or *fare worse* in consequence of this change? Suppose this taxing work to go on, and the receivers of taxes to increase, *'till one half* of the whole of the produce of all the labour be taken in taxes. What misery must the *payers of taxes* then begin to endure? It is certain, that they must be punished in two ways; first by an addition to the hardness of their work, and next by a reduction of their former food and clothing. They must, under such circumstances, necessarily become skinny, sick, ragged and dirty. For, you will observe, that those who would *live upon the taxes,* would each of them eat and drink and wear ten times as much as one of the poor mortals who were left to labour and to pay taxes. As these poor creatures would be unable to lay up any thing against a day of sickness or old age, a poor-house must be built to prevent them from actually dying by the road-side, and a part of the taxes must be laid out to support them in some way or other till they expired, or, if children, till they should be able to work.

There can be no doubt, that such would be the effect of heavy taxation in this case; and the same reasoning applies to *millions of families,* only the causes and effects are a little more difficult to trace. Now, you will observe, that I do not say, that *no taxes* ought to be collected. Our vile enemies impute this to me; but, my friends, I have never said it or thought it. In a large community of men, there must be laws to protect the weak against the strong; there must be administrators of the laws; there must be persons to hold communications with foreign powers; there must be, in case of necessary wars, a public force to carry on such wars. All these require taxes of some sort; but, when the load of taxes becomes so heavy as to produce *general misery* amongst all those who pay and who do not receive taxes, then it is that taxes become an enormous evil.

This is our state at present. It is the sum taken from those who labour to be given to those who do not labour, which has produced all our present misery. It has been proved by me, but, which is better for us, it has been expressly acknowledged by Mr. PRESTON, who is a lawyer of great eminence, the owner of a large estate in Devonshire, and a Member of Parliament for a *Borough,* that the labourer who earns 18 pounds a year, pays 10 pounds of it in taxes. I have before observed, but I cannot repeat it too often, that you pay a tax on your shoes, soap, candles, salt, sugar, coffee, malt, beer, bricks, tiles, tobacco, drugs, spirits, and, indeed, on almost every thing you use in any way whatever. And, it is a monstrous cheat in the corrupt writers to attempt to persuade you, that *you* pay *no taxes,* and, upon that ground to pretend, that you have no right to vote for Members of Parliament. In the single article of *salt,* it is very clear to me, that every one of our labourers who has a *family,* pays more than *a pound* every year. The salt is sold in London at 20s. a bushel, wholesale; but, if there was no tax, it would not exceed perhaps 3s. a bushel. Every labourer with a family must consume more than a bushel, which does not amount to more than *the third of half a pint a day;* and, you will bear in mind, there is salt in the bacon, the butter, and the bread, besides what is used in the shape of salt.

Now, is it not clear, then, that you do pay taxes? And, is it not also clear, that the sum, which you pay in taxes is just so much taken from your means of purchasing food and clothes? This brings us back to the cause of your *want of employment* with sufficient wages. For, while you pay heavy taxes, the Landlord, the Farmer, the Tradesman, the Merchant, are not exempt. They pay taxes upon all the articles which they use and consume, and they pay direct taxes besides, on their houses, lands, horses, servants, &c. Now, if they had not to pay these taxes, is it not clear, that they would have more money to expend on labour of various kinds; and, of course, that they would purchase more *Stockings* and more *Lace* than they now purchase? A farmer's wife and daughters, who would lay out 10 pounds in these articles, cannot so lay it out, if it be taken away by the tax-gatherer; and so it is in the case of the Landlord and the Tradesman. I know a country town, where a couple of hundred pounds used to be expended on a *fair day*, in cottons, woollens, gloves, linen, &c. and where, at the last fair, not *fifty* pounds were expended. The country-shopkeeper not wanting the goods to the *same* amount as before, the London wholesale dealer does not want them to that amount; and as he does not want them from your employers, they do not want your labour to the same *amount* as before. So that they are compelled to *refuse you work,* or, to give you work at *low wages,* or, to give away to you their property and means of supporting themselves and their families, which, in reason and justice cannot be expected.

Then there is another very injurious effect produced by this load of taxes. The goods made by you cannot be *so cheap* as if you and your employers had not so heavy taxes to pay. Thus, foreign nations, which are not so much loaded with taxes, can afford to make the goods themselves as cheap, or cheaper, than you can make them. Formerly, when our taxes were light, the Americans, for instance, could not afford to make Stockings, Broad Cloth, Cutlery, Cotton Goods, Glass Wares, Linens. They now make them all, and to a vast extent! They have machinery of all sorts, manufactories upon a large scale, and, what is quite astonishing, they, who, before our wars against the French people, did not grow *wool* sufficient in quantity for their hats and saddle-pads, grow now fine wool sufficient for their own manufactories of cloth, and to *export to Europe*!

This change has been produced wholly by the late wars, and more especially by our Orders in Council and by our impressment of Native American Seaman, which last produced *the war with America,* to carry on which, both parties, the INS and OUTS, most cordially joined. That war finished what the Orders in

Council had begun. It *compelled* the Americans to manufacture; and, in order to protect their own manufactories, the government of that country has naturally passed laws to check the import of ours. Thus it is, my good friends, that the manufacturers of England, Scotland, and Ireland, have lost a considerable part of the custom of *ten millions of farmers and farmers' wives and children*. I foresaw this consequence in 1811; and I most earnestly, at that time, in a series of Letters to the Prince Regent, besought the government not to enter into that fatal war. It was, however, entered into; my advice was rejected, and the manufacturers and merchants of this kingdom are now tasting the bitter fruit of that disgraceful war, which, after having cost about fifty millions of money, was given up in the teeth of a solemn declaration to the contrary, without having effected any one of the objects for which it was professed to have been begun and prosecuted.

Thus, then, my fellow-countrymen, it is not *machinery;* it is not the grinding disposition of your employers; it is not improvements in machinery, it is not extortions on the part of Bakers and Butchers and Millers and Farmers and Corn-Dealers and Cheese and Butter Sellers. It is not to any causes of this sort that you ought to attribute your present great and cruel sufferings; but wholly and solely to the great burden of taxes, co-operating with the bubble of paper-money. And now, before I proceed any further, let me explain to you how the paper-money, or funding system has *worked* us all. This is a very important matter, and it is easily understood by any man of plain good sense, who will but attend to it for a moment.

Before the wars against the French People, which wars have ended in replacing our king's and country's *old enemies,* the family of *Bourbon,* on the thrones of France, Spain and Naples, and which have restored the Inquisition that Napoleon had put down; before those wars, the chief part of the money in England, was *Gold and Silver*. But, even the first war against the people of France cost so much money, that bank-paper was used in such great abundance that, in 1797, people became alarmed, and ran to the Bank of England to get real money for the notes which they held. Then was fulfilled the prophecy of

Mr. PAINE. The Bank *could not pay their notes;* the Bank Directors went to PITT and told him their fears. He called a Council, and the Council issued an *order* to the Bank to *refuse* to pay their promissory notes in specie, though the notes were all payable to the *bearer* and on *demand*. The parliament *afterwards* passed an Act to *protect* Pitt, the Council, and the Bank Directors *against the law*, which had been violated in these transactions!

From this time, there has been little besides paper-money. This became plenty, and of course wages and corn and every thing became *high in price*. But, when the *peace* came, it was necessary to reduce the quantity of paper-money; because, when we came to have intercourse with foreign nations, it would never do to sell a one-pound note at *Calais*, as was the case, for about *thirteen shillings*. The Bank and the Government had it in their power to lessen the quantity of paper. *Down came prices* in a little while; and if the *Debt* and *Taxes* had come down too in the same degree, there would have been no material injury; but, they did not. Taxes have continued the *same*. Hence our ruin; the complete ruin of the great mass of farmers and tradesmen and small landlords; and hence the misery of the people.

But, some of the taxes have been *taken off*. Yes; about 17 millions out of 70, or about a *fourth* part. But, the paper-money has been diminished in a greater degree, and of course, farm-produce in the same degree as paper-money. Bread and Corn sell pretty high, owing to a bad harvest; but we must take *all* the produce of a farm, and you will soon see how the farmer has been ruined.

BEFORE.

	£	s.	d.
A load of Wheat	33	0	0
A Cart Colt 2 years old	38	0	0
A Cow	22	0	0
A South Down Ewe	1	18	0
A Steer for fatting	15	0	0
	£109	18	0

NOW

A load of Wheat	.	.	.	19	0	0
A Cart Colt 2 years old	.	.	8	0	0
A Cow	.	.	.	7	0	0
A South Down Ewe	.	.	0	18	0
A Steer for fatting	.	.	6	0	0

£40 18 0

Thus, our produce has fallen off 69*l*. out of £100. 18s. od. and our taxes have been reduced only 17*l*. in every 70*l*. This has been the effect of the paper-money bubble. I speak this with a certain knowledge of the facts. I myself have 8 beautiful Alderney Heifers, with calf, for which I cannot obtain 4*l*. each. Four years ago I could have sold just such for 16*l*. each. I have 12 Scotch Steers, for which I cannot obtain 5*l*. each. Just such ones, at Barnet fair, only in 1813, I saw sold for 13*l*. *each*. This has been the effect of paper-money; and by this cause have thousands upon thousands of farmers been already wholly ruined, while thousands upon thousands more are upon the threshold of the jail.

Here, then, we have the real causes of your sufferings, of the sufferings of all the labourers, all the farmers, all the tradesmen, and, in short, of every class, *except those who live* upon the taxes.

If, as I observed before, *the taxes had been lowered* in the same degree as the farm produce, the distress would not have been much greater than before; that is to say, if the sum total of the year's taxes had been reduced from 70 millions to about 26 millions. But this could not be done, while the interest of the DEBT was paid in full at 5 per cent. while an army of 150 thousand men was kept up; and while all the pensions and sinecures and the Civil List were kept up to their former amount; and, besides these, all the pay of the Naval and Military People and all others, living, in any way, upon the taxes.

And why should such an army be kept up? There was a time, when a man would have been looked upon as mad, if he had proposed to keep up any standing soldiery at all in time of peace. But, why not reduce *pay* and *salaries*? The JUDGES, for instance, had their salaries *doubled* during the war, and so had the *Police Justices* and many others. When the Whigs (the *famous* Whigs!) were in office, they augmented the allowances of the Junior branches of the Royal Family from 12 thousand pounds each to 18 thousand pounds each, per year. The allowance to the King, Queen, &c. called the Civil List, was augmented enormously. Now, you will observe, that all these augmentations were made upon the express ground, that the *price* of *Provisions* had risen. Well, provisions *fall,* and down come the *wages of journeymen* and *labourers*; and why, in the name of reason and of justice, should not the *salaries of the Judges,* and the pay and allowances of all others in public employ *come down too?* What reason can there be for keeping all these *up,* while *your wages* have come down?

Then, as to the DEBT, why should those who have lent their money to the government to carry on the wars; why should they continue to be paid in full at 5 per cent. interest in the present money? It is the bubble of paper-money; it is the bubble which they have helped to make, which has reduced my Alderney Heifers from 16*l.* value to 4*l.* and why am I and you and all the rest of us to pay them as much as we used to pay them? The greater part of them *lent* their money to the government, when the pound note was not worth more than half what it is worth now, if we take all circumstances into view; and, what right, then, have they to be paid in full in the money of the present day? Yet, they are paid in full, and I am compelled to give them as much tax out of the price of a Heifer worth 4 pounds, as I used to give them out of the price of the Heifer worth 16 pounds. You will see, and you will *feel* most severely, that *corn* is *now dear.* But, this is owing to the *short crop* and *bad harvest.* This high price is no good to the farmer; but a most terrible evil. If he should get 15*s.* a bushel for his wheat instead of 7 or 8*s.* he will receive *no more money;* because he will not have more than *half the quantity* to sell. If I sell a hog at 15*s.* a score instead of 8*s.* I do not gain by the high price; because I am, from the shortness of my crop of corn and the badness of the corn, not able to fat more than half as many hogs as I should have been able to fat, if the crop had been good and the harvest fine. So that, as you will clearly see, as to the *present* high price of corn and bread, that it cannot be any benefit at all to the farmer, and cannot at all tend to enable him to pay the enormous taxes that now press him out of existence.

Thus have I laid before you the *real causes* of your sufferings. You see, that they are deep rooted, of steady growth, and that they never can end but in consequence of some very *material change* in the mode of managing the nation's concerns. They have arisen from the *taxes* and *loans;* those arose out of the *wars*; the wars arose out of a desire to keep down *Reform;* and a desire to keep down Reform arose out of the *Borough System,* which excludes almost the whole of the people from voting at elections. It is a maxim of the English Constitution, that *no man shall be taxed without his own consent.* Nothing can be more reasonable than this. But, as I have shown, we are *all* taxed; you pay away half your wages in taxes; but, do you *all vote for Members of Parliament?* If the Members of Parliament, for the last fifty years, had been chosen *by the people at large,* and *chosen annually,* agreeably to the old laws of the nation, do you believe, that we should have expended one thousand millions in taxes raised during the wars, and another thousand millions which is now existing in the shape of DEBT? This is not to be believed; no man *can* believe it. And, therefore, as the want of such a Parliament is the real root of all our sufferings, the only effectual remedy is to obtain such a parliament. A parliament, *annually chosen by all the people,* seeing that they *all* pay taxes.

In 1780 the late Duke of Richmond brought a bill into the House of Lords to restore the people to their right of having such a parliament; PITT co-operated in this work with the Duke of Richmond; and PITT expressly declared, in a speech in Parliament, that, until the parliament was reformed, it was " *impossible* for English Ministers to be *honest.*" Therefore, this is no *new scheme*; it is a measure long contended for and well digested; it may be carried into effect with perfect safety to every rank in society; and, it is my firm persuasion, that it is the *only* means of preserving order and peace. Indeed, I am of opinion, that it is the *hope* of seeing this measure adopted; that it is the *expectation* that it will be adopted, which *now* preserves that tranquillity in the country, which is so honourable to the understanding and the hearts of the people. God send that this expectation may not be *disappointed*!

In order, that it may not, the people of every class should assemble and petition the *Parliament* for reform. No matter how many or how few, no matter whether in Counties, Cities, Towns, Villages, or Hamlets. We have all *a right to petition;* to perform that right is a sacred *duty;* and to obstruct it a heinous *crime.* But in these petitions, the *only* essential *object* should be *a Reform;* for, though the want of it has produced numerous and great evils, still this is all that need be petitioned for, seeing that a Reform would cure all the evils at once. Trade, commerce, manufactures, agriculture, all would soon revive, and we should again see our country free and happy. But, without a Reform, it is impossible for the nation to revive, and, I believe, it is impossible to prevent utter confusion.

How vain, how stupid, then, are all the schemes of the writers on the side of Corruption for *making employment* for the poor! And how base all their attempts to persuade the people, that their sufferings can be alleviated by what are called "*charitable subscriptions*," which are in fact, only so many acts of *insolence* towards the numerous and unhappy sufferers, who are paying, in the shape of *taxes,* one half of the little that they earn by their labour!

These corrupt writers, in order still to cajole and deceive the people (who, thank God! are no longer to be deceived), recommend to the Landlords and farmers to *make employment* for the poor by causing commodious *roads, footpaths,* and *causeways* to be undertaken; by causing *shell-fish to be gathered for manure;* by causing *lime, chalk, marle,* &c. to be gotten and prepared; by causing *land to be drained and embankments made*! What folly, or what an impudent attempt to deceive! Why, these are some of the very things that the poor would be employed in if the Landlords and Farmers *had money* to give in wages; and, if they have not money to give in wages, how are they to have money to bestow in these works at all?

As to the "*charity subscriptions,*" the people seem to understand the object of them perfectly well. LORD COCHRANE sent them forth to the nation, *stripped of their mask,* for which we are deeply indebted to him, and which debt of gratitude we are not so base as not to pay. The people of GLASGOW led the way in their indignation against the *Soup-shop and its Kettle.* At WIGAN, at OLDHAM, and several other places, where Meetings of the *Subscription Tribe* have been held, the people have told them, that they want not Soup and Old Bones and Bullock's Liver; but they want their *rights.* Indeed, these attempts to hold pretended *charitable* meetings are full of *insolence.* Those who are enabled to work, or to find work, have *a legal right* to be supported out of the taxes raised on the rich and on *all Houses and all Lands.* Why, then, are they to be held out as *beggars?* Why are self-erected bodies to insult them with their pretended *charity?* It is not the poor, who have brought the nation into its present state. It is not they who have ruined so many farmers and tradesmen. The *law* says that they shall be relieved; and, why are they to look to any other relief than this, until the state of the nation can be amended?

But, before I conclude, let me beg your attention to a very curious fact or two as to the employment of the taxes which you and all of us pay. In No. 18 of the Register, which contains an Address to *Journeymen and Labourers* in general, I noticed, that, in the account, which was laid before Parliament in the year 1815, there was a charge for money paid to suffering *French and Dutch Emigrants,* and also to the *Poor* Clergy of the *Church of England.* But, I observed, that I did not know whether any such charges were contained in the accounts laid before parliament this *year,* 1816. I have that account before me now, and what will be your feelings, how will you feel towards the Soup-Kettle Fraternities, when you are told, that there are, in this last account, a charge of *seventy-five thousand pounds* for the Relief of French and Dutch Emigrants, and of *one hundred thousand pounds* for the *poor* Clergy of the Church of England! This is, you will observe, quite a *new* thing. Never till the time of Perceval was any minister bold enough to take money, or to get the parliament to vote money *out of the taxes,* paid by the poor as well as the rich, to be given to the *poor* Clergy of a Church, whose dignitaries and beneficed people are bursting with wealth, and who receive in various ways, *more than five millions a year*! What! And have these Subscription gentry the impudence to look you in the face while these things exist? Have they the impudence to talk of their *charity* towards you, while they say not a word against seeing *you taxed* to help to make up the immense sums thus given in *charity* to the French and Dutch Emigrants and to the Clergy of the Church of England? Put these pithy questions to the insolent Societies of the Soup Kettle, and tell me what they can say in their defence. What! Are you to come crawling, like sneaking Curs, to lick up alms to the amount of *forty or fifty* thousand pounds round the brim of a Soup Kettle, while you are taxed with the rest of us to the amount of *one hundred and seventy-five thousand pounds* in order to give *relief* to French and Dutch Emigrants and to the *poor Clergy* of the Church of England! I do hope, that there are none of my countrymen who will be so base. I trust that they have yet English blood enough left in their veins to make them reject *such alms* with scorn and indignation.

If I had room, I would lay before you an account of some of the other articles of expense, to defray which you are taxed; but, as I intend, within three or four weeks, to shew you how *all* the taxes are expended, I shall now conclude this long letter by expressing my hope, that it will be proved by your subsequent conduct not to have been written wholly in vain.

For past errors I make all possible allowance. We all fall into errors enough naturally; and, no wonder that you should have adopted erroneous notions, seeing that the corrupt press has, for so many years, been at work to deceive and mislead you. This base press, knowing what would be the inevitable consequence of your seeing the *real causes* of your calamities, has incessantly laboured to blind you, or to direct your eyes towards an imaginary cause. Machines, Bakers, Butchers, Brewers, Millers; any thing but the *taxes* and the *paper-money*. In all acts of violence, to which you have been led by these vile hire-lings, you have greatly favoured the cause of corruption, which is never so much delighted as at the sight of *troops* acting against the people. Let me, therefore, most earnestly beseech you to think seriously on these matters; to stay the hand of vengeance against your townsmen and countrymen, and to harbour that feeling to the latest hour of your lives against all that is corrupt and detestable. I have taken the liberty freely to offer you my advice, because I have full confidence in your good sense and your public spirit. The hirelings have endeavoured to exasperate you by their revilings and menaces; I, knowing that brave men are not to be abused or bullied into compliance, have endeavoured to gain you by an appeal to your sense of honour and of justice. The hirelings call aloud for sending forth penal statutes and troops to put you down; I send you the most persuasive arguments my mind can suggest and all the kindest wishes of my heart.

And, with these wishes, I hope I shall always remain,

Your Friend,

WM. COBBETT.

To the Cotton-Lords

P.R. LI., c. 65. *To the Cotton-Lords. On their petition to the honourable House, praying that illustrious and pure Assembly to take measures, for causing an acknowledgment, by England, of the freedom and independence of the Spanish colonies in America: and also on the complaints of the Cotton-Lords against the Corn Bill.* 10-7-24.

MY LORDS,
SEIGNEURS of the Twist, sovereigns of the Spinning-Jenny, great yeomen of the Yarn, give me leave to approach you with some remarks on your Petition to that House which is so well worthy of receiving your prayers. It seems to have been made for you, and you for it. One of its last labours was to pass an act for amending an act passed in " the *thirteenth* year of his *present Majesty* ". The King must be delighted to find, that he has already reigned *thirteen years*! However, here is solid ground of confidence for you; for, if the great big House can make *four* years into *thirteen,* it really may make Catholics love the rulers of Ireland, and induce the Spaniards of America to set their king, and even their priests, at defiance, merely for the sake of having their carcasses covered with your cottons, with your

calicoes, so " well worth the money, Ma'am! see, Ma'am, how *strong* they are! "

*   *   *   *   *   *

To be sure *you* must naturally have a contempt for men who seek *profit,* you scorn all profit, generous souls! If we are to judge by your *tenderness* for the little creatures that swallow the cotton-fuz. " Curse all profit," say you : it is pure tenderness; mere compassion; humanity, (Manchester humanity!); it is philanthropy; it is the milk of human kindness that makes us raise the heat in our factories to *eighty-four degrees!* Indeed! why do you wish to have the poor little creatures so hot? Agreed, since you swear so hard; since you curse all *profit*; since you call God to witness that it is for the sake of humanity that you have raised the heat to eighty-four degrees. Granted that you are as disinterested with regard to the use of this heat, as you are with regard to the independence of the Spanish colonies. Grant it. But, why make the places so *very hot?* Our summer-heat is only seventy-five degrees; and yet you shut these poor little cotton-fuz creatures up in eighty-four degrees of heat. Pray, my Lords, reduce your heat to fifty or sixty degrees; reduce your hours of working to eight in a day for these poor little creatures; show us the petitions that you presented on the subject of the Manchester woundings and killings of the sixteenth of August; show us petitions of yours on the subject of the Oldham Inquest, or on the subject of the Grand-Jury findings in the years 1819 and 1820; or, hold your babbling tongues with regard to South America. The Morning Chronicle of to-day, in lamenting the fall in the price of the funds, observes, that it arises from the Spanish colonists having incurred the displeasure of tyrants, " because they have ventured to *shake off their chains* and resume the rights of mankind." Now, in the first place, there is no shaking off of chains in the case. This is a figurative expression; and by chains every man of sense understands *oppression* to be meant. And what is oppression? What is *tyranny?* Put both the names together, and what do they amount to? I am not asking for their grammatical sense. I am asking you what the *things* amount to. Why, in the end, they destroy people; they actually kill people. But what is the way in which they produce the killing? Why, this is the way they work : they take away the money of the rich : they take away their houses, lands, and all sorts of property. They take away the earnings of the labourer and make him poor. They make him work like a horse to get a quarter of a belly full of victuals. They go on making him poorer and poorer, till they put him into gravel-pits with haybands twisted round his legs instead of stockings. They put a ragged sack over his shoulders in place of a coat. They strip him of his kettles and beer-barrels, and make him drink water. They strip even the women half-naked, and bring whole parishes to the verge of death from starvation. They compel kind and tender parents to drive their children to live in heat of eighty-four degrees and to swallow cotton-fuz : they compel these parents thus to act, in order to avoid more immediate death from starvation. Now, these are " *chains,*" Mr. Morning Chronicle; and did you ever hear of chains like these being in use in the Spanish colonies? What do you mean by the people having broken their chains, then? I push you to the point : tell me *what chains.* But, if the loan-jobbing villains were to keep possession of the governments of those countries, there would soon be real chains enough : there would soon be *death* from starvation; a thing that the Spanish colonies never yet saw.

Growth of Manufactures

P.R. LII., c. 451. *To the Landowners. On the evils of collecting Manufacturers into great masses.* 20-11-24.

IT is the natural tendency of a system of loans and funds to draw money into great masses; to rob the most numerous class, and still to keep heaping riches upon the few. The Devil of Funding covers the country with his imps, the tax-gatherers. These latter draw away the substance of the people, and bring it to be deposited in great parcels. Thus collected into great parcels, it is made the means of commanding the common people to stoop in abject submission to the few.

Before this infernal system was known in England; before this system, which has corrupted every thing, was known in this country, there were none of those places called Manufactories.

To speak of these places with any degree of patience is impossible. It is to be a despicable hypocrite, to pretend to believe that the slaves in the West Indies are not better off than the slaves in these manufactories. However, I have first to speak of the great injury which these factories, as they are called, have done *the land*.

The occupations of the people of a country consist, in a great part, of the rearing of *food* and of *raiment*. Every thing of which food and raiment are composed, is produced by *agriculture*. To the carrying on of agriculture a great part of the labour of the whole of the people is necessary. The *men* and the stout boys are, and must be, the principal workers upon the land. At particular seasons, women and girls do something in the fields, and also the little boys. But, during the far greater part of the year, there is no work in the fields for the women and girls. When things are in their proper state, they are employed, at these times of the year, in *preparing materials for the making of raiment* : and, in some instances, actually making articles of raiment. In the "*dark ages*," when I was a boy, country labourers' wives used to spin the wool, and knit the stockings and gloves that were wanted in the family. My grandmother knit stockings for me after she was blind. In those "*dark ages*," the farmers' wives and daughters and servant maids, were spinning, reeling, carding, knitting, or at something or other of that sort, whenever the work of the farm-house did not demand them.

The manufacturing which was thus divided amongst the millions of labourers' wives and children, while it was a great blessing to the labouring people themselves, was, also, a great benefit to the landowner. Agriculture cannot be carried on without men and boys. But, to have these men and boys, you must have *women* and *girls;* and if you have these without their having profitable employment, you must have them a burden upon the land. They must be kept by the parish rates, instead of being kept by their own labour.

The lords of the loom, enabled by the funding system, and encouraged and assisted by this foolish Government in all sorts of ways, have drawn away from the land all this profitable and suitable employment for the women and girls. Some will say, that the women and girls may follow the employment to the factories. That is impossible. They cannot do that. They must remain with the men and the boys, or there will be nobody at all to carry on the labours of agriculture.

* * * * * *

This is one great cause of pauperism, and of the degradation of the people. The women and girls must be where the men and boys are; and a wise government would have taken care that they should not lose their employment. This is, however, only to say, that a wise government would not have made a funding system, and that it would have done none of those things, by which the country has been brought into its present state. The man who invented the funding system should have been burnt alive the moment he opened his lips upon the subject. It has totally eradicated happiness in this country; and it must, at last, bring dreadful punishment upon somebody; upon some of its upholders and abettors.

When MALTHUS and his crew are talking of an increase in the population, they have their eye upon the masses which their greedy upstart lords of the loom have drawn together; and the horrible condition of which masses I shall more particularly mention by-and-by. They overlook the depopulation which has taken place in order to create this abominable crew of upstarts, who, in order to support their injustice and tyranny, which are wholly without a parallel, except, perhaps, in the cases connected with the game, procured laws to be passed, called *combination laws*, such as never were heard of before in any country in the world.

MALTHUS and his crew of hardhearted ruffians; those cool calculators of how much *" national wealth "* can be made to arise out of the misery of millions, wholly overlook the frightful *depopulation* which has taken place in consequence of the destruction of *seven-eighths*, at least, of the farm-houses, and a similar destruction of cottages, in consequence of the enclosure of wastes. This destruction has, in part, arisen from the total ruin of the agricultural manufactories. These profitable labours having been taken from the women, girls, and little boys, it became hardly possible for a large family to live upon a small farm. The profit of the small farm received a great addition from the fruit of the labours of spinning, knitting, and the like; but, when these were taken away by the lords of the loom; when flagrant impolicy had thrown all these profits into the hands of a very few persons, who had converted the manufacturing labourers into the slaves that we shall presently see them, the little farm itself did not afford a sufficiency of means to maintain a considerable family. The occupiers of such farms became poor; became unable to pay their rents, and, in a short time, were driven from their healthy habitations; were huddled into sheds and holes, became mere labourers, and a large part of them paupers. MALTHUS and his crew never look at this cause of depopulation. The landowner naturally sought to get rent for his land, and he could now get it from nobody but one who had money sufficient to hold nine or ten farms. The women, girls and little children, having now lost their natural employment for the greater part of the year, became a mere burden upon the land; and the farmer and landowner resorted to all sorts of expedients to diminish that burden. To diminish the burden there were no means but that of reducing the number of the labouring class of country people as much as possible. The man and the boy were necessary to agriculture, agriculture could not have them without the women and the girls; it became necessary, therefore, to do without the men and the boys as much as possible.

To do without them, all sorts of schemes were resorted to. To make horses perform that which was before performed by men, was one of the methods pursued, and with most destructive success. So that, at last, the agricultural parts of the country have been stripped of a very large part of their population. Every scheme that the ingenuity of greediness could devise has been put in practice; but, after all, there remains a mass of pauperism and misery which the law-makers themselves declare is frightful to behold; and, whatever else their reports may contain; however widely they may differ from one another; and however completely each may be at variance with itself, every one declares that the *evil is constantly increasing*.

While this is the case, and while the country is going on becoming more and more depopulated, and more and more miserable, the great towns, and particularly the manufacturing districts, are daily increasing in numbers. If the people, thus drawn together in masses, were happily situated there might be the less ground for lamentation; but, so far from this being the case, these masses are still more miserable than the wretches left behind them in the agricultural districts.

Some of these lords of the loom have in their employ thousands of miserable creatures. In the cotton-spinning work, these creatures are kept, fourteen hours in each day, locked up, summer and winter, in a heat of from EIGHTY TO EIGHTY-FOUR DEGREES. The rules which they are subjected to are such as no negroes were ever subjected to. I once before noticed a statement made on the part of these poor creatures, relative to their treatment in the factories of Lancashire. This statement is dated on 15th of February 1823, and was published at Manchester by J. PHENIX, No. 12, Bow-street, in that blood-stained town. This statement says, that the heat of the factories is from *eighty to eighty-four degrees*. A base agent of the Cotton-Lords, who publishes a newspaper at Stockport, has lately accused me of exaggeration, in having stated the heat at *eighty-four degrees*.

Now, the statement of which I am speaking was published at Manchester; and does any man believe that such a statement would have been published there, if it had not been founded on fact? There was a controversy going on at the time of the publishing of this statement. I read very carefully the answer to this statement; but this answer contained no denial of the heat being from *eighty to eighty-four degrees*.

Now, then, do you duly consider what a heat of *eighty-two* is? Very seldom do we feel such a heat as this in England. The 31st of last August, and the 1st, 2d and 3d of last September, were very hot days. The newspapers told us that men had dropped down dead in the harvest fields, and that many horses had fallen dead upon the road; and yet the heat during those days never exceeded eighty-four degrees in the *hottest part of the day*. We were retreating to the coolest rooms in our houses; we were pulling off our coats, wiping the sweat off our faces, puffing, blowing and panting, and yet we were living in a heat nothing like eighty degrees. What, then, must be the situation of the poor creatures who are doomed to toil day after day, for three hundred and thirteen days in the year, fourteen hours in each day, in an average heat of eighty-two degrees? Can any man, with a heart in his body, and a tongue in his head, refrain from cursing a system that produces such slavery and such cruelty?

Observe, too, that these poor creatures have no cool room to retreat to, not a moment to wipe off the sweat, and not a breath of air to come and interpose itself between them and infection. The " door of the place wherein they work, *is locked, except half an hour,* at tea-time, the workpeople are not allowed to send for water to drink, in the hot factory; even the *rain water is locked up,* by the master's order, otherwise they would be happy to drink even that. If any spinner be found with his *window open,* he is to pay a fine of a shilling "! Mr. MARTIN of Galway has procured acts of parliament to be passed to prevent *cruelty to animals.* If horses or dogs were shut up in a place like this, they would cerainly be thought worthy of Mr. MARTIN'S attention.

Not only is there not a breath of sweet air in these truly infernal scenes; but, for a large part of the time, there is the abominable and pernicious stink of the GAS to assist in the murderous effects of the heat. In addition to the noxious effluvia of the gas, mixed with the steam, there are the *dust,* and what is called the *cotton-flyings* or *fuz,* which the unfortunate creatures have to inhale; and, the fact is, the notorious fact is, that well constituted men are rendered old and past labour at forty years of age, and that children are rendered decrepid and deformed, and thousands upon thousands of them slaughtered by consumptions, before they arrive at the age of sixteen. And, are these establishments to boast of? If we were to admit the fact, that they compose an addition to the population of the country; if we were further to admit, that they caused an addition to the pecuniary resources of the Government, ought not a government to be ashamed to derive resources from such means?

*   *   *   *   *   *

When the pay, the miserable pittance of pay, gets into the hands of these poor creatures, it has to be laid out at a SHOP. That shop is, generally, directly or indirectly, the master's. At this shop the poor creatures must lay out their money, or they are very soon turned off. The statement that I have just mentioned relates an instance, where, " If any workman's wife purchase but a trifling matter at another shop, the shopkeeper tells the *book-keeper,* and the latter says to the workmen, that the master *will not allow of such work,* and that they must tell their wives neither to go to another shop nor *give saucy language to the shop-keeper"*!

It must be manifest to every one, that, under such circumstances, the *pay* is nearly nominal. The greedy master takes back again as much of it as he pleases. Another mode of despoiling the poor creatures is this : The master is the owner of cottages, or, rather, holes, which the work-people have to rent. The statement says, " That cottages of exceedingly small dimensions are let to the workmen at NINE POUNDS A-YEAR. But though the rent is by the year, it is stopped from him at the end of every fortnight. A *cellar* is *two shillings and sixpence a-week;* and if a house or cellar be empty, and a workman come to work, and have another house or cellar already, he must *pay rent for the empty one,* whether he occupy it or not."

Nine hundred and ninety-nine thousandths of the people of England have not the most distant idea that such things are carried on, in a country calling itself free; in a country whose Minister for Foreign Affairs is everlastingly teasing and bothering other Powers to emulate England in *" her humanity,"* in abolishing the slave trade in the blacks. The blacks, when carried to the West Indies, are put into a paradise compared with the situation of these poor white creatures in Lancashire, and other factories of the North. And yet, the Editor of the Morning Chronicle is incessantly singing forth the blessings of the manufacturing districts. Bad as is the situation of the labourers in the agricultural counties, it is heaven itself compared with that of these poor creatures. In Norfolk and Suffolk, and particularly in the latter county, the labourers have been greatly subdued; but, I am quite satisfied that the Cotton-Lords, if they had to do with the people from Surrey, from Kent, from Sussex, from Hampshire, from Berkshire, or from any of the Western counties, would be obliged to content themselves with a much lower degree of heat, and much smaller profits.

Then, the immoralities engendered in these pestiferous scenes are notorious. They were very well described by TIMOTHEUS, in a letter first published in a Manchester paper, and re-published in the Register, in August last. "Here," as that writer observes, "the sexes are huddled together, while man is separated from wife, and child from father, for full three-fifths of the waking hours of their lives." All experience proves, that the congregating of people together in great masses, is sure to be productive of impurity of thought and of manners. The country lad, who becomes a soldier, has a new soul in him by the time that he has passed a year in a barrack-room. Even in great schools, all experience tells us how difficult it is to prevent contagious immoralities. This is universally acknowledged. What, then, must be the consequences of heaping these poor creatures together in the cotton-factories? But, what more do we want; what other proof of the corrupting influence of these assemblages; what more than the following regulation, which I take from the list of fines, imposed at the factory of TYLDESLEY, in Lancashire?

Any two Spinners, *found together* in the *necessary*, each man . . . 1s.

I challenge the world to produce me so complete a proof of familiarity with the most shocking immorality. One is almost ashamed to put the thing upon paper, though for the necessary purpose of exposing it to just indignation. To what a pitch must things have come; how familiar people must have become with infamy, before a master manufacturer could put such a thing into writing, and stick it up in his factory! What hotbeds of vice and corruption! Here we have, in the heart of England, hatched the heat of the East, and hatched all its loathsome and infamous vices along with it: and yet these manufactories are to be *our boast*, and we are to applaud the Government for having upheld and cherished them!

Want of Employment

P.R. LXIV., c. 712.   *Want of Employment.   Eating System.*   15-12-27.

ON all hands it is agreed that there is a great want of employment for the labouring class of the people. The cause of
this, that is to say, the original cause, has been the weight of the
taxes, and the operation of the paper-money monopoly; these
have driven occupiers of manufactories and of farms to those
measures which shift the weight from their own shoulders to
those of the defenceless class of labourers. These measures have
been, the invention of machines of various descriptions, for the
purpose of diminishing the quantity of manual labour, and of
reducing the wages of the labourers to the lowest possible degree
consistent with their bare existence; and even that would have
been kept from them, and a resort to the rights of nature, on the
parts of the labourers, must have taken place long ago, had it
not been for the Poor Laws. An insurrection of hunger must
have put an end to the Government itself, had it not been for
those laws.

The schemes, the models, the discussions verbally as well as
in print, most in vogue amongst the *" Agriculturalists,"* as the
nonsensical phraseology of the day terms them, have all turned
upon that most *" desirable "* thing, diminishing the wages of
labour; or, in other words, deducting from the share the labourer
formerly received from the produce of the earth : wind, water,
fire, and all the arts and sciences, have been pressed into the
service, for the purpose of effecting this object; till at last a
Scotchman formally announces a scheme of *ploughing the land
by steam,* and of greatly augmenting the produce of the earth
that way; forgetting, as Scotchmen do, upon such occasions, that
he would destroy the people for whom the produce of the earth
is wanted; that our King would have machines and not men for
his subjects; and that the country, which would be wholly defenceless, would bring invaders out of mere charity to eat the
Scotchman's " surplus produce." Every thing that can be done by
wheels, by iron, by steel, by wood, by horses, has been done by
them, as it were for the purpose of starving the labouring classes
out of existence.

No wonder that a " *want of employment* " should form a great feature of this unhappy era : no wonder that starvation presents itself, in all its horrid forms in every part of the kingdom, and that the present dress, and make, and countenances of the English labouring people, should make all ancient descriptions of them appear to have been the cruelest of irony. At last it has come to this, that the great political philosophers, including certain bodies of men, who ought to know better, but whom I do not think it very prudent to name; that all these, may be divided into two classes, the NASTY and the STUPID. The former class of philosophers wish to *put an end to the breeding* of the labouring people; the latter seem content to let them breed on, and to get rid of the stock, as soon as fit for removal, by a sort of transportation; which they call emigration. In the end, the whole of the schemers appear to be in a desperate dilemma; all their remedies, one after the other, prove to be abortive, and the evil goes raging on, from bad to worse, seeming to threaten in the end a total breaking up of the community.

I have observed above, that the taxation, the funding system, and the necessary accomplishments of these form the original cause of this great, this enormous evil. But, the immediate cause, consists of these things : the substituting of machine and of horse labour, for manual labour; the driving of the single men, boys and young women from the farm houses; the paying of wages out of poor rates; and, lastly, the accursed practice of sending the produce of the land, or, rather, the diminishing the quantity of that produce, and sending a large part of the money which the rest brings, to be expended upon articles, almost wholly useless in themselves, and brought from foreign countries. What a disgraceful fact, how monstrously disgraceful to the understandings of the English Land-holders, that the single article of *tea,* which, every one allows, has in it no nourishment at all, should cost the people of England more every year than the article of MALT. This fact alone would be enough, if there were no other, to account for the miseries of the people.

I do not pretend that any *general* change can be effected for the better until the change of the system shall come; but I know this, that if a change of the system would come, very little good would be effected for the people at large, unless, with that change of system, there came a change as to the *habits* of the people. I have no scruple to say, that it is my sincere conviction, that if the taking off of the malt tax did not cause the tea-kettle and the tea-tackle to be kicked out of the houses of the poor or labouring classes, even the taking off that tax would be of very little service to the country. Even a parliamentary reform would effect no great good, unless the reformed parliament set itself resolutely to work to eradicate the vicious habits, which taxation and a want of wisdom have introduced. I am firmly convinced that this system must be changed; that the parliament must be reformed; that wise and humane measures must and will be adopted : and though I know, that all my reasoning, adding thereunto my example, are not likely to produce any general immediate effect, I am nevertheless persuaded, that that reasoning and that example will cause much talk and much discussion; and that such discussion will tend to prepare men's minds for the change of habit which it is my great object to introduce.

I was aware, that a change, such as I had resolved to put in practice, would necessarily produce a great deal of acrimonious feeling among Big Brewers, East and West Indians, and all the shopkeeping tribe, who live at their ease, and waddle about in the villages as fat as hogs, by tricking the poor starving labourers out of their money, for tea, sugar, coffee; and others, for stuff that they call beer. This race of beings have in a great measure set aside the markets and the fairs. Every labouring creature is constantly in their debt, and he purchases at the rate that men sell to insolvents, or to persons suspected of insolvency. In many places, the money-wages are paid to the shopkeeper, who knows nothing of the money but its name. Upon this race of shop-keepers and beer-sellers my scheme is open and desperate war; and war, too, in which they are *sure* to be beaten. Through them I drive at the East and West Indian, and the Big Brewer; but the lower order of these grinders of the labourers feel the attack first, and are therefore more sharp-sighted and more keen in their resentment, than those for whom they are the receivers.

Factory Bill

P.R. LXXXI., c. 180. *Factory Bill*. 20-7-33.

AT about one o'clock this morning, the House of Commons divided on the Factory Bill of Lord ASHLEY, and defeated his bill, in fact, by 238 votes against 93. The MILL-OWNERS, as they call them in Yorkshire and Lancashire, thus carried their point so far. I shall give a more full account of the matter another time. It is now six o'clock and I did not get to bed till half-after-two; and this must be printed and published this afternoon. I think it right, to prevent misrepresentation, to report what I said upon the subject, especially as it was so very little. I attempted to speak four or five times during the evening; but did not get an opportunity. The debate was closing at half-after twelve; and the main argument of the opponents of Lord ASHLEY was, that if two hours' labour from these children, under eighteen years of age, were taken off, the consequences, on a *national scale,* might be " truly dreadful"! It might, and would, destroy manufacturing capital; prevent us from carrying on competition with foreign manufacturers, reduce mills to a small part of their present value; and break up, as it were, the wealth and power of the country; render it comparatively feeble; and expose it to be an easy prey to foreign nations. What I said, was that which here follows, as near as I can recollect, word for word. " Sir, I will make but one single observation upon this subject; and that is this : that this *'reformed'* House has, this night, made a *discovery* greater than all the discoveries that all former Houses of Commons have ever made, even if all their discoveries could have been put into one. Heretofore, we have sometimes been told that our ships, our mercantile traffic with foreign nations by the means of those ships, together with our body of rich merchants; we have sometimes been told that these form the source of our wealth, power, and security. At other times, the land has stepped forward, and bid us look to it, and its yeomanry, as the sure and solid foundation of our greatness and our safety. At other times, the Bank has pushed forward with her claims, and has told us, that great as the others were, they were nothing without ' PUBLIC CREDIT,' upon which, not only the prosperity and happiness, but the very independence of the country depended. But, Sir, we have this night discovered, that the shipping, the land, and the Bank and its credit, are all nothing worth compared with the labour of three hundred thousand little girls in Lancashire! Aye, when compared with only an eighth part of the labour of those three hundred thousand little girls, from whose labour, if we only deduct two hours a day, away goes the wealth, away goes the capital, away go the resources, the power, and the glory of England! With what pride and what pleasure, sir, will the right honourable member opposite (Mr. P. Thomson), the honourable member for MANCHESTER behind me, go northward with the news of this discovery, and communicate it to that large portion of the little girls whom they have the honour and the happiness to represent!"

Strange to say, our Chancellor of the Exchequer really appeared to be *angry* with me for this! For, having complimented the mill-owners on the "*strong minds,*" of which they had given proof, he was "*free to confess,*" that in the speech of the *honourable member for Oldham* he found a very *striking contrast*" with the effusions of those strong minds!

NINE

THE LAWS OF POLITICAL ECONOMY

Political Economy

P.R. LIV., c. 116. " *Liberal* " *Press.* 9-4-25.

"**R**ECEIVED doctrines of *Political Economy*." Received *by whom*? I know of nobody but the empty-headed dupes of the Scotch Jews who *receive* them. And, what is this " *Political Economy* "? This writer speaks of it as if it were an *Act of Parliament,* or, some great *public cause,* or *institution.* Who would think, that he meant a heap of rubbishy paragraphs, written by a man who " made half a million of money by *watching the turn of the market,*" and another such a heap, written by a Parson, who proposed to starve the *working people,* to check *their breeding children*? Who would think, that he meant the nasty, beastly, and blackguard stuff, that a Scotchman at Sheffield and Leeds is reading, in the way of *lectures,* to the working men, in order to induce them to *insist upon their wives using the proper means to prevent them from having children*?

Overproduction

P.R. XL., c. 721. *Letters to Landlords. On the Agricultural Report and Evidence.* 29-9-21.

THEY speak of " *redundant* production," and observe, that this admits of no " *adequate remedy,*" except that of diminution of supply or increase of demand. They further observe that " *no relief* " from exportation can be expected, till there be a scarcity abroad, or a " *failing crop here,* either of which will restore the markets to their natural level." They speak of the " *inconvenience* " arising from " *abundance,*" and, observe, that this cannot be " *alleviated* " by any legislative provision. Now, was ever language like this made use of before, in any part of the world, since the world was a world? Did ever man before hear of *abundance* being an *inconvenience*? Did ever man before hear the word *redundant* applied to the products of the earth? Did ever man before hear of a *remedy* being wanted for an *abundant crop*? Did ever man hear, since the world began, of a wished for *alleviation* of the effects of *abundance*? It required this state of things; it required the nation to be under the effect of the measures of PITT and his successors; it required the existence of a system of paper money to put it into men's minds to venture upon paper such combinations of words. Instead of prayers for gentle showers; for plenty and for cheapness, we ought, according to these notions, to pray for floods, blights, parching droughts, blasting winds, the fly, caterpillars, grubs, wire-worm, lice and locusts. Sunshine in harvest ought to be hateful to our sight; and, oh! what pleasure to see the wheat growing in the ear, or coming home to the yard soaked and sopped in the wagon! *Redundant production*! No *remedy* for this! Redundant means *too much*. Remedy means the *getting rid of an evil*. And these words we have lived to see applied to the harvests of England! But, the system of paper money is full of monstrousness. It destroys the very mind and thoughts. It makes good evil. Like Satan, it says, "Evil be thou my good." However, it is waste of words to talk thus. This question presses itself upon every mind: What! how wretched; how troubled; how unnatural; how every thing abominable, must that state of things be, where abundant harvest can be called a *redundancy*, and where men can talk of a *remedy* for such *redundancy*!

To Parson Malthus

P.R. XXXIV., c. 1019. *To Parson Malthus, On the Rights of the Poor, and on the cruelty recommended by him to be exercised towards the Poor*. 8-5-19.

PARSON,

I have, during my life, detested many men; but never any one so much as you. Your book on POPULATION contains matter more offensive to my feelings even than that of the Dungeon-Bill. It could have sprung from no mind not capable of dictating acts of greater cruelty than any recorded history of the massacre of St. Bartholomew. Priests have, in all ages, been remarkable for cool and deliberate and unrelenting cruelty; but it seems to have been reserved for the Church of England to produce one who has a just claim to the atrocious pre-eminence. No assemblage of words can give an appropriate designation of you; and, therefore, as being the single word which best suits the character of such a man, I call you *Parson*, which, amongst other meanings, includes that of Borough-monger Tool.

It must be very clear to every attentive reader of your book on *Population*, that it was written for the sole purpose of preparing before-hand a justification for those deeds of injustice and cruelty, of which the *Parish Vestry Bill* appears to be a mere prelude. The project will fail; the tyrants will not have the *power* to commit the deeds, which you recommend, and which they intend to commit. But, that is no matter. It is right that the scheme should be exposed; in order that, as we ought to take the will for the deed, we may be prepared to do justice to the schemer and to the intended executors of the scheme.

In your book you shew, that, in certain cases, a *crowded* population has been attended with great evils, a great deal of unhappiness, misery and human degradation. You then, without any reason to bear you out, predict, or leave it to be clearly inferred, that the same is likely to take place in England. Your principles are almost all false; and your reasoning, in almost every instance, is the same. But, it is not my intention to waste my time on your abstract matter. I shall come, at once, to your practical result; to your recommendation to the Borough-mongers to pass laws to *punish the poor for marrying*.

I have in my possession a list of 743 parsons (of the Church of England I mean) who have taken an active part in the Dungeon and Oliver proceedings, either as justices of the peace, or as suppressors, unlawfully, of my publications. They have threatened hawkers; they have imprisoned many; they have starved the families of not a few; they have threatened book-sellers; they have, in many instances (not less than twenty that have come to my knowledge) caused "*Paper against Gold*" to be excluded from *reading rooms*, though that is a work which

ought to be read by every one, high as well as low, rich as well
as poor. I must hate these execrable Parsons; but, the whole mass
put together is not, to me, an object of such perfect execration as
you are. You are, in my opinion, a man (if we give you the
name) not to be expostulated with; but to be punished. And, I
beg the public to regard this paper of mine as intended merely
to prove, that you deserve the severest punishment that outraged
laws can inflict upon you.

The bare idea of a *law* to punish a labourer and artizan for
marrying; the bare idea is enough to fill one with indignation
and horror. But, when this is moulded into a distinct proposal
and strong recommendation, we can hardly find patience
sufficient to restrain us from breaking out into a volley of curses
on the head of the proposer, be he who he may. What, then,
can describe our feelings, when we find that this proposition
does not come from an *Eunuch;* no, nor from a *Hermit;* no,
nor from a man who has condemned *himself* to a life of *Celibacy,*
but from a *Priest* of a church, the origin of which was the in-
continence of its Clergy, who represented views of chastity as
amongst the damnable errors of the Church of Rome, and have,
accordingly, fully indulged themselves in carnal enjoyments:
what can describe our feelings, when we find that the proposition
comes from a Priest of this luxurious, this voluptuous, this
sensual fraternity, who, with all their piety, were unable to
devote their own vessels to the Lord!

But, before I proceed further, let us have your proposition
before us in your own insolent words; first observing, that, at
the time when you wrote your book, the Borough-mongers began
to be alarmed at the increase of the *Poor rates.* They boasted of
wonderful *national prosperity;* wonderful ease and happiness;
wonderful improvements in agriculture; but, still the poor-rates
wonderfully increased. Indeed, they seemed to increase with
the *increase* of the Borough-mongers' *national prosperity;* which
might, I think, very fairly be called the eighth wonder of the
world.

Being in this puzzle, the Borough-mongers found in a Priest
the advocate of a method to rid them of their ground of alarm.
You, overlooking all the *real causes* of the increase of the paupers,

assumed, without any internal proof, and against all experience, that *the giving of relief* is the cause of the evil; and then you came to your proposition of a *remedy*. The words, the infamous words, are as follows :

" To this end I should propose a regulation to be made, declaring, that *no child* born from any marriage taking place after the expiration of a year from the date of the law : and no illegitimate *child* born two years from the same date, should ever be entitled to parish assistance. After the public notice, which I have proposed, had been given, to the punishment of nature HE should be left; the punishment of severe want : all parish assistance should be rigidly denied him. HE should be taught that the laws of nature had doomed him and *his family* to starve; that HE had no claim on society for the smallest portion of food; that if HE and *his family* were saved from suffering the utmost extremities of hunger, he would owe it to the pity of some kind benefactor, to whom HE ought to be bound by the strongest ties of gratitude."

*   *   *   *   *   *

You talk of the *" punishment of nature"*; you talk of " the *laws of nature* having doomed him and his family to *starve"*. Now, in the first place, the laws of nature; the most imperative of all her laws, bid him *love* and seek the gratification of that passion in a way that leads to the procreation of his species. The laws of nature bid man as well as woman desire to produce and preserve children. Your prohibition is in the face of these imperative laws; for you punish the illegitimate as well as the legitimate offspring. I shall not talk to you about *religion,* for I shall suppose you, being a Parson, care little about that. I will not remind you, that the articles of the Church, to which articles you have *sworn,* reprobate the doctrine of celibacy, as being hostile to the word of God; that the same article declares that it is lawful for all Christian men to marry; that one of the Church prayers beseeches God that the married pair may be fruitful in children; that another prayer calls little children as arrows in the hand of the giant, and says that the man is happy who has his quiver full of them; that the scriptures tell us that LOT's neighbours were consumed by fire and brimstone, and that ONAN was stricken dead; that adultery and fornication are held, in the New Testament, to be deadly sins: I will not dwell upon any thing in this way, because you, being a Parson, would laugh in my face. I will take you on your own ground: the *laws of nature*.

The laws of nature, written in our passions, desires and propensities; written even in the organization of our bodies; these laws compel the two sexes to hold that sort of intercourse, which produces children. Yes, say you: but nature has *other laws,* and amongst those are, that man shall live by *food,* and that, if he cannot obtain food, he shall *starve*. Agreed, and, if there be a man in England who cannot find, *in the whole country,* food enough to keep him alive, I allow that *nature has doomed him to starve*. If, in no shop, house, mill, barn, or other place, he can find food sufficient to keep him alive; *then,* I allow, that the laws of nature condemn him to die.

"Oh!" you will, with Parsonlike bawl, exclaim, "but he must not commit *robbery* or *larceny*!" Robbery or Larceny! what do you mean by that? Does the law of *nature* say any thing about robbery or larceny? Does the law of nature know any thing of these things? No: the law of nature bids man to take, whenever he can find it, whatever is necessary to his life, health, and ease. So, you will quit the law of nature *now,* will you? You will only take it as far as serves your purpose of cruelty. You will take it to sanction your barbarity; but will fling it away when it offers the man food.

Your muddled Parson's head has led you into confusion here. The *law of nature* bids a man *not starve* in a land of plenty, and forbids his being punished for taking food, wherever he can find it. Your law of nature is sitting at Westminster, to make the labourer pay taxes, to make him fight for the safety of the land, to bind him in allegiance, and when he is poor and hungry, to cast him off to starve, or, to hang him if he takes food to save his life! That is your law of nature; that is a Parson's law of nature. I am glad, however, that you blundered upon the law of nature; because that is the very ground, on which I mean to start in endeavouring clearly to establish the *Rights of the Poor;* on which subject I have, indeed, lately offered some observations to the public, but on which subject I have not dwelt so fully as its importance seemed to demand; especially at a time, when the Poor ought to understand clearly what their rights are.

When nature (for God and religion is out of the question with Parsons); when nature causes a country to exist and people to exist in it, she leaves the people, as she does other animals, to live as they can; to follow their own inclinations and propensities; to exert their skill and strength for their own advantage, or, rather, at their pleasure. She imposes no shackles other than those which the heart and mind themselves suggest. She gives no man dominion over another man, except that dominion which grows out of superior cunning or bodily strength. She gives to no man any portion of the earth or of its fruits for his own exclusive enjoyment. And, if any man, in such a state of things, cannot get food sufficient to keep him alive, he must die; and, it may truly enough, *then,* be said, that "the laws of nature have *doomed* him to be starved."

But, when this state of things is wholly changed; when the people come to an agreement to desist, *for their mutual benefit,* from using their cunning and strength at their sole will and pleasure. When the strong man agrees to give up the advantage which nature has given him, in order that he may enjoy the greater advantage of those regulations which give *protection to all,* he surely must be understood to suppose, as a condition, that no state of things is ever to arise, in which he, without having broken the compact on his part, is to be refused, not only protection from harm, but even the bare means of existence.

The land, the trees, the fruits, the herbage, the roots are, by the law of nature, the common possession of all the people. The social compact, entered into for their mutual *benefit* and *protection;* not Castlereagh's "*social system,*" which means the employment of spies and blood-money men and the existence of mutual suspicion and constant danger to life and limb. The social compact gives rise, at once, to the words *mine* and *thine.* Men exert their skill and strength upon particular spots of land. These become *their own.* And, when laws come to be made, these spots are called the *property* of the owners. But still the property, in land especially, can never be so *complete* and *absolute* as to give to the proprietors the right of withholding the means of existence, or of animal enjoyment, from any portion of the people; seeing that the very foundation of the compact was, the *protection* and *benefit* of the whole. Men, in agreeing to give up their rights to a common enjoyment, of the land and its fruits, never could mean to give up, in any contingency, their right to *live* and to *love* and to seek the gratification of desires necessary to the perpetuating of their species. And, if a contingency arise, in which men, without the commission of any crime on their part, are unable, by moderate labour that they do perform, or are willing to perform, or by contributions from those who have food, to obtain food sufficient for themselves and their women and children, there is no longer *benefit* and *protection* to the whole; the social compact is at an end; and men have a right, thenceforward, to act agreeably to the laws of nature. If in process of time, the land get into the hands of a comparatively small part of the people, and if the proprietors were to prevent, by making parks, or in any other way, a great part of the land from being cultivated, would they have a right to say to the rest of the people, you shall *breed no more;* if you do, *nature* has doomed you to starvation? Would they have a right to say, " We leave you to the *punishment of nature*? " If they were fools enough to do this, the rest of the people would, doubtless, snap them at their word, and say, " Very well, then; *nature* bids us live and love and have children, and get food for them from the land; here is a pretty park, I'll have a bit here; you take a bit there, Jack; " and so on. What! say the proprietors, would you take our *property*? No : but, if you will neither give us some of the fruits without our labour, nor give us some of them for our labour, we will use some of the land, for starved we will not be. " Why do you *love* and *have children* then? " Because nature impels us to it, and because our right to gratify the passion of love was never given up either expressly or tacitly.

But there are the *helpless;* there are those who are *infirm;* there are babies and aged and insane persons. Are the proprietors to support them? To be sure they are; else what *benefit,* what *protection,* do these receive from the Social Compact? If these are to be refused protection, why is the feeble and infirm rich man to be protected in his property, or in any other way? Before the Social Compact existed, there were no sufferers from *helplessness.* The possession of every thing being in common, every man was able, by extraordinary exertion, to provide for his helpless kindred and friends by the means of those exertions. He used more than ordinary industry; he dug and sowed more than ordinary; all the means which nature gave were at his command according to his skill and strength. And, when he agreed to allow of proprietorship, he understood, of course, that the helpless were, in case of need, to be protected and fed by the proprietors. Hence the *Poor,* by which we ought always to mean the *helpless* only, have a right founded in the law of nature, and necessarily recognized by the compact of every society of men. Take away this right; deny its existence; and then see to what a state you reduce the feeble shadow of a man, who calls himself a land-owner. The constables and all the whole *posse* of the county are to be called forth to protect *him.* The able and hearty labourer is to be *compelled* to fight for this frail creature; but if the father of this labourer become *helpless,* this father is to be handed over to the *punishment of nature;* though nature would enable the son to provide most amply for the father, if there were not laws to restrain the son from using for the supply of the father that same strength which he is compelled to use in the defence of the feeble proprietor! Oh, no! Mr. Parson! If we are to be left to the *punishment of nature,* leave us also to be rewarded by nature. Leave us to the honest dame all through the piece: she is very impartial in rewards as well as in her punishments: let us have the latter, and we will take the former with all our hearts. Their Borough-mongerships were extremely angry with the SPENCEANS for their talking about a common partnership in the land; but the Spenceans have as much right as you to propose to recur to a state of nature; yet *you* have not yet been *dungeoned.*

* * * * * *

To suppose such a thing possible as a Society, in which men, who are able and willing to work, cannot support their families, and ought, with a great part of the women, to be *compelled* to lead a life of celibacy, for fear of having children to be starved; to suppose such a thing possible is monstrous. But, if there should be such a Society, every one will say, that it ought instantly to be dissolved; because a state of nature would be far preferable to it. However, the *laws of England* say, that no person shall be without a sufficiency of food and raiment; and, as we shall see, this part of our laws is no more than a recognition of those principles of the social compact, of which I have just been speaking.

TEN

EMIGRATION, AND AMERICA

The United States of America

P.R. XXVIII., c. 68. *To Correspondents in the United States of America.*
22-7-15.

THE happiness of America arises *chiefly* not from the *great* learning possessed by any part of her citizens, but from the enlightened state of the minds of the *whole population*. This has arisen from the means of education which *all* possess. These means arise, not so much from the superior industry of Americans (for they labour less, far less, than the people of England) as from the cheapness of their Government, which may *safely* be cheap, because it is strong in the good sense, the information, freedom, and happiness of the people. Next to your enlightened state of mind, comes, as a cause of your happiness, that *moderation* in the desire to amass wealth, which is the natural consequence of an absence of titles and family distinctions. All the money of Peru would not place either of your sons above the son of your poorest neighbour. Since, therefore, no great end is to be obtained by the possession of wealth, men are less likely to use unjustifiable means in obtaining it, as well as less likely to apply it to a corrupt use, or, to heap it on one child to the ruin of all the rest. Hence that equal distribution of property; hence that stubborn spirit which makes the labourer refuse to call his employer *master;* hence that consciousness of self-worth, which makes meanness and crimes so rare; and hence, in the Americans, that fidelity to their country and their colours, and that contempt for their enemies, which naturally must produce, and which already have produced, such wonderful effects.

On Emigration to America

P.R. XXVIII., c. 397.　*To Correspondents, on the Subject of Emigration to America.*　30-9-15.

SEVERAL persons have addressed me with a view of obtaining information, necessary to them, having an intention to emigrate to America. I should very willingly comply with their requests; but, in the first place, it must be obvious to them, that I cannot have the *time* to do it. In the second place, it is impossible for me to know the particular circumstances and capacities of the parties applying so thoroughly as to be able to give them advice. And, in the third place, I shall never *advise* any person to go to America, or to any other foreign country, unless I am personally acquainted with such person, and am pretty certain that he would better himself by such a removal. What I have *written* about America all my readers know. With that information, and with other information that they may acquire, they must judge for themselves.—There can be no doubt of the happiness of a country, which so rapidly increases in population and resources, while the expences of government are so trifling. A people, whose population is now nearly as great as that of England and Scotland, and whose government, debt and all, does not demand more than a twelfth part of the sum from them that ours demands from us, *must* be happy. But, whether Englishmen, going amongst that people, would be happier than they are at home, must be left for the decision of their own judgment. It is very certain, that to go to America with the view of living an *idle* life would produce sad disappointment. Sinecure-placemen, pensioners, grantees, venal news-paper writers and reviewers, puffers, parasites, and quacks in every department, will certainly act wisely in remaining at home. Gentlemen who teach religion, if they have benefices or tolerable good chapels, may remain safely here. They would not better their lot by emigration to America. Lawyers, whether in silk or camlot gowns, will do well to remain; for, though there is a great deal of *law-work* in America, the native growth of lawyers are very sharp and eloquent. And, besides, they wear neither *gowns* nor *wigs* nor *bands,* which form no small part of the possessions of the English bar. For *medical* men, there is always room, and always will be as long as people continue to die. The truth is, that of the three *professions* this is the best. I mean, it contains the best men, and the wisest and cleverest men. The priest or the lawyer may thrive by subserviency. Religion and law accommodate themselves to *times* and *politics;* but, he who has a broken leg or an affection of the liver, thinks of nothing but the *skill* of the surgeon or physician that he employs. Besides, the very nature of the researches and the observations of medical men make them despise superstition. Hence it is, that we very rarely meet with one of them, whose mind is not independent. These may safely go to a country, where the population is continually increasing, and where skill joined to diligence is sure to meet with due reward. The *big-bellied farmers,* that require a stout horse, or a strong gig, to carry them about their fields to see what their men are doing, had better remain here till low-prices and the tax-gatherer have sweated them into a reasonable bulk and weight; for, though the land in America produces very fine things, it will not produce much without *labour;* and, as labourers for hire are very scarce, the farmer must *labour himself,* or, his sons and daughters must labour for him. But, of all the classes of the community *Borough-mongers* would profit least from emigration to America. In the State of Massachusetts there did seem to be a party that wished for the introduction of a *Noblesse.* Yet, I question whether our Lords would, even in that State, find a change for the better, because the aristocrats of Massachusetts seem to have been hankering after titles for *themselves.* But the *Borough-mongers* would be like fish out of water in reality. All their jargon about close-boroughs and open-boroughs and burgage-tenures and pot-wallopers, all their bargaining and trafficking would vanish for ever. They ought not emigrate by any means. Neither ought the Voters at Sarum, Gatton, Honiton, and such places, move an inch. They will find no country like Old England. All Corporations, if they know when they are well off, will stick fast. Tax-gatherers grow out of National Debts and standing armies as naturally as toadstools grow out of the rotten stumps of trees; and, though ours are astonishingly expert, in the first place their trade is a thriving one here, and, in the next place, there is only an army of six thousand men in America, and the debt, compared to ours, is a mere nothing. Military and Naval Officers would gain no *Knightships* in America, and their numerous wives, whose eyes our 'Squires' dames are ready to tear out, would never be *Ladies*: would never once hear the dulcet sound of "*your Lady-ship*," though they were to hang the whole of their tawdry wardrobe upon their backs from morning till night. The makers of Hanoverian whiskers, of muffs, tippets, and trifles for dragoons, and of stimulant draughts and corsets for worn out bucks, had better remain in England. The Masters of Work-houses, whose virtue and piety, like that of Don Manuel Ordonnez, are such, that they universally "grow *rich* in taking care of the concerns of the *poor*," ought not to quit a country where their trade is so flourishing; and, those useful members of society, informers, thief-catchers, jailors and hangmen, would emigrate from plenty to starvation. In stating these discourage-ments to emigration, I wish to be understood as bearing no emnity towards America; and, if any American choses to draw a different conclusion, I must leave him to the enjoyment of his error.

WILLIAM COBBETT.

Emigration

P.R. LXVII., c. 660. *Emigration.* 23-5-29.

MANY persons apply to me for advice upon this subject; and I will here say that which may save trouble to myself and others in future. I speak not of the poor people who *have no money,* and who do not like to remain here to be starved to death. They would prefer *transportation* to remaining here; but, if they have a choice, I would advise such to go to *Canada;* for, they can thence *walk into the United States,* and become freemen, never to care about borough-mongers more, and never more to have their earnings devoured by sinecure men and women and by parsons, army, and dead-weight. If a man have *money,* and have, of course, a choice of countries to which to go, and if he can hesitate for one moment between the *United States* and an *English Colony,* I despise the slave; and, I desire, that no wretch of this description will ever trouble me with applications for advice. *France,* or the *United States,* is the country. The former for people who can live upon their means, and have no families that it is necessary to bring up to work; and the latter for people who wish to live and to rear up families by the means of trade, manufactures, or agriculture. Those of this last description are most numerous. But first, let me speak of *France.* The climate is as good as ours at any rate; the country is as healthy; and, as *to expense of living,* this is precisely the fact : a man, who has *here* a house with twelve windows, who keeps only one horse and one dog, who has a garden, and in whose house only *one bottle of wine a day is drunk,* pays more in assessed taxes, poor-rates, and indirect *taxes alone,* than would furnish him with *three times as much of these things and other useful things in France.* In other words, out of a thousand pounds a-year that it costs a man to live in England, he might lay by *seven hundred in France,* and live better into the bargain. However, if his delight be to read the base old Times newspaper, and to pull off his hat and crouch to borough-mongers, who or whose spawn suck his blood, he will do well to remain where he is.—As to the *UNITED STATES,* if a man have no money, he must be prepared for mechanical or labouring *work* : if he have money, let him not think of *back woods* and *land for nothing;* for he will find that " *nothing* " to be an enormously high price. A couple or three thousand pounds will *purchase* and *stock* a nice snug farm in Long Island, with house, out-buildings, orchard, woodland, and every thing in order. Such a farm can, in that beautiful and happy island, be purchased and stocked for less than it would take to carry a family, and just squat it down, in *Van Diemen's Land;* and between this latter place and the *back woods of America* there is little difference, except that in the latter you dare *call your soul your own,* and in the former you dare not. For my part, I can form an idea of nothing so pleasant, as an English farmer, with two or three thousand pounds in his pocket, going and settling *at once* in Long Island or near it. Oh! how happy he must feel when he looks back at what he has left behind him! How he must pity the poor devils who are still compelled to pull off their hats to the borough-mongers and their numerous spawn. What a change to see no beggar; to hear of no pauper; never to hear the sound of the words, "*want of employment;*" and to look upon a man as mad, who raves about "*surplus population!*" What a change to behold the poorest of labourers eat meat three times a-day, and to see a whole people who do not deem it a trespass, if the stranger gather their fruit, or even if he come and sit down in their houses! What a change to behold these things, and never to see or hear of an insolent cock parson, strutting about and devouring the fruits of men's labour! Who can refrain from praying for the prosperity of such a country? Who can refrain from wishing success to its government?

ELEVEN

THE LIBERTY OF THE PRESS

Liberty of the Press

P.R. XIX., c. 481. *The Liberty of the Press.* 27-2-11.

THE Liberty of the Press is a mere name, and has no existence in reality, where any man cannot, without harm or risk to himself, publish the *truth* respecting the public character, conduct, and measures of men in public office, men paid for conducting or managing the affairs of the nation, let those men be whom they may, in what office they may, whether in the state, the law, the church, the army, or the navy, or any other department.

State of the Press

P.R. XI., c. 546. *To the Free and Independent Electors of the City and Liberties of Westminster.* 11-4-07.

IT is not to these trammels, in which the press is held, these perils which surround every man who ventures to write and publish truth, that I am, at present, solicitous to draw your attention; but, to the corruption and baseness of the press itself, and the way in which it has been rendered an enemy to real freedom. Of this we have an instance sufficiently striking in the Morning Chronicle alone. For twenty years that paper, the property of the very same person who now owns it, was the eulogist and champion of the party of Mr. Fox. When Mr. Fox and his party came into power, that proprietor, Mr. Perry, had a place given him; and thus for his party-labours was he remunerated at our expence. The True Briton and Sun newspapers were set up with the public money; and, when Mr. Heriot, the person who conducted them for so many years, and whose sole and settled business was to eulogize Pitt and his minions, retired from the business, he had five or six hundred pounds a year of the public money settled upon him for life, in what is called a double-commissionership of the Lottery, which salary, *if at all necessary,* should have gone to reward some man, who had rendered undoubted services to the country. Mr. Walter, the proprietor of the Times news-paper, did receive for many years, if he does not still receive, a pension of six hundred pounds a year from the public purse in consequence of his devoting his paper to the minister Pitt. The Anti-Jacobin weekly news-paper, in which those famous " young friends," Messrs. Canning and Frere wrote, was set up at the public expence; and Mr. William Gifford, whom they employed to assist them and to edit the paper, had, first, a patent place of a hundred a year bestowed upon him; next he was made a double commissioner of the Lottery, and, since, in addition, pay-master of the Gentlemen-Pensioners, making in all about a thousand a year for life at our expence; and, never in his whole life time, though he is a very modest, and, I believe, a very worthy man, has he ever rendered any service to the country. I will pass over the particulars relating to the " Pilot " and the " Royal Standard," weekly papers set up by the Addington administration to oppose my Register; but, I cannot help pointing out to you the nature of the influence arising from advertisements in *all* the papers. This is the great source of emolument; and this source flows from all the public offices as well as from Lloyd's and all its numerous connections according to the *politics* of the paper through which it runs. Some papers, the Morning Post in particular, are the property of companies of traders or speculators. The thing is regarded merely as a money speculation, is to be made the most of, and, of course, the most profitable politics will be always preferred. In all the daily papers, paragraphs from individuals, or bodies of men, are inserted for payment, no matter what they contain, so that the proprietor be not exposed to the lash of the law. The price is enormous, not less than half-a-guinea an inch; of course, the rich villain has the whole of the daily press for his defender or apologist, while the oppressed or slandered man, if he be poor, has no means whatever of appealing to the justice of the public.

ENGLISH LIBERTY OF THE PRESS,

As illustrated in the Prosecution and Punishment of
WILLIAM COBBETT.

P.R. XXII., c. 111.   *English Liberty of the Press, as illustrated in the Prosecution and Punishment of William Cobbett.*   25-7-12.

IN order that my countrymen and that the world may not be deceived, duped, and cheated upon this subject, I, WILLIAM COBBETT, of Botley, in Hampshire, put upon record the following facts; to wit : That, on the 24th June, 1809, the following article was published in a London news-paper, called the COURIER :—" The Mutiny amongst the LOCAL MILITIA, which broke out at Ely, was *fortunately* suppressed on Wednesday, by the arrival of four squadrons of the GERMAN LEGION CAVALRY from Bury, under the command of General Auckland. Five of the ringleaders were tried by a Court-Martial, and *sentenced to receive* 500 *lashes each,* part of which punishment they received on Wednesday, and a part was remitted. *A stoppage for their knapsacks* was the ground of the complaint that excited this mutinous spirit, which occasioned the men to surround their officers, and demand what they deemed their arrears. The first division of the German Legion halted yesterday at Newmarket on their return to Bury."—That, on the 1st July, 1809, I published, in the Political Register, an article censuring, in the strongest terms, these proceedings; that, for so doing, the Attorney General prosecuted, as seditious libellers, and by Ex-Officio Information, me, and also my printer, my publisher, and one of the principal retailers of the Political Register; that I was brought to trial on the 15th June, 1810, and was, by a Special Jury, that is to say, by 12 men out of 48 appointed by the Master of the Crown Office, found guilty; that, on the 20th of the same month, I was compelled to give bail for my appearance to receive judgment; and that, as I came up from Botley (to which place I had returned to my family and my farm on the evening of the 15th), a Tipstaff went down from London in order to seize me, personally; that, on the 9th of July, 1810, I, together with my printer, publisher, and the newsman, were brought into the Court of King's Bench to receive judgment;

that the three former were sentenced to be imprisoned for some months in the King's Bench prison; that I was sentenced to be imprisoned for two years in Newgate, the great receptacle for malefactors, and the front of which is the scene of numerous hangings in the course of every year; that the part of the prison in which I was sentenced to be confined is sometimes inhabited by felons, that felons were actually in it at the time I entered it; that one man was taken out of it to be transported in about 48 hours after I was put into the same yard with him; and that it is the place of confinement for men guilty of unnatural crimes, of whom there are four in it at this time; that, besides this imprisonment, I was sentenced to pay a thousand pounds TO THE KING, and to give security for my good behaviour for seven years, myself in the sum of 3,000 pounds, and two sureties in the sum of 1,000 pounds each; that the whole of this sentence has been executed upon me, that I have been imprisoned the two years, have paid the thousand pounds TO THE KING, and have given the bail, Timothy Brown and Peter Walker, Esqrs. being my sureties; that the Attorney General was Sir Vicary Gibbs, the Judge who sat at the trial Lord Ellenborough, the four Judges who sat at passing sentence Ellenborough, Grose, Le Blanc, and Bailey; and that the jurors were, Thomas Rhodes of Hampstead Road, John Davis of Southampton Place, James Ellis of Tottenham Court Road, John Richards of Bayswater, Thomas Marsham of Baker Street, Robert Heathcote of High Street Marylebone, John Maud of York Place Marylebone, George Baxter of Church Terrace Pancras, Thomas Taylor of Red Lion Square, David Deane of St. John Street, William Palmer of Upper Street Islington, Henry Favre of Pall Mall; that the Prime Ministers during the time were Spencer Perceval, until he was shot by John Bellingham, and after that Robert B. Jenkinson, Earl of Liverpool; that the prosecution and sentence took place in the reign of King George the Third, and that, he having become insane during my imprisonment, the 1,000 pounds was paid to his son, the Prince Regent, in his behalf; that, during my imprisonment, I wrote and published 364 Essays and Letters upon political subjects; that, during the same time, I was visited by persons from 197 cities and towns, many of them as a sort of deputies from Societies or Clubs; that, at the expiration of my imprisonment, on the 9th of July 1812, a great dinner was given in London for the purpose of receiving me, at which dinner upwards of 600 persons were present, and at which Sir Francis Burdett presided; that dinners and other parties were held on the same occasion in many other places in England; that, on my way home, I was received at Alton, the first town in Hampshire, with the ringing of the Church bells; that a respectable company met me and gave me a dinner at Winchester; that I was drawn from more than the distance of a mile into Botley by the people; that, upon my arrival in the village, I found all the people assembled to receive me; that I concluded the day by explaining to them the cause of my imprisonment, and by giving them clear notions respecting the flogging of the Local Militia-men at Ely, and respecting the employment of German Troops; and, finally, which is more than a compensation for my losses and all my sufferings, I am in perfect health and strength, and though I must, for the sake of my six children, feel the diminution that has been made on my property (thinking it right in me to decline the offer of a subscription), I have the consolation to see growing up three sons, upon whose hearts, I trust, all these facts will be engraven.

TWELVE

JOURNEYMEN AND LABOURERS

Address to the Journeymen and Labourers

P.R. XXX., c. 433. *To the Journeymen and Labourers of England, Wales, Scotland and Ireland.* 2-11-16.

FRIENDS AND FELLOW COUNTRYMEN,

Whatever the Pride of rank, of riches or of scholarship may have induced some men to believe, or to affect to believe, the real strength and all the resources of a country, ever have sprung and ever must spring, from the *labour* of its people; and hence it is, that this nation, which is so small in numbers and so poor in climate and soil compared with many others, has, for many ages, been the most powerful nation in the world : it is the most industrious, the most laborious, and therefore, the most powerful. Elegant dresses, superb furniture, stately buildings, fine roads and canals, fleet horses and carriages, numerous and stout ships, warehouses teeming with goods; all these, and many other objects that fall under our view, are so many marks of national wealth and resources. But all these spring from *labour*. Without the Journeyman and the labourers none of them could exist; without the assistance of their hands, the country would be a wilderness, hardly worth the notice of an invader.

As it is the labour of those who toil which makes a country abound in resources, so it is the same class of men, who must, by their arms, secure its safety and uphold its fame. Titles and immense sums of money have been bestowed upon numerous Naval and Military Commanders. Without calling the justice of these in question, we may assert that the victories were obtained by *you* and your fathers and brothers and sons in co-operation with those Commanders, who, with *your* aid have done great and wonderful things; but, who, without that aid, would have been as impotent as children at the breast.

With this correct idea of your own worth in your minds, with what indignation must you hear yourselves called the Populace, the Rabble, the Mob, the Swinish Multitude; and with what greater indignation, if possible, must you hear the projects of those cool and cruel and insolent men, who, now that you have been, without any fault of yours, brought into a state of misery, propose to narrow the limits of parish relief, to prevent you from marrying in the days of your youth, or to thrust you out to seek your bread in foreign lands, never more to behold your parents or friends? But suppress your indignation, until we return to this topic, after we have considered the *cause* of your present misery and the measures which have produced that cause.

The times in which we live are full of peril. The nation, as described by the very creatures of the government, is fast advancing to that period when an important change must take place. It is the lot of mankind, that some shall labour with their limbs and others with their minds; and, on all occasions, more especially on an occasion like the present, it is the duty of the latter to come to the assistance of the former. We are all equally interested in the peace and happiness of our common country. It is of the utmost importance, that in the seeking to obtain those objects, our endeavours should be uniform, and tend all to the same point. Such an uniformity cannot exist without an uniformity of sentiment as to public matters, and to produce this latter uniformity amongst you is the object of this address.

As to the *cause* of our present miseries, it is the *enormous amount of the taxes,* which the government compels us to pay for the support of its army, its placemen, its pensioners, &c. and for the payment of the interest of its debt. That this is the *real* cause has been a thousand times proved; and, it is now so acknowledged by the creatures of the government themselves. *Two hundred and five* of the Correspondents of the Board of Agriculture ascribe the ruin of the country to *taxation.* Numerous writers, formerly the friends of the Pitt System, now declare, that taxation has been the cause of our distress. Indeed, when we compare our present state to the state of the country previous to the wars against France, we must see that our present misery is owing to no other cause. The taxes then annually raised amounted to about 15 millions: they amounted last year to 70 millions. The nation was then happy: it is now miserable.

The writers and speakers, who labour in the cause of corruption, have taken great pains to make the *labouring classes* believe, that *they* are *not taxed;* that the taxes which are paid by the landlords, farmers, and tradesmen, do not affect *you,* the journeymen and labourers; and that the taxmakers have been *very lenient* towards *you.* But, I hope, that you see to the bottom of these things now. You must be sensible, that, if *all* your employers were *totally* ruined in one day, you would be *wholly* without employment and without bread; and, of course, in whatever *degree* your employers are deprived of their means, they must withhold means from you. In America the most awkward common labourer receives five shillings a day, while provisions are cheaper in that country than in this. Here a carter, boarded in the house, receives about seven pounds a year; in America he receives about thirty pounds a year. What is it that makes this difference? Why, in America the whole of the taxes do not amount to more than about *ten shillings* a head upon the whole of the population; while in England they amount to nearly *six pounds* a head! *There,* a journeyman or labourer may support his family well and save from thirty to sixty pounds a year: *here,* he amongst you is a lucky man, who can provide his family with food and with decent clothes to cover them, without any hope of possessing a penny in the days of sickness, or of old age. *There* the chief Magistrate receives 6000 pounds a year: *here* the civil list surpasses a million of pounds in amount, and as much is allowed to each of the *Princesses* in one year, as the chief Magistrate of America receives in two years, though that country is nearly equal to this in population.

* * * * *

In proceeding now to examine the *remedies* for your distresses, I shall first notice some of those, which foolish, or cruel and insolent men have proposed. Seeing that the *cause* of your *misery* is the *weight of taxation,* one would expect to hear of nothing but a *reduction of taxation* in the way of remedy; but, from the friends of corruption, never do we hear of any such remedy. To hear them, one would think, that *you* had been the guilty cause of the misery you suffer; and that you, and you alone, ought to be made answerable for what has taken place. The emissaries of corruption are now continually crying out against the *weight* of the *poor-rates,* and they seem to regard all that is taken in that way as a *dead loss to the Government*! Their project is, to deny relief to all who are *able to work*. But what is the use of your being able to work, if no one will, or can, give you work? To tell you that you must work for your bread, and, at the same time, not to find any work for you, is full as bad as it would be to order you to make bricks without straw. Indeed, it is rather more cruel and insolent; for Pharaoh's task-masters did point out to the Israelites that they might go into the fields and get *stubble*. The COURIER newspaper, of the 9th of October, says, " we must thus be *cruel* only to be *kind*." I am persuaded, that you will not understand this kindness, while you will easily understand the cruelty. The notion of these people seems to be, that every body that receives money out of the taxes have a *right* to receive it, *except you*. They tremble at the fearful amount of the poor-rates : they say, and very truly, that those rates have risen from *two and a half* to *eight* or *ten* millions since the beginning of the wars against the people of France; they think, and not without reason, that these rates will soon swallow up nearly all the rent of the land. These assertions and apprehensions are perfectly well founded; but how can *you* help it? You have not had the management of the affairs of the nation. It is not *you* who have ruined the farmers and tradesmen. You want only food and raiment : you are ready to work for it; but you cannot go naked and without food.

But the complaints of these persons against you are the more unreasonable, because they say not a word against the sums paid to *Sinecure Placemen* and *Pensioners*. Of the five hundred and more correspondents of the Board of Agriculture, there are scarcely ten, who do not complain of the weight of the *poor-* rates, of the immense sums taken away from them by the *poor,* and many of them complain of the *idleness* of the poor. But not one single man complains of the immense sums taken away to support *Sinecure Placemen,* who do *nothing* for their money, and to support pensioners, many of whom are *women* and *children,* the wives and daughters of the nobility and other persons in high life, and who can do nothing, and never can have done any thing, for what they receive. There are of these places and pensions all sizes, from *twenty pounds* to *thirty thousand* and nearly *forty thousand pounds a year*! And, surely, these ought to be done away before any proposition be made to take the parish allowance from any of you, who are unable to work, or to find work to do. There are several individual placemen, the profits of *each* of which would maintain *a thousand families.* The names of the *Ladies* upon the pension list would, if printed one under another, fill a sheet of paper like this. And is it not, then, base and cruel at the same time in these Agricultural Correspondents to cry out so loudly against the charge of supporting the unfortunate *Poor,* while they utter not a word of complaint against the Sinecure Places and Pensions?

The unfortunate journeymen and labourers and their families have a *right,* they have a *just claim,* to relief from the purses of the rich. For, there can exist no riches and no resources, which they by their labour, have not *assisted to create.* But, I should be glad to know how the sinecure placemen and lady pensioners have assisted to create food and raiment, or the means of producing them. The labourer who is out of work, or ill, to-day, may be able to work, and set to work to-morrow. While those placemen and pensioners never can work; or, at least, it is clear that they never *intend* to do it.

* * * * * *

Mr. PRESTON, whom I quoted before, and who is a *Member of Parliament* and has a large estate, says, upon this subject, "Every family, even of the poorest labourers, consisting of five persons, may be considered as paying in *indirect taxes,* at least *ten pounds a year,* or more than half his wages at seven shillings a week!" And yet the insolent hirelings call you the *mob,* the *rabble,* the *scum,* the *swinish multitude,* and say, that your voice is nothing; that you have no business at public meetings; and that *you* are, and ought to be, considered as nothing in the body politic! Shall we *never* see the day when these men will change their tone! Will they never cease to look upon you as brutes! I trust they will change their tone, and that the day of the change is *at no great distance*!

The weight of the Poor-rate, which must increase while the present system continues, alarms the Corrupt, who plainly see, that what is paid to relieve you *they* cannot have. Some of them therefore, hint at your *early marriages* as a great evil, and a *Clergyman* named MALTHUS, has seriously proposed measures for *checking* you in this respect; while one of the Correspondents of the Board of Agriculture complains of the INCREASE *of bastards,* and proposes *severe punishment* on the parents! . How hard these men are to please! What would they have you do? As some have called you the *swinish multitude,* would it be much wonder if they were to propose to serve you as families of young pigs are served? Or, if they were to bring forward the measure of Pharaoh, who ordered the midwives to kill all the male children of the Israelites?

But, if you can restrain your indignation at these insolent notions and schemes, with what feelings must you look upon the condition of your country, where the increase of the people is now looked upon as a curse! Thus however, has it always been, in all countries, where taxes have produced excessive misery. Our Countryman, Mr. GIBBON, in his history of the *Decline and Fall of the Roman Empire,* has the following passage, " The horrid practice of *murdering their new-born infants* was become every day more frequent in the provinces. It was the effect of *distress,* and the distress was principally occasioned by the *intolerable burden of taxes,* and by the *vexations as well as cruel prosecutions of the officers of the Revenue* against their insolvent debtors. The less opulent or less industrious part of mankind, instead of rejoicing at an increase of family, deemed it an act of paternal tenderness to release the children from the impending miseries of a life which they themselves were unable to support."

But that which took place under the base emperor Constantine will not take place in England. You will not murder your new-born infants, nor will you, to please the corrupt and the insolent, debar yourselves from enjoyments to which you are invited by the very first of nature's laws. It is, however, a disgrace to the country, that men should be found in it capable of putting ideas so insolent upon paper. So then, a young man, arm-in-arm with a rosy-cheeked girl, must be a spectacle of evil omen! What! and do they imagine, that you are thus to be *extinguished*, because some of you are now (without any fault of yours) unable to find work. As far as you were wanted to labour, to fight, or to pay taxes, you were welcome, and they boasted of your numbers; but now that your country has been brought into a state of misery, these corrupt and insolent men are busied with schemes *for getting rid of you*. Just as if you had not as good a right to live and to love and to marry as they have! They do not propose, far from it, to check the breeding of Sinecure Placemen and Pensioners, who are supported in part by the taxes which you help to pay. They say not a word about the *whole families* who are upon the pension list. In many cases, there are sums granted in trust for *the children* of such a Lord or such a Lady. And, while labourers and journeymen who have large families too, are actually paying taxes for the support of these Lords' and Ladies' children, these cruel and insolent men propose that they shall have no relief, and that their having children ought to be *checked*! To such a subject *no words* can do justice. You will *feel* as you ought to feel; and to the effect of your feelings I leave these cruel and insolent men.

There is one more scheme to notice, which, though rather less against nature, is not less hateful and insolent; namely, *to encourage you to emigrate to foreign countries*. This scheme is distinctly proposed to the government by one of the Correspondents of the Board of Agriculture. What he meant by *encouragement* must be to *send away* by force, or by *paying for the passage;* for a man who has *money* stands in no need of relief. But, I trust, that not a man of you *will move*, let the *encouragement* be what it may. It is impossible for *many* to go, though the prospect may be ever so fair. We must stand by our country, and it is base not to stand by her, as long as there is a chance of seeing her what she ought to be. But, the proposition is, nevertheless, base and insolent. This man did not propose to *encourage* the Sinecure Placemen and Pensioners to emigrate; yet, surely, you who help to maintain them by the taxes which you pay, have as good a right to remain in the country as they have! You have fathers and mothers and sisters and brothers and children and friends as well as they; but, this base projector recommends, that you may be encouraged to leave your relations and friends for ever; while he would have the Sinecure Placemen and Pensioners remain quietly where they are!

No: you will not leave your country. If you have suffered much and long, you have the greater right to remain in the hope of seeing better days. And I beseech you not to look upon yourselves as the *scum;* but, on the contrary, to be well persuaded, that a great deal will depend upon *your exertions;* and, therefore, I now proceed to point out to you what appears to me to be the line of conduct which Journeymen and Labourers ought to pursue in order to obtain *effectual relief,* and to assist in promoting tranquility and restoring the happiness of their country.

*   *   *   *   *   *

We have seen that the cause of our miseries is the *burden of taxes* occasioned by wars, by standing armies, by sinecures, by pensions, &c. It would be endless and useless to enumerate all the different heads or sums of expenditure. The *remedy* is what we have now to look to, and that remedy consists wholly and solely of such a *reform* in the Commons' or People's House of Parliament, as shall give to every payer of *direct taxes* a vote at elections, and as shall cause the Members to be *elected annually*.

In a late Register I have pointed out how easily, how peaceably, how fairly, such a parliament might be chosen. I am aware, that it may, and not without justice, be thought wrong to deprive those of the right of voting, who pay *indirect* taxes. Direct taxes are those which are directly paid by any person into the hands of the taxgatherer, as the assessed taxes and rates. Indirect taxes are those which are paid indirectly through the maker or seller of goods, as the tax on soap and candles or salt or malt. And, as no man ought to be taxed *without his consent,* there has always been a difficulty upon his head. There has been no question about the *right* of every man, who is free to exercise his will, who has a settled place in society, and who pays a tax of *any sort,* to vote for Members of Parliament. The difficulty is in taking the

votes by any other means than by the *Rate Book;* for if there be
no *list* of tax-payers in the hands of *any person,* mere menial
servants, vagrants, pick-pockets and scamps of all sorts might not
only come to poll, but they might poll in several parishes or
places, on one and the same day. A corrupt rich man might
employ scores of persons of this description, and in this way
would the purpose of reform be completely defeated. In
America, where one branch of the Congress is elected for *four*
years and the other for *two years,* they have still adhered to the
principle of *direct taxation,* and in some of the states, they have
made it necessary for a voter to be worth a hundred pounds. Yet
they have, in that country, duties on goods, custom duties and
excise duties also; and, of course, there are many persons. who
really *pay taxes,* and who, nevertheless, are not permitted to vote.
The people do not complain of this. They know that the
number of votes is so great, that no corruption can take place,
and they have no desire to see livery servants, vagrants and pick-
pockets take part in their elections. Nevertheless, it would be
very easy for a *reformed parliament,* when once it had taken
root, to make a just arrangement of this matter. The most likely
method would be to take off the indirect taxes, and to put a small
direct tax upon every master of a house, however low his situation in life.

But, this and *all other good things,* must be done by a *reformed
parliament.*—We must have *that first,* or we shall have nothing
good; and, any man, who would, *before hand* take up your time
with the detail of what a reformed parliament ought to do in this
respect, or with respect to any changes in the form of government, can have no other object than that of defeating the cause
of reform, and, indeed, the very act must show, that to *raise
obstacles* is his wish.

Such men, now that they find you justly irritated, would
persuade you, that, because things have been perverted from
their true ends, there is *nothing good* in our *constitution and
laws.* For what, then, did Hampden die in the field, and Sydney
on the scaffold? And, has it been discovered, at last, that England has *always* been an enslaved country from top to toe? The
Americans, who are a very wise people, and who love liberty

with all their hearts, and who take care to *enjoy* it too, took special care not to part with any of the great principles and laws which they derived from their forefathers. They took special care to speak with reverence of, and to preserve Magna Charta, the Bill of Rights, the Habeas Corpus, and not only all the body of the Common Law of England, but most of the rules of our courts, and all our form of jurisprudence. Indeed, it is the greatest glory of England that she has thus supplied with sound principles of freedom those immense regions, which will be peopled, perhaps, by hundreds of millions.

I know of no enemy of reform and of the happiness of the country so great as that man, who would persuade you that we possess *nothing good,* and that *all* must be torn to pieces. There is no principle, no precedent, no regulations (except as to mere matter of detail), favourable to freedom, which is not to be found in the Laws of England or in the example of our Ancestors. Therefore, I say we may ask for, and we want *nothing new*. We have great constitutional laws and principles, to which we are immoveably attached. We want *great altera-tion,* but we want *nothing new*. Alteration, modification to suit the times and circumstances; but the great principles ought to be and must be, the same, or else confusion will follow.

* * * * * *

I have no room, nor have I any desire, to appeal to your passions upon this occasion. I have laid before you, with all the clearness I am master of, the causes of our misery, the measures which have led to those causes, and I have pointed out what appears to me to be the only remedy—namely, a reform of the Commons', or People's House of Parliament. I exhort you to proceed in a peaceable and lawful manner, but at the same time, to proceed with zeal and resolution in the attainment of this object. If the *Skulkers* will not join you, if the " decent fire-side " gentry still keep aloof, proceed by yourselves. Any man can draw up a petition, and any man can *carry* it up to London, with instructions to deliver it into trusty hands, to be presented whenever the House shall meet. Some further information will be given as to this matter in a future Number. In the meanwhile, I remain   Your Friend,

Wm. COBBETT.

Mr. Cobbett's Taking Leave of his Countrymen

P.R. XXXII., c. 417. *Mr. Cobbett's Taking Leave of his Countrymen.*
5-4-17.

THE Country Gentlemen who have now been amongst our most decided Adversaries, will very soon be compelled, for their own preservation, to become our friends and fellow-labourers. Not a fragment of their property will be left, if they do not speedily bestir themselves. They have been induced to believe, that a Reform of the Parliament would expose them to plunder or degradation; but they will very soon find, that it will afford them the only chance of escaping both. The wonder is, that they do not see this already, or, rather, that they have not seen it for years past. But, they have been blinded by their foolish pride; that pride, which has nothing of mind belonging to it, and which, accompanied with a consciousness of a want of any natural superiority over the Labouring classes, seeks to indulge itself in a species of vindictive exercise of power. There has come into the heads of these people, I cannot very well tell how, a notion, that it is proper to consider the Labouring Classes as a *distinct cast.* They are called, now-a-days, by these gentlemen, " *The Peasantry.*" This is a new term as applied to Englishmen. It is a French word, which, in its literal sense, means *Country Folks.* But, in the sense, in which it is used in France and Flanders and Germany, it means, not only country people, or country folks, but also a *distinct and degraded class of persons,* who have no pretensions whatever to look upon themselves, in any sense, as belonging to the same *society,* or *community,* as the *Gentry;* but who ought always to be " *kept down in their proper place.*" And, it has become, of late, the fashion to consider the Labouring Classes in England in the same light, and to speak of them and treat them accordingly, which never was the case in any former age.

The writings of MALTHUS, who considers men as *mere*

animals, may have had influence in the producing of this change; and, we now frequently hear the working classes called " the *population,*" just as we call the animals upon a farm " the *stock.*" It is is curious, too, that this contumely towards the great mass of the people should have grown into vogue amongst the Country Gentlemen and their families, at a time when they themselves are daily and hourly losing the estates descended to them from their forefathers. They see themselves stript of the means of keeping that hospitality, for which England was once so famed, and of which there remains nothing now but the *word* in the dictionary; they see themselves reduced to close up their windows, live in a corner of their houses, sneak away to London, crib their servants in their wages, and hardly able to keep up a little tawdry show; and, it would seem, that, for the contempt which they feel that their meanness must necessarily excite the common people, they endeavour to avenge themselves, and at the same time to disguise their own humiliation, by their haughty and insolent deportment towards the latter : thus exhibiting that mixture of poverty and of pride, which has ever been deemed better calculated than any other union of qualities to draw down upon the possessors the most unfriendly of human feelings.

It is curious, also, that this fit of novel and ridiculous pride should have afflicted the minds of these persons at the very time that the working classes are become singularly enlightened. Not enlightened in the manner that the sons of Cant and Corruption would wish them to be. The conceited creatures in what is called high life, and who always judge of men by their clothes, imagine that the working classes of the people have their minds quite sufficiently occupied by the reading of what are called " *religious and moral tracts.*" Simple, insipid dialogues and stories, calculated for the minds of children seven or eight years old, or for those savages just beginning to be civilized. These conceited persons have no idea that the minds of the working classes ever presume to rise above this infantine level. But these conceited persons are most grossly deceived : they are the " *deluded* " part of the community; deluded by a hireling and corrupt press, and by the conceit and insolence of their own minds. The working classes of the people understand well what they read; they dive into all matters connected with politics; they have a relish not only for interesting statement, for argument, for discussion; but the powers of *eloquence* are by no means lost upon them; and, in many, many instances, they have shewn themselves to possess infinitely greater powers of describing and of reasoning, than have ever been shewn generally by that description of persons, who, with MALTHUS, regard them as mere animals. In the report of the Secret Committee of the House of Lords, it is observed, that, since the people have betaken themselves to this reading and this discussing, " *their character seems to be wholly changed.*" I believe it is indeed! For it is the natural effect of enlightening the mind to change the character. But, is not this change for the better? If it be not, why have we heard so much about the efforts for instructing the children of the poor? Nay; there are institutions for teaching *full-grown persons* to read and write; and a gentleman, upon whose word I can rely, assured me, that, in a school of this sort, in Norfolk, he actually saw one woman teaching another woman to read, and that both teacher and pupil had *spectacles upon their noses*! What, then! Has it been intended, that these people, when taught to read, should read nothing but Hannah MORE'S " *Sinful Sally,*" and Mrs. TRIMMER's Dialogues? Faith! The working classes of the people have a relish for no such trash. They are not to be amused by a recital of the manifold blessings of a state of things, in which they have not half enough to eat, nor half enough to cover their nakedness by day or to keep them from perishing by night. They are not to be amused with the pretty stories about " the *bounty of Providence* in *making brambles* for the purpose of tearing off pieces of the sheep's wool, *in order* that the little birds may come and get it to line their nests with, to keep their young ones warm! " Stories like these are not sufficient to fill the minds of the working classes of the people. They want something more solid. They have had something more solid. Their minds, like a sheet of paper, have received the lasting impressions of undeniable fact and unanswerable argument; and it will always be a source of the greatest satisfaction to me to reflect, that I have been mainly instrumental in giving those impressions, which, I am very certain will never be effaced from the minds of the people of this country.

Cobbett on his Addresses

P.R. XXXIII., c. 419. *To Henry Hunt, Esq. Letter III. On the Terrible Scenes, Exhibited at DERBY in October and November, 1817; and Particularly on the Conduct of LAWYER CROSS of Manchester.* 11-4-18.

IT is well known that the main drift of my Address to the Journeymen and Labourers and of my other publications following that Address, I say it is well known, and the content of those publications will *prove* it, that the main drift of them was to *prevent* riot and acts of violence of all sorts. It is well known, that, while the papers in the pay of the government, were goading on the poor to assail the shops of Bakers and Butchers and the barns and stacks of Farmers, I was using my paper so as to prevent these and all other acts of unlawful violence. At the time when I began to address myself more immediately to the Labouring Classes, there had been riots in Cambridge-shire, ending in a terrible series of executions. There had been riots in Wales. There had recently been riots in Somersetshire, in Surrey, in Monmouthshire, in Suffolk. Riots were hourly expected in Staffordshire and Lancashire. And, in Nottinghamshire and the neighbouring counties, there had been rioting going on for more than five years, which, with all its new and terrific powers, the government, with an army and a band of spies to assist it, had been unable to suppress.

This was the state of things, when the *Cheap Register* first made its appearance. An hostility to the use of *machines* was one ground of these riots. A mistaken notion in the mess of the Labouring Classes led them to attack and destroy property of that description. I, therefore, at the risk of loss of popularity, or, rather, trusting to the good sense of the people, bent all the force of my mind against this erroneous notion; I proved to them, that machines were beneficial *to them* as well as to their country generally; I proved to them, that they could not be benefitted by the destruction of machines; I proved to them, that Bakers, Butchers, Millers and Farmers could *not be benefitted* by *high prices;* I proved to them, that *riot must make matters worse.*

And, the effect, the wonderful effect was, that all riot and disposition to riot *ceased throughout the kingdom,* though the misery of the people had been increasing all the while. These facts are well known; they are recorded in the publications themselves, which publications will be read with delight ages after the carcass of this Manchester Lawyer shall have been food for maggots, and after his name shall have been forgotten, except as far as my exposure and reprobation of him shall tend to perpetuate a recollection of it. True it is, indeed, that his memory will *live;* and so does that of Judas Iscariot.

From the very first appearance of the Cheap Register, *until* the passing of the *Absolute-Power-of-Imprisonment Act* and the *Gagging* and *New Treason Laws,* not a riot took place in any part of the kingdom, except at one place in Scotland, where the people had been *too loyal* to permit any Meeting for Reform. There the people rioted and broke open Bakers' and Grocers' shops. But, the moment that the Dungeon and Gagging-Laws were passed, rioting began. When the people, in answer to their humble petitions, were menaced with the dungeon and the gallows; then they, of course, ceased to have any hope from a peaceable and supplicating line of conduct. This, no one will deny, is a true state of the case; and, this being a true state of the case, it follows, of course, that the Manchester Lawyer has been guilty of the foulest of calumny.

THIRTEEN

THE REPRESSION AND THE SPY SYSTEM

Flogging Soldiers

P.R. XIX., c. 641. *Flogging Soldiers.* 16-3-11.

THE public have seen by the reports of the debates in the House
of Commons, that there is some alteration introduced into
the MUTINY ACT of this year, relative to the odious punishment of *flogging*. It is stated, that the JUDGE ADVOCATE
said, in introducing a clause the object of which was to make this
alteration, that the court-martial would, by it, have *the power*
of inflicting the punishment of imprisonment in lieu of that of
flogging.—The words were : " that in proposing this amendment, he by no means intended to defeat the ends of punishment.
It would only give to Courts Martial *an alternative,* where they
should think it necessary, to imprison, instead of resorting to any
corporal infliction.''—That is to say, *to flogging.* Why do you
mince the matter? Why not name the thing? *Flog is flog,* and
flogging is the active participle of the verb to *flog.* *Flog,
flogging, flogged.* That is the word; and, it means, in this sense
of it, to whip the naked back (and, sometimes, *other parts*) of
a soldier, with a thing called a *cat;* that is to say, with nine strong
whip-cords, about a foot and a half long, with nine knots in each,
and which cords are fastened, like the thong of a whip, to the
end of a stick about two feet long. With this cat-o'-nine-tails
the soldier, being tied up to a thing for the purpose, by his hands
and thighs, is flogged, out in the open field, or parade, while the
regiment are drawn up round him.—This is the plain, un-
adorned, unexaggerated thing; and its name is *flogging.* Why,
then, call it by any other name? Why call it *" corporal infliction? ''* These words may mean any thing touching the
body. The word *flogging* we all understand; and, as to *delicacy*
of expression, if the word *be* indelicate, what must the *thing*

be?—As to flogging upon parts *lower down* than the back, I do
not know that it is now practised; but, I saw it done once myself,
in a meadow of the Bush Inn at Farnham, by the Surrey Militia;
and, though I was then but a little boy, I remember that an
officer, who was an enormously fat man, beat the Drummer with
his stick, because he did not flog the soldier hard enough.

The Spy-System

P.R. XXXII., c. 900.   *Letter to Peter Walker, Esq. of Worth, in the
County of Sussex. On the Spy-System.* 25-10-17.

THE *Spy-System,* or, as a worthy Lancashire friend of ours
called it, the " *Spoy-System,*" used to be treated by me with
ridicule. He, however, insisted, that it was, and long had been,
on foot and in great vigour; and you observed, not many weeks
before I left England, that, as there *were no treasons,* treasons
would be *made,* and traitors would be *hired.* Your opinions have
now been proved to be correct. The traitors have been *hired,*
and the fact is *openly avowed* by the base employers. Indeed
they could not deny it. The proofs were at hand. They had
been caught in the fact.

What a picture, then, does their System *now* present? You
used to say, that I turned an abstruse point about on every side,
and at both ends, till, at last, the dullest eyes saw it. So these
Spy-Employers seem to be turning their System about. They
appear to be resolved to keep on, 'till it shall be impossible for
even their own creatures to have impudence enough left to say
one word in their favour. They seem to be determined to
exhaust their whole stock of inventions to provide for themselves
implacable and everlasting hatred.

What! Was the country *too quiet* for them? Yes, and you
will remember with what *particular malignity* they spoke of these
essays of mine, the main object of which was *to prevent* disorder
and riot. Amongst the endless abuse, heaped upon me by those
choice tools of corruption, *Walter* and *Stewart,* there was none
equal to that which was drawn forth by my endeavours to put an
end to the destruction of machines and to the attacks on bakers
and butchers. These were the things, which these ruffians

wanted to see continued; because, against acts like these all good men would naturally say, that *force* must be employed. Nothing, therefore, was so painful to these plot-makers as to see the people really enlightened as to the *cause* of their sufferings. This was that *change* in the character of the people, which was so feelingly spoken of in the First Report of the Secret Committee of the House of Lords. The people had met by twenties and thirties and forties of thousands, and they had *talked sense,* and had *quietly separated.* Mr. BENBOW, who is a shoe-maker, and whom, I see, SIDMOUTH has in one of his dungeons, was talking with me upon some point (I forget what), and, in order to maintain his opinion, he pulled *a Volume of Blackstone out of his pocket.* This was that *dreadful* change of character, of which the Borough-mongers were so much afraid. And well they might be afraid of it, unless they had meant to yield the people their rights; for, it amounted to a proof, that the people now understood those rights, and that they were never again to be deceived.

But, as it was not easy to resort to a military system without some apparent reason, it was necessary to hatch plots. CASTLE's plots are now blown into the air. But, they wanted plots in country as well as town. The people, full of indignation at the cruel acts which had been adopted, were, of course, brooding resentment; and, we now see, that the hired Spies were sent expressly to blow this into a flame. If a man, very deeply injured by another, were to be instigated by a third party to go and assist the third party in killing the cruel man, who would be the *real murderer?* And, what would you say to a fourth party, who should have hired the third for the purpose? But, the present case is still worse; for here the cruel man hires the third party to instigate the suffering party to *attempt* the deed, and then to betray the suffering party into his hands. Not content with the injuries he has inflicted already, the cruel man, in this case, knowing that his victim cannot forgive him, seeks to take *his blood,* and to take it, too, by the most base, cowardly, and detestable of means.

However, my friend, it is still *inconsistent* in any one to disapprove even of the *Spy-System,* unless he, at the same time, *be an advocate for Reform;* or, unless he wishes, indeed, to exchange the Dungeon and Spy-System for the more honest system of openly avowed military despotism and *martial-law;* for, to prevent a Reform there must be *force* continually in activity. It is nonsense to talk of *hushing things up.* What is it to the mass of the people what the thing is *called,* which makes them poor and miserable? What is it to a farmer, whether he be put into jail by the tax-gatherer, or by Sidmouth? What is it to the labourer, whether he starve in a hut, or in a dungeon? So long as you pay *twenty* English shillings for a bushel of that very salt, for which, when landed here, I pay *two shillings and sixpence,* what is it to you whether the soldiers, the spies, or the great Borough-monger families and their dependents swallow the *seventeen shillings and sixpence?*

Oliver the Spy

P.R. XXXIII., c. 589. *Letter II to Messrs. Benbow, Evans, Sen., Evans, Jun., John Roberts, John Smith, Francis Ward, John Johnson, John Knight, Samuel Brown, John Baguelly, and the rest of those who have acted the same noble part.* 23-5-18.

THERE was not a man amongst them who did not know, and well know, that it was OLIVER, who was the immediate cause of the rising in Derbyshire. There was not a man amongst them who did not know, that the discontent was created by the tyrannical Bills, and that it was worked into a rising by OLIVER. And yet, they could *unanimously* pass an address, which ascribed it to me and to others, who had taken an active part in the cause of Reform; they could, thus, unanimously, vote this, which originated in the false and base mind of LAWYER CROSS, whose *defence,* to make the thing complete, is complimented by that wonderful patriot, SIR SAMUEL ROMILLY, who, as if that were not enough, called the Derby men, *poor, ignorant creatures.* Faith, SIR SAMUEL was deceived; for the Derby men knew very well what they were about; they were betrayed; they were deceived; but they knew what they were about very well, and all the grounds upon which they proceeded. They knew well, that according to law as well as reason, *Resistance of Oppression* is a RIGHT, and not a CRIME. They *might* be wrong, as to whether oppression did, or did not, exist;

but, in their *doctrine* they were perfectly right. Their measures, too, were efficient, had they not been *betrayed*. Even here their humanity was the cause of their defeat. OLIVER was suspected, and so strongly suspected *that a rope,* as I have been assured, *was ready prepared for his neck;* and, he would have carried intelligence to the Devil at once, instead of to LORD SIDMOUTH, if justice had not spoke and said: "He *may* be innocent. *It is better to run any risk, than put an innocent man to death."*

The Gagging Acts

P.R. XXXII,. c. 1049.   *To Earl Fitzwilliam.*   22-11-17.

FOR my part, I think it much better that the Despotism should should exist in its present shape than that things should fall back into the state of 1816. Things are now come to a certain known point. We now understand that it is force, sheer force to which we yield. The struggle is open and avowed; and when men fall, they have, at any rate, the compassion of their country-men, and of all the good part of mankind. Before this revolution, it was a non-descript sort of thing. Men were destroyed in estate and in person; and the world hardly knew why or how. Some how or other, they were destroyed, and that was all that was known. There was such a mixed medley of Liberty of the Press and truth being a libel; of trial by Jury and of Juries chosen by the master of the Crown Office; of Habeas Corpus Act and of commitment for want of bail in cases of libel, the party being too poor to find bail; of compulsion to come to trial, and of power of the Attorney General not to bring on the trial but just when he pleased, and to stop the trial, if he pleased, after the Jury was empannelled, without consent of Court, and then bring it on again when he pleased, to the end of a man's life. All this mixed medley has now given place to one plain, simple act of Parliament, giving absolute power to the Ministers, to take any man that they please, native or foreigner, to put him into a jail that they please, and any dungeon that they please, to treat him there in any manner that they please, to deny access to him by any human being, and to keep him to that state just as long as they please. This is a plain simple thing, that scorns all hypocrisy; and it plainly tells the people that " thus it is that you shall be as long as we have the power of keeping you so."

This is something to be understood. We all understand it. All the world understands it; and the only question now is, how long this can go on. My opinion is that three years will be the utmost period of its duration. Four is the very outside that I give it, and even two is more than I think it very likely to last. Your Lordship and the rest of you have found it difficult enough to get this new system into play; but you will find it much more difficult to get rid of it.

Death of Castlereagh

P.R. XLIII., c. 385. *To Joseph Swann.* 17-8-22.

TO JOSEPH SWANN,

Who was sentenced by the Magistrates of Cheshire to FOUR YEARS AND A HALF imprisonment in Chester Gaol, for selling Pamphlets and being present at a Meeting for Parliamentary Reform; who was imprisoned many Weeks, for WANT OF BAIL, before his Trial; who has now TWO YEARS OF HIS IMPRISONMENT UNEXPIRED; and who, when Imprisoned, had a Wife and four helpless Children.

Kensington, 15 August, 1822.

MR. SWANN,
CASTLEREAGH HAS CUT HIS OWN THROAT, AND IS DEAD! Let that sound reach you in the depth of your dungeon; and let it carry consolation to your suffering soul! Of all the victims, you have suffered most. We are told of the poignant grief of *Lady Castlereagh;* and, while he must be a· brute indeed, who does not feel for her, what must he be, who does not feel for *your wife* and your four helpless children, actually torn from you when you were first thrown into the dismal cells?

* * * * * *

As to compassion; as to *sorrow*, upon this occasion, how base a hypocrite I must be to affect it! nay, how base a hypocrite to disguise, or attempt to disguise, my satisfaction! Can I forget Ireland; can I forget Mr. FINNERTY; can I forget NAPOLEON, Marshal NEY! can I forget the QUEEN, who, though she suffered so much, though she suffered to the breaking of her heart, never thought of the dastardly act of putting an end to her existence. The ruffians who continue to praise this man, tell us that the history of his life is found in the measures of the Government for the last twenty-seven years; and that is true enough; it is found in all the various acts that have been passed to shut the Irish up in their houses from sunset to sunrise, and to transport them without trial by jury. It is found in the Power-of-imprisonment Bill of 1817. It is found in those terrible Six Acts, one of which prescribes that the printer of a newspaper shall enter into bail even before he begins to print; which prescribes that this very pamphlet in which I am now addressing you, shall be so loaded with paper and with price, as to make it difficult to effect its circulation. It is found in another of those Acts, which was intended to transport men, and which does banish men for life, for a second time uttering that which has a tendency to bring into contempt those who pass such a law. His history is in the figure of eight and eight cyphers, which represent the amount of the National Debt. It is written in those measures which have reduced the most industrious and enterprising farmers in the world to a state of beggary, and have plunged no small number of them into despair, real insanity, and self-destruction. It is written in a mass of pauperism, hitherto wholly unknown to England, and it is written in starvation to Ireland amidst over-production. As to his family and connexions, look at the immense sums which they are now receiving out of the fruit of the people's labour. And as to any compassion that we are to feel for them, we will feel it when an end to the sufferings of the Reformers and their families will leave us a particle of compassion to bestow on any body else. The mention of the anguish of Lady CASTLEREAGH only reminds me of the anguish of poor Mrs. JOHNSON, who, brought to a death-bed by long and racking anxiety on account of her husband, harassed, persecuted, thrown into a dungeon at a hundred miles from her, merely for having *been present* at a Meeting never before deemed unlawful; when I hear Lady Castlereagh's anguish mentioned I forget, for the time, the enormous sinecure of her father, but I remember that exemplary and affectionate wife, Mrs. Johnson, who, brought to her death-bed by the means just mentioned, earnestly prayed that she might *see* her husband before she closed her eyes for ever; and I remember, that that prayer was *rejected by Castlereagh and his colleagues,* though the husband tendered bail to any amount and offered to submit to any length of imprisonment as the price of permission to receive the last sigh of his dying wife.

I have now peerformed my duty; a duty towards the Public; towards the Reformers more especially; and, Joseph Swann, particularly towards you. I anxiously hope that you may come alive, and in health, out of your dungeon. I admired your conduct at the time when the sentence was passed upon you. You did not talk of cutting your throat; but, darting a look at those who passed the sentence, you exclaimed: " Is that *all*? I though you had a *bit of rope* in your pockets for me! " Your children are in misery now; but be of good cheer; they may live to see the day when they will not have to mourn over a father in a dungeon. I am,

Your faithful Friend and

Most obedient Servant,

Wm. COBBETT.

FOURTEEN

PARLIAMENT AND REFORM

Letter to Honiton Electors

P.R. IX., c. 833. *To the Electors of Honiton. Letter II.* 7-6-06.

GENTLEMEN;—Perceiving that Mr. Cavendish Bradshaw has, since by your voice he was constituted one of the guardians of the public purse, taken care to obtain a place by the means of which he will draw into his own pocket some thousands a year out of that purse, and this, too, at a time when the load of indispensible taxes is pressing his honest and industrious constituents to the earth; perceiving this, and being fully persuaded, that, whenever the electors of any place re-choose representatives under similar circumstances, the cause is not so much in their own disposition as in the apathy and lukewarmness of those independent men who may have the ability to rescue them from such hands; with this truth being deeply impressed, I did, upon hearing of the approaching vacancy, use my efforts to prevail upon other men of this description to afford you an opportunity of evincing your good sense and uprightness, and, having failed in those efforts, I have thought it my duty to afford you this opportunity myself; it being manifestly true, that, unless men of independence and of public spirit will offer themselves as candidates, to rail at electors for choosing and re-choosing the dependent and the mercenary is, in the highest degree, unreasonable and unjust.—As to professions, Gentlemen, so many and so loud, upon such occasions, have they been; so numerous are the instances, in which the foulness and shamelessness of the apostacy have borne an exact proportion to the purity and solemnity of the vow; so completely, and with such fatal effect, have the grounds of confidence been destroyed, that, it is now become necessary, upon all occasions like the present, to give a pledge, such as every man can clearly understand, and

such as it is impossible to violate without exposing the violator
to detection and to all the consequences of detected hypocrisy
and falsehood; and, such a pledge I now give in declaring, that,
whether you elect me or not, I never as long as I live, either
for myself, or for, or through the means of, any one of my
family, will receive, under any name, whether of salary, pension
or other, either directly or indirectly, one single farthing of the
public money; but, without emolument, compensation, or
reward of any kind or in any shape, will, to the utmost of my
ability, watch over and defend the property, the liberties and
the privileges of the people, never therefrom separating, as I
never yet have, the just and constitutional rights and prerogatives
of the crown.——This declaration, Gentlemen, is not made without due reflection as to the future as well as to the present, as
to public men in general as well as to myself. It proceeds, first,
from an opinion, that the representatives of the people ought
never to be exposed to the temptation of betraying their trust;
secondly, from long observation, that those who live upon the
public are amongst the most miserable of men; and, thirdly,
from that experience in the various walks of life, which has
convinced me of the wisdom of Hagar, who prayed for neither
riches nor poverty; not riches, lest he should forget God; not
poverty, lest he should be tempted to steal; and, to receive the
public money unjustly, is not only stealing, but stealing of the
worst and basest sort, including a breach of the most sacred trust,
accompanied with the cowardly consciousness of impunity.
From reflections like these, Gentlemen, it is, that the declaration
now made has proceeded, and, when I depart, in word or in
deed, from this declaration, may I become the scorn of my
country; wherein to be remembered with esteem, I prize beyond
all the riches and all the honours of this world.——But,
Gentlemen, as it is my firm determination never to receive a
farthing of the public money, so it is my determination equally
firm, never, in any way whatever, to give one farthing of my
own money to any man, in order to induce him to vote, or to
cause others to vote, for me; and, being convinced, that it is this
practice of giving, or promising to give, money, or money's
worth, at elections; being convinced, that it is this disgraceful,

this unlawful, this profligate, this impious practice, to which are to be ascribed all our calamities and all the dangers that now stare us in the face, I cannot refrain from exhorting you to be against all attempts at such practices, constantly and watchfuly upon your guard. The candidates who have resorted to such means have always been found amongst the most wicked of men; men, who, having, by a life of adultery or of gambling, or of profligracy of some other sort, ruined both their character and their fortunes, have staked their last thousand upon an election, with the hope of thereby obtaining security from a jail, and of selling their vote for the means of future subsistence drawn from the sweat of the people at a hundred-fold; and thus expecting to pocket the profit of the corrupt speculation, sneering at their bribed and perjured constituents, as Satan is said to have sneered at the reprobate with whom he had bargained for his soul. —Far from you, Gentlemen, be credulity so foolish! Far from you, disgrace so deep, infamy so indelible! Far from you, so flagrant a violation of the law, so daring a defiance of the justice and the power and the wrath of God! But, were it otherwise, and did I find in Honiton but as many righteous men as were found in Sodom and Gomorrah, I would tender them my hand to lead them from the rest. Very different, however, are my hopes; these hopes forbid me to believe it possible, that there should be, collected upon one spot, four hundred Englishmen, having the eyes of all England upon them, who will not, by their votes, freely and cordially given, sanction the great principle upon which I now stand; and, in these hopes, I will, if I have life, do myself the honour to meet you on the day of election.

In the mean while,

I am, with great respect, Gentlemen,

Your most humble and most obedient servant,

WM. COBBETT.

1st of June, 1806.

Cobbett and Parliament

P.R. XLIX., c. 67.   To Sir Thomas Beevor, Bart.   On his proposition for placing Mr. COBBETT in the House of Commons.   10-1-24.

SO early as the year 1809, I was of opinion, that *to place me in parliament* would be very beneficial to the country. If I had been in parliament at the close of the war against Bonaparte, in the year 1814; or, in 1816; or, in 1819; or, in 1822; if I had been in parliament at either of these epochs, things could not have been as they are now. The *cash-measures* never could have been taken; the land and labour could not have been oppressed as they now are; the debt could not have been what it now is; the nation could not have been so cowed down as to suffer France to counter-revolutionize and to take possession of Spain; and that state of peril, in which the very independence of the country is now likely to be placed, could not have existed.

I have never wished to be in parliament for my *own sake;* for, the habits of my life, my mode of living, my taste, and my pursuits other than public pursuits, all forbid me to enter the House at Westminster. To gain *money* by being placed in that house is *impossible,* unless upon the supposition that I should consent to be set down for the most infamous of all mankind; and, as to *fame,* what do I want with more than I have? Would the words, WILLIAM COBBETT gain any thing by having tacked to the end of them the M.P. which are seen at the tail of *Coke, Wodehouse, Wilberforce, Horace Twiss,* and the endless tribe of the *Lord Johns* and *Lord Charleses*? For *myself,* or for any one related to me *by blood,* I value a seat in parliament no more than I value a dead leaf or a straw. I should deem it *no honour at all.* Your good opinion; your openly, and in the most formal manner, declaring that opinion, I deem a great honour. But, the seat itself, constituted as the House now is, I should deem no honour at all; and, I have never desired it except for the benefit of the country.

Radical Reform

P.R. XLII., c. 530.   *Visit to Farnhâm.*   1-6-22.

THE toast expresses a wish that we should have an *efficient* Reform. For my own part, I prefer the word *radical* reform. The word Radical has been interpreted to mean, amongst other horrid things, sedition and rebellion. But what does it mean? It means something belonging to or appertaining to the root; and if we have an evil to remove, is it not necessary to go to the root of it? Can we remove it without going to the root of it? There may be those who, having their pastures infested by docks, prefer the cutting of them off just beneath the ground, to the digging of them clean up. I am for the latter mode. In Politics as well as in Husbandry, I am for going to the root, and therefore am for a *radical* reform.

Prorogation of Parliament

P.R. LXIII., c. 65.   *King's Speech.*   7-7-27.

THE Parliament, God and King be praised, is prorogued; that is to say, their talkings, their everlasting talkings, are, for a while, at least, put a stop to. Any thing, no matter what, that would effect this, must be pleasing to me; for, to have in one's mind constantly the reflection, that one is living in the *same world* where this everlasting talking (and *such* talking!) is going on, would, of itself, be bad enough; but, when to this abstract misery is added the real, the practical evil of one's being *obliged to pay for this talking,* and that, too, at an enormous price, we must exclaim, as Old STERN-PATH MAN is said to have done, when he got from Castlereagh's brother the application for a pension, " *this is too bad!* " However, they are *gone,* God be thanked, for a while, at any rate; and poor CANNING's back is, for some months (unless a " late panic " should come), relieved from the pressings of the sharp knees of Burdett.

Preston Election

P.R. LXIV., c. 201. *The Poor Man's Friend.* To the Electors of Preston.
20-10-27.

I SHALL *have no subscription for this election; and I shall spend no money of my own.* I want no place, as STANLEY did and does; I want nothing from the taxes; I am content with my own earnings; but I am not content to expend one farthing of those earnings upon persons who will not perform their own duty; who will not do their obvious duty towards their wives, their children, their neighbours, and their country, without being paid for it. I will be under no control of anybody; I will be a free representative of free and honest men, or I will be no representative at all.

I would have you see this matter, from the beginning to the end, in its true light. I scorn the man, I despise the man who imagines that I am in pursuit of gain for myself or for any of my family. What do I want? What can this Government give me, King and all taken together? Nothing, so help me God, that I would accept of. If there were a REFORM *of the* PARLIAMENT, I would give any assistance in my power to the King or his Council. Without such reform, all the titles, all the wealth, every thing that the King and the Parliament have to bestow, I would reject with scorn. I hereby distinctly pledge myself, that as I never have, in the whole course of my life, touched the public money in any shape, so I never will, unless in the way of bare payment of expenses for loss of time, that might be due to me for services actually and personally rendered to the country, the country having first a REFORM in PARLIAMENT! I go further than this : I labour : I practice frugality; I rise early; I eat the bread of carefulness; not for the sake of myself, however, but for the sake of others; my food and drink is very little other than that of a ploughman in a good old-fashioned farm house : no man exceeds me in anxiety to make suitable and comfortable provision for every one dependant upon me : I have expended a considerable part of my earnings upon poor brothers and their children, and upon unfortunate labouring people, whom I thought demanded this alienation from the stock of my family. I have done all this with the greatest cheerfulness :

I have had the greatest pleasure in contemplating the prospect of seeing well off every one looking up to the result of my labours : I have sons that I love as much as any man ever loved his children; but, I here most solemnly declare, that if either of those sons should ever accept any post of profit, or any distinction, commonly thought or called " honourable," under this Government, the Parliament still remaining unreformed, that son never should again be under the same roof with me if I could help it. I am convinced that my country is ill-treated; I behold its fallen state; I detest the wretch, be he who he may, who can behold the miseries of the people without feelings of indignation : I see ruin and starvation spread over this once happy land; I feel all the disgrace of the projects of emigration committees : I see the magistrates of New York inflicting punishments on the mariners who, with English bribes in their pockets, have landed English paupers upon the American shore : and if I see and feel all this, I know that it arises from a want of reform in the Parliament; and if a son of mine were to lend his hand to wield the scourge upon my suffering country, he never should be again considered as my son; I should distinctly state to you that I do not suspect and never have suspected (God forbid), that any son of mine would be guilty of such baseness. On the contrary, I should not be afraid to pledge my life upon their faithful adherance to the principles of their father. But, young men get connected; and that, too, in a way, where the temptation may become very powerful. I have duly thought of all this matter. My own character; my own happiness; their happiness too, and, above all things, my duty to my country, call upon me to make this declaration, from which I never can flinch without being knocked on the head with impunity by any two or three fellows that may choose to perform the just but disagreeable job.

Then, it would be base and bootlessly base in me to participate in any shape or manner in the taxes squeezed out of the people. What do I want in this world but the things that I have? I have a house at Fleet Street, I have another at Kensington, I have another at Barn Elm, which is only about half a mile over Hammersmith Bridge, and at about the distance of three and a half miles from Kensington. These are all good houses, too :

they are furnished with every necessary. At Barn Elm I have now a farm of nearly a hundred acres, the richest land I believe in this whole world, except those marshes which bring diseases along with their riches.. What more than this can I want? I have horses at my will : always not less than half a dozen men to start at my call : I feed more hungry, meritorious people than any lord in the kingdom : God has blessed me with health and strength very rare at my age : I am enabled to set a great example of enterprize, industry, early rising, perseverance, to all around me. What more can I want? Has ambition its calls upon me? What can it suggest beyond the farm which I have? Beyond the real power which I possess of upholding my friends and beating down my enemies. What can ambition suggest, beyond the circumstance of my very name exacting attention whenever it is pronounced; beyond that of the innumerable persons, who testify their joy and even their gratitude at being permitted to shake me by the hand? What can I want more than these? What can the KING of CANNING and of STANLEY; what can he who promoted these men, and who gave titles to WALTER SCOTT, COUTTS TROTTER, CHARLES LONG, and base DUDLEY; what can he bestow that would be accepted of by a man like me, who despises from the bottom of his soul what is called *wealth* : a man in whom it is no affectation to eat fat bacon and drink small beer at seven o'clock in the morning for breakfast, and who would not, if he could do it, even out of his resources, make his children what is called rich, it being his firm conviction, grounded on long experience and observation, that riches, especially great riches, produce misery in ten cases, where they produce happiness in one? What has the King or any king to bestow upon such a man? I think much of the office of the King; I think much of my DUTY towards him; I have always inculcated due obedience to his authority : but favours from him I want none; I set less value upon them, and infinitely less value than upon a single plant of five beds of sassafras trees which I now have growing in my garden at Kensington.

Plan of Reform

P.R. LXX., c. 553. *Plan of Parliamentary Reform, addressed to the Young Men of England.* 30-10-30.

OF *what description ought the Reform to be?* Having brought ourselves to the thorough conviction, at which conviction indeed ninety-nine hundredths of the people had arrived long ago, that a *Reform of the Parliament is necessary,* the next question to be answered, is, that which I have just asked: namely, of what description the reform ought to be. Things have now come to that pass, that some sort of reform will be proposed, I dare say, even by the minister himself. It is said that this will be the case; but, to hope that he will propose the sort of Reform which the circumstances of the nation require, would be to be one's own dupe. Be this as it may, however, it becomes me, it is my duty indeed to lay before you my opinions upon the subject; to state to you distinctly *my plan of Reform,* or, more properly speaking, the plan which I think the nation ought to insist upon. To suppose that the country is going to be contented with the pitiful project of giving two members to Birmingham, and two to each of three other great towns, would argue almost insanity. The thing is scoffed at even by those who have been forward to talk of a moderate reform; and if the bawling lawyer who has put himself forward as the hero of this project, be not frightened from it before the day of trial, he will become the byword and scoffing-stock even of the clowns in the villages, who, clownish as they are, all understand the matter too well to be imposed upon by means like these, even for one single moment. It is hard to say what, amongst all the contrivances that will be hatched for the purpose of giving the name and withholding the substance of reform; amongst all the schemes that will be tried to cajole and deceive the people; amongst all the great variety of projects that will probably be presented to our view; it is hardly possible to guess at what precise point of shadow, shutting out the substance, the projectors will rest; but, let us suppose, that, alarmed at present appearances; let us suppose that, bearing in mind the deeds of the working people of Paris and of Brussels, and estimating the effect of those deeds upon the minds of the mass of the people in England; let us suppose that, at last, and at the eleventh hour, it be resolved to do something; and let us even suppose that it be in the midst of daily-increasing dangers resolved to abolish the infernal boroughs of every description, and to give the people their fair choice, only confining the right of voting to householders. This is a great deal too much for any man to suppose; but let us suppose it, for the argument's sake; let us suppose that they are, at last, willing to give a vote to every man that occupies a house, whether he pay direct taxes or not. Then, this does not satisfy me. It ought not to satisfy you, and it will not give peace and happiness and freedom to the country. The reform which would be just, and which you ought to demand, is as follows :

1. That a new Parliament shall be chosen every year.

2. That every man, having attained the age of eighteen, shall have a vote, and that no man shall have more than one vote.

3. That no man shall be excluded, whether pauper, soldier, sailor, or any-thing else, if he be of sane mind, and is not branded by sentence of a court of justice for some indelible crime which renders him incapable of giving evidence in a court of justice in civil matters.

4. That there be no pecuniary qualification for members, and that the only qualifications necessary shall be, that the member be a native of the county, that he have resided in it three years previous to being elected; and that each member be twenty-one years of age.

5. That the mode of choosing the members be by ballot.

What will Reform do?

P.R. LXXII., c. 4.   *To the Labourers of England.* 1. *Observations to Labourers on the subject of Parliamentary Reform.* 2-4-31.

IT may be asked, Will a reform of the Parliament give the labouring man a cow or a pig; will it put bread and cheese into his satchell instead of infernal cold potatoes; will it give him a bottle of beer to carry to the field instead of making him lie down upon his belly to drink out of the brook; will it put upon his back a Sunday coat and send him to church, instead of leaving him to stand lounging about shivering with an unshaven face and a carcass half covered with a ragged smock-frock, with a filthy cotton shirt beneath it as yellow as a kite's foot? Will parliamentary reform put an end to the harnessing of men and women by a hired overseer to draw carts like beasts of burden; will it put an end to the practice of putting up labourers to auction like negroes in Carolina or Jamaica; will it put an end to the system which caused the honest labourer to be fed worse than the felons in the jails; will it put an end to the system which caused almost the whole of the young women to incur the in-delible disgrace of being on the point of being mothers before they were married, owing to that degrading poverty which prevented the fathers themselves from obtaining the means of paying the parson and the clerk : will parliamentary reform put an end to the foul, the beastly, the nasty practice of separating men from their wives by force, and committing to the hired overseer the bestial superintendence of their persons day and night; will parliamentary reform put an end to this which was amongst the basest acts which the Roman tyrants committed towards their slaves? The enemies of reform jeeringly ask us, whether reform would do these things for us; and I answer distinctly that IT WOULD DO THEM ALL!

Address to the Electors of Manchester

P.R. LXXIII., c. 641. *To the Electors of Manchester.* 10-9-31.

GENTLEMEN,

In all cases where men are about to form engagements with each other, it is, before all things, necessary for them to start with a clear understanding with regard to what each party shall do, in consequence of the engagement.

I will therefore clearly state to you the things which I will do (God giving me life and health), if you choose me for one of your representatives. I have always found, that the short way to arrive at any just object, in the accomplishment of which you stand in need of the co-operation of others, is to declare to those others, at the outset, openly and explicitly *what the object is;* and therefore I will now, in the most open and plain manner, state the things which I wish to see accomplished, and which, if you send me to the Parliament, I will use my utmost endeavours to cause to be accomplished; and which things are as follows:

1. To put an end to all pensions, sinecures, grants, allowances, half-pay, and all other emoluments now paid out of the taxes, except for such public services as, upon a very scrupulous examination, shall be found fully to merit them; and to reduce all salaries to the American standard.

2. To discharge the standing army, except such part of the ordnance and artillery as may be necessary to maintain the arsenals at the seaports in a state of readiness for war; and to abolish the military academies, and dispose of all barracks and other property now applied to military uses.

3. To make the counties, each according to its whole number of members of parliament, maintain and equip a body of militia, horse as well as foot and artillery, at the county-expense, and to have these bodies, as they are in America, mustered at stated periods; so that, at any time, a hundred thousand efficient men may be ready to come into the field, if the defence of the kingdom require it.

4. To abolish tithes of every description; to leave to the clergy the churches, the church-yards, the parsonage houses, and the *ancient* glebes; and, for the rest, leave them to the voluntary contributions of the people.

5. To take all the rest of the property, commonly called church-property; rents, and real property of every kind, now possessed by bishops, chapters, or other ecclesiastical bodies, and all the misapplied property of corporate bodies of every sort; and also all the property called crown-lands, or crown-estates, including that of the Duchies of Cornwall and Lancaster; and sell them all, and apply the proceeds to the discharge of the Debt which the late parliaments contracted with the fundholders.

6. To cease, during the first six months after June 1832, to pay interest on a fourth part of the Debt; second six months, to cease to pay interest on another fourth; and so on for the other two fourths; so that no more interest on any part of the Debt would be paid, after the end of two years.

7. To divide the proceeds of all the property mentioned in paragraph No. 5, and also in paragraph No. 2, in due proportion, on principles of equity, amongst the owners of what is called *stock*, or, in other words, the *fundholders*, or persons who lent their money to those who borrowed it in virtue of acts of the late parliaments; and to give to the fundholders, out of the taxes, nothing beyond these proceeds.

8. To make an equitable adjustment with respect to the pecuniary contracts between man and man, and thereby rectify, as far as practicable, the wrongs and ruin inflicted on thousands upon thousands of virtuous families by the arbitrary changes made by acts of the late parliaments, in the value of the money of the country.

9. To abolish *all internal taxes* (except on the land), whether direct or indirect, including stamp-taxes of every description; and to impose such a postage-charge for letters as to defray the *real expenses* of an economical and yet efficient post-office establishment, and no more; so that the postage would be merely a *payment* for the conveyance of letters, and not a tax.

10. To lay just as much custom-house duty on importations as shall be found conducive to the benefit of the navigation, commerce, and manufactures of the kingdom, viewed as a whole, and not to lay on one penny more.

11. To make effectual provision, in every department, for the maintenance of a powerful navy; to give such pay and such an allotment of prize-money to the seamen as to render impressment wholly unnecessary; to abolish the odious innovation of *naval academies*, and re-open the door of promotion to skill and valour, whether found in the heirs of nobles, or in the sons of the loom or of the plough; to abolish all military *Orders*, and to place the navy next in honour to the throne itself.

12. To make a legal, a *fixed*, and a generous allowance to the king, and, through him, to all the branches and members of his family; to leave to him the unshackled freedom of appointing all his servants, whether of his household or of

his public ministry; to leave to him the full control over his palaces, gardens, and parks, as land-owners have over their estates; to take care that he be not worried with intrigues to purloin from him that which the people give him for his own enjoyment; so that he may be, in all respects, what the Chief of a free people ought to be, his name held in the highest honour, and his person held sacred, as the great guardian of the people's rights.

13. To make an accurate valuation of all the houses, lands, mines, and other real property, in each county in the whole kingdom; to impose a tax upon that property, to be paid quarterly, and in every county on the same day, and in such manner as to cost in the collection, or, rather, payment, not more than *four hundred pounds* a year in any one county; to make the rate and amount of this tax vary with the wants of the state, always taking care to be amply provided with means in case of war, when war shall be demanded by the safety, the interest, or the honour of the kingdom.

Now, gentlemen, if sent to Parliament by you, or by any-body else, these things I will endeavour to accomplish; and, by argument unanswerable, I am ready to maintain the *justice,* and *expediency,* and the *easy practicability* of them all; and these I will maintain in the series of addresses of which this is the first. These things done, the yearly expenditure of the kingdom comes far within the sum of ten millions; and I do most solemnly assure you, that if I had no hope to see that result of my efforts, not one single day more of my life should be passed in the smoke and stench of this WEN, amidst the din of long-coaches and short-coaches and omnibuses and hacks and cabs and vans by day, and the bawlings of gens d'armerie and the squallings of prostitutes by night.

Here is no mention of Corn Bills, Sturges Bourne's Bills, New-Treason laws, Soldier-seducing death laws, Justices' Power-to-transport laws, horrid Six-Acts, and the like; and they need no mention here; for as the limbs of the tree die when the root is cut off, so these will disappear when that taxation, from which they have all naturally proceeded, shall cease to exist. Those of you, if there be any of you who have done me the honour to read my writings during the last twenty years, will know that hardly one month of that long space of time has passed without my observing that it was folly to complain of particular acts of severity on the part of the Government; that it was folly to complain of any of the sufferings that we had to endure, and, at the same time, to acknowledge, expressly or tacitly, that it was necessary to raise on us sixty millions in taxes in a year; for that it was impossible to raise these without the use of means which must cause suffering, the natural violent effects of which were to be prevented only by measures of severity, at the bare thought of the possibility of their children enduring which our fathers would have died with shame.

Turn your eyes for a moment towards HAMPSHIRE, not my native county, for I was born at a few miles from the skirts of it; but a county, for many reasons, particularly dear to me : turn your eyes towards that beautiful county; and there behold seventy-three wives brought to a state of widowhood; two hundred and ninety-four children made fatherless; the hearts of a hundred and fifty-seven parents half broken; and these, by the transportation of a hundred and thirty-five men, the very worst offences of the most violent of whom would not, forty years ago, have been deemed worthy of so much as six months' imprisonment. Look at WILLIAM SUTTON, a labouring lad of eighteen, *condemned to death,* and transported for life, for having been one of three or four others, who, in a half drunken freak, threatened a man, until he gave them *four copper pennies*! Look at HENRY COOK, condemned to death *and executed,* for having *hit* BINGHAM BARING on the collar of his coat and the rim of his hat, without producing any wound or leaving any mark, or doing him any harm whatsoever. But, a relation of the whole history would drive one mad! Having put the words upon the paper, shame to think that I am an Englishman would, if any one were in the room, prevent me from lifting up my eyes and looking him in the face! But, gentlemen, it is inconsistent to complain of this; it is even *unjust* to complain of it, if we acknowledge that this system of taxation ought to endure; for, without such law and such acts the system cannot be carried on. To pay such taxes and to avoid pinching the working people to the point of starvation is impossible. First the employers are pressed by the hand of taxation; they press the working people; the working people, to avoid death by starvation, break out into acts of violence; to prevent or punish these, new and harder laws are necessary; Ellenborough's act made it death to wound with pointed or sharp-cutting instruments with intent to kill; this act, *improved* by Lord Lansdown, makes it *death* to strike with *any instrument,* whether a wound *be inflicted or not* : on this law, COOK, of Mitcheldever, was hanged : on this law any man of us may be hanged, if we strike another man or woman, who has the means of preferring a bill of indictment against us, charging us with intent to murder. So that we may, in the language of Scripture, truly say, that, " in the midst of life we are *in death.*" And this is in that England, the laws of which were, for so many, many ages, famed throughout the world for their tender regard for human liberty and human life!

But, gentlemen, we fret and torment ourselves, we " walk in a shadow and disquiet ourselves in vain," as long as this system of taxation shall continue. The hanging of the poor woman at Manchester, in 1812, for snatching some potatoes from a cart to carry home to her starving children; the hanging of the boy, who was so insensible of his situation, that, at the gallows, he cried for help to his " *Mammy* "! Gracious God! the blood runs cold through my veins as I write! But again and again, I say, it is base hypocrisy, or it is contemptible folly at the best, to complain of these laws, and to affect to lament these transactions, if we neglect to do our best to put an end to that system of taxation, to support which such laws and such transactions are absolutely necessary.

The Labourers and Reform

P.R. LXXVI., c. 652. *To the Electors of England. Letter I. Reform Festivals.* 16-6-32.

I HAVE always been of opinion that we owe the Reform Bill more to the COUNTRY LABOURERS than to all the rest of the nation put together; because if they had remained quiet under their sufferings; if they had not resolved not to be reduced to potatoes, and if they had not acted *as they did,* in order to preserve themselves from this state of horrible degradation, WELLINGTON would not have been turned out, GREY would not have come in, the Parliament would have acted upon WELLINGTON's insolent declaration, and we should have had no Reform Bill at all; though, in time, we must have had a terrible and violent revolution. Every man, therefore, who really wishes for the settlement of our difficulties to terminate in peace, must feel gratitude towards these country labourers. I feel this gratitude in a peculiar degree; because, taking England throughout, I know more of their toils, their sufferings, and their virtues, than any other man. I therefore shall spend my day of triumph amongst them; and for the reasons that I am about to give, I shall do it in Hampshire, and in a hamlet called SUTTON SCOTNEY, which is in the parish of WONSTON, and which is situate at about seven miles from WINCHESTER, seven miles from STOCKBRIDGE, seven miles from ANDOVER, seven miles from WHITCHURCH, twelve miles from BASINGSTOKE, fourteen miles from ODIHAM, twelve miles from ALTON, and seven miles from ALRESFORD. And which little hamlet is on the road from London to Salisbury, going through Basingstoke and Stockbridge. At SUTTON SCOTNEY the labourers of ten parishes met, when they sallied forth on November 1830, to remonstrate with the farmers, the parsons, and the landowners, with regard to the wages that had reduced them to a state of half-starvation. But this spot is more dear to me, and it ought to be dear to every Englishman, for a reason other than this. It was at this spot that was signed, that *petition for parliamentary reform,* which the labourer, JOSEPH MASON, carried to the King, at Brighton, in the month of October 1830, the interesting circumstances relating to which, are as follows.

The general notion in London has been, that the country labourers are ignorant creatures; that they have no sentiment at all relative to political rights and liberties; that, like cattle, they know when they are hungry, and that their risings and committing acts of violence, resemble, in point of motive, the feelings which animate cows, or oxen, when they break out of a barren field to get into a rich pasture. Such, too, are the opinions which our Ministers and members of Parliament have entertained towards these producers of the food and the wool and the wood of the country. Proceeding upon these opinions, they have adopted schools without number, and the distribution of millions of pamphlets, the main object of all which has been, to persuade the labourers, that God never intended anything but potatoes for them to eat, and, that it is grievously sinful in them not to be content with such diet, though they see the fields and the meadows covered with corn and with cattle, created by their own labour. It has also been fashionable, amongst even the working classes, to look upon the country labourers, particularly those here in the South, as being totally ignorant with regard to public matters, and as being utterly unable to be made to understand anything about the political causes of their misery; and of course not knowing the least in the world about Parliamentary Reform.

Such opinions were never entertained by me for any one moment of my life. I, from my childhood, have known the country labourers well; and, in conversation as well as in writing, I have always maintained, that they well understood the *nature of their wrongs,* and the *causes of their misery;* and that the day would come, when they would endure that misery no longer.

Burning of the Parliament House

P.R. LXXXVI., c. 262. *Burning of the Parliament House!* 1-11-34.

BUT my friend, the HERALD, has made one observation, upon which, distant as I am, and agitated as the reader will naturally suppose my mind to be, I cannot refrain from offering a remark or two. My insipid friend says, "that the MOB" (meaning *the people of London*), when they *saw the progress of the flames,* raised a SAVAGE shout of EXULTATION." Did they indeed? The *Herald* exclaims, "O, UNREFLECTING people!" Now perhaps the "MOB" exulted because the "MOB" was really a *reflecting* "mob." When even a dog, or a horse, receives any treatment that it does not like, it always shuns *the place* where it got such treatment : shoot at and wound a hare from out of a hedge-row, she will always shun that spot : cut a stick out of a coppice, and beat a boy with it, and he will wish the coppice at the devil : send a man, for writing notorious truth, out of the King's Bench to a jail, and there put him half to death, and he will not cry his eyes out if he happen to hear that court is no more. In short, there is always a connexion in our minds, between sufferings that we undergo and *the place* in which they are inflicted, or in which they originate. And this "*unreflecting* mob" might in this case have reflected, that in the building which they then saw in flames, the following, amongst many other things, took place. They might have reflected, that it was in this House,

That the act was passed for turning the Catholic priests, who shared the tithes with the poor, out of the parishes, and putting Protestant parsons in their place, who gave the poor no share at all of the tithes.

That this was the VERY FIRST ACT that was passed after this building became the Parliament House!

That the all-devouring church of England was BORN in this very House.

That, soon after the people became *compelled to beg or starve,* in this same House an act was passed to put an iron collar on a beggar's neck, and to make him a slave for life.

That, it was in this House, that the aristocracy (who had got the abbey lands and great tithes), solemnly *renounced the damnable errors of the Catholic religion,* in the reign of Edward the Sixth.

That, it was in this same House, that they solemnly recanted, and received pardon and absolution from the Pope, in the reign of Queen Mary, bargaining to keep the abbey lands and great tithes.

That, it was in this same House, that the same aristocracy chopped about *when* ELIZABETH *came,* and again solemnly renounced the damnable idolatry of popery.

That, it was in this same House, that the act was passed for plundering the guilds and fraternities of their prescriptive property.

That, it was in this same House, that all the tyrannical and bloody penal laws were passed against those who faithfully adhered to the religion of our fathers.

That, it was in this same House, that the Riot Act and the Septennial Act were passed.

That, it was in this same House, that the sums were voted for carrying on a war to subjugate the Americans.

That, it was in this same House, that the new treason-laws, new game-laws, new trespass-laws, and new felony-laws were passed.

That, it was in this same House that the million and half of money was voted to be given to the parsons of the church of England, over and above their tithes to enormous amount.

That, it was in this same HOUSE, that the Act of William and Mary was passed, providing for the contingent accession of the House of Hanover; that, in that act, which was entitled an Act for Preserving the Religion and Liberties of England, it was provided, that, in case of the accession of the family, no one having *a pension* from the crown, or holding any place of *trust* or *emolument* under it, *civil or military, should be capable of sitting in the House of Commons.*

That, it was in this same HOUSE, that this part of that act was REPEALED; and that the House of Commons now contains great numbers of *pensioners,* and of persons living on public money, military as well as civil.

That, it was in this same HOUSE, that THIRTY-FOUR MILLIONS of money were voted for *the army alone* in the year of the battle of Waterloo!

That, it was in this same HOUSE, that seven hundred thousand pounds were voted to Wellington.

That, it was in this same HOUSE, that the POWER-OF-IMPRISONMENT-BILL, and the other bills of that sort, were brought in by Sidmouth and Castlereagh, and passed in 1817.

That, it was in this same HOUSE, that CANNING was cheered, when he made a jest of the groans of the aged and innocent Ogden, one of the victims of those bills,

That, it was in this same HOUSE, that it was, in 1819, voted that the House would *not inquire* into the massacre at Manchester.

That, it was in this same HOUSE, that Liverpool, in 1820, brought in the Bill of Pains and Penalties against the Queen of Geo. IV.

That, it was in this same HOUSE, that the members stood up, bare-headed, and with clapping of hands, received Castlereagh, when he returned from Paris after the *death of Marshal Ney,* and the breaking up of the *museums.*

That, it was in this same HOUSE, where CASTLEREAGH brought in, and the House passed, the SIX ACTS, in 1819.

That, it was in this same HOUSE, that were passed the laws for enabling the landowners to SELL wild animals, called GAME, and to enable the justices to TRANSPORT poor men, who should, by night, be found in pursuit of those animals.

That, it was in this same HOUSE, that the Bills establishing the Police, were passed and that the Bourbon-like detected spy POPAY was suffered to go unpunished and his employers unreproved.

That, it was in this HOUSE, that botheration BROUGHAM, in 1820, *defended the employment of spies* by the government.

That, it was in this same HOUSE, where CASTLEREAGH was the *leader,* for many years, up to the 6. of August, 1822; and he CUT HIS OWN THROAT, at North Cray, in Kent, on the 12. of that month, a Kentish coroner's jury pronouncing that he was INSANE, and had been so for *some weeks;* he being also Secretary of State for Foreign Affairs, and acting as such for the Home and Colonial Departments *at the very time when he cut his throat.*

That, it was in this same HOUSE, that *a million and a half of money* was, in the regency and reign of George IV., voted out of the taxes to be given to the clergy of the church of England, over and above their tithes and other enormous revenues.

That, it was in this same HOUSE, that about *three millions* of the people's money were voted for SECRET SERVICES, in the two last reigns, and in the present reign.

That, it was in this same HOUSE, *more than a hundred millions of money* have been voted, in the two last reigns and in the present reign, to pensioners, sinecurists, grantees, allowance-people, and the like.

That, it was in this same HOUSE, that the reasonable and just proposition, made by me, to cause the great landowners to pay as heavy stamp-duties as the *little ones,* and to cause the *land* to pay as heavy duties as *personal property,* was *rejected.*

That, it was in this same HOUSE, that my motion for a repeal of the MALT-TAX was rejected by the reformed Parliament

That, it was in this same HOUSE, that the IRISH COERCION BILL was passed, amidst cheers to insult Mr. O'Connell.

That, it was in this same HOUSE, that a petition from the electors of SANDWICH, complaining that Sir Thomas TROUBRIDGE, one of the members, had obtained his commission in the navy by criminal means, was, *while the facts were not denied*, rejected by the *" reformed House of Commons."*

That, it was in this same HOUSE, that my resolution against Sir ROBERT PEEL was " EXPUNGED " upon a motion, put by Lord ALTHORP WITHOUT NOTICE, and amended by the Speaker without the leave of the House.

That, it was in this same HOUSE, that the sums were voted for the new palaces, and for the famous *gateway*!

That, it was in this same HOUSE, that were passed the *Cash-Payment-Suspension Act* of 1797; PEEL's Act, in 1819; the Small-Note Bill of 1822; the Panic Act of 1826, which, at last, leaves the taxes unredeemed, while the wheat is brought down to forty shillings a quarter.

That, it was in this same HOUSE, that the BANK, the PAPER-MONEY, and the FUNDS were enacted.

That, it was in this same HOUSE, that LOANS were voted,

which, at last, have created a debt, the bare yearly interest of which amounts to *thirty millions of sovereigns in gold*!

That, it was in this same HOUSE, that a vote to take off a *part* of the tax on the people's daily drink was *rescinded*.

That, it was in this same HOUSE, that Sturges Bourne's Bills were passed, *giving plurality of votes,* at vestries, to the RICH, and authorizing the employment of HIRED OVERSEERS.

That, it was in this same HOUSE, the Special Commissions of 1830 were approved of.

That, it was in this same HOUSE, that the petitions on behalf of the poor DORSETSHIRE MEN were unattended to.

That, it was in this same HOUSE, that the "*Poor-law Amendment Bill,*" brought in by Lords ALTHORP and BROUGHAM, was passed, in 1834.

That, it was in this same HOUSE, now consumed by FIRE, that the vault (*now let down by fire*) resounded with PRAISES on *the* MAGNANIMOUS "*Alexander,*" when he had *burnt to ashes* a city with three hundred thousand people in it; and, beyond all doubt, with not less than *a thousand women in child-birth,* to say nothing of the sick, the decrepit, the aged, and the infants!

Oh! God of mercy! Might not those, whom the insipid and time-serving wretch of the *Morning Herald* abuses; might not that people of London, whom the base crew of REPORTHERS, reeking with the heat of gin, and always eager to libel their own suffering country; might not the people of London, instead of being "*unreflec*ting," have DULY REFLECTED on the hundreds of things, of which I have, from mere memory, mentioned only a *small part*? These things are always present to *my mind*. Why should they not be present to the minds of the people of London?

Whigs, Tories, and Shoy-hoys

T.T., p. 65. *To the Working People of England and Scotland*. 1-9-30.

FROM this time, which is now four-and-twenty years ago, I have been abhorred by these factions, and have most severely

suffered in consequence of that abhorrence; but I have de-
molished the factions, and the words Tory and Whig now excite
ridicule and contempt at the bare sound of them. The words
" *opposition,*" and " *gentlemen opposite,*" are become equally
contemptible. The people have long looked upon the whole as
one mass of fellows fighting and scrambling for public money;
some fighting to keep it, and others scrambling to get at it; some
dogs in possession of the carcase, and some growling and barking
because they cannot get a share. Seeing the people despising
both these factions, *a third* has started, to whom I have always
given the name of SHOY-HOYS; and now I will tell you why.
A shoy-hoy is a sham man or woman, made of straw or other
stuff, twisted round a stake, stuck into the ground, and dressed
in clothes of man or woman, with arms, legs, head, and everything, and with a stick or gun put into its hand. These shoy-
hoys are set up for the purpose of driving birds from injuring the
corn or the seeds, and sometimes to frighten them from cherries,
or other fruit. The people want a reform of the parliament, and
there has for a long time (about fifteen or sixteen years) been a
little band, who have professed a desire to get parliamentary
reform. They have made motions and speeches and divisions,
with a view of keeping the hopes of the people alive, and have
thereby been able to keep them quiet from time to time. They
have never desired to *succeed;* because success would put an end
to their hopes of emolument; but they have amused the people.
The great body of the factions, knowing the reality of their views,
have been highly diverted by their sham efforts, which have
never interrupted them in the smallest degree in their enjoyment
of the general plunder. Just as it happens with the birds and
the shoy-hoys in the fields or gardens. At first, the birds take
the shoy-hoy for a *real* man or woman; and, so long as they do
this, they abstain from their work of plunder; but after having
for some little while watched the shoy-hoy with their quick and
piercing eyes, and perceived that it never moves hand or foot,
they totally disregard it, and are no more obstructed by it than if
it were a post. Just so is it with these political shoy-hoys; but,
their demerits are not, like the field shoy-hoys, confined to the
doing of no good; they *do mischief;* they really, like my friend

the Frenchman's safety-valve, assist the factions in the work of plunder; which I remember an instance of, indeed, in the curious case of a horticultural shoy-hoy, which case very aptly illustrates the functions of these political deceivers. The birds were committing great ravages upon some turnip-seed that I had at Botley. "Stick up a shoy-hoy," said I to my bailiff. "That will do *no good, sir;*" "It can do *no harm,* and therefore, stick one up." He replied by telling me, that he had, that morning, in the garden of his neighbour MORELL, who had stuck up a shoy-hoy to keep the sparrows from his peas, actually seen a sparrow settled, with a *pod,* upon the *shoy-hoy's hat,* and there, as upon a dining table, actually pecking out the peas and eating them, which he could do with greater security there where he could look about him and see the approach of an enemy, than he could have done upon the ground, where he might have been taken *by surprise.* Just exactly such are the functions of our political shoy-hoys. The agricultural and horticultural shoy-hoys deceive the depredating birds but a very short time; but they continue to deceive those who stick them up and rely upon them, who, instead of rousing in the morning, and sallying upon the depredators with powder and shot, trust to the miserable shoy-hoys, and thus lose their corn and their seeds. Just thus it is with the people, who are the dupes of all political shoy-hoys. In Suffolk, and other eastern counties, they call them *mawkeses.* Mawkes seemes to be the female, and shoy-hoy the male, of this race of mock human beings; and I suppose that the farmers in the east, from some cause or other, look upon the female as the most formidable of the two. At any rate, our political shams are of the masculine gender, and therefore shoy-hoy is the proper name for them.

FIFTEEN

THE THING

Honours to Mr. Pitt

P.R. IX., c. 133. *Summary of Politics: Honours to Mr. Pitt.* 1-2-06.

AND, first, our notice is attracted by an admission, said to have been made, with respect to the *great talents* of Mr. Pitt. But, of what *sort* were these talents? For, Kemble has great talents, and Cooke has great talents, in their way, and in his way, so had Katterfelto. Mr. Pitt never gave *proof* of any talents, except as a debater. He was a great debater; a person of wonderful readiness and dexterity in conducting a contest of words; a most accomplished, a truly incomparable *advocate.* But, that was *all;* and that, from the use which he made of it, was pernicious to his country. His eloquence was frothy; it was always unsubstantial; it very rarely produced conviction; but, its object was answered by the plausibility of it, which furnished the means of a justification, or rather which protected against an unbearable sense of shame, those who, from motives of self-interest, gave him their support. In all matters of state, rightly so denominated, he was conspicuous for nothing but the imbecility of his plans, and the fondness of his expectations, arising from that arrogance which had been born with him; and which had been nursed up by the flattery of the supple slaves, with whom he was, and loved to be, continually surrounded. In all his schemes, whether of war or of peace or of interior economy, you trace the shallow mind, which was no where more conspicuous than in his schemes of taxation and finance, which was so glaring in the pamphlet published under the name of Old Rose in 1799, and which has been so ably exposed in the work of Lord Lauderdale. Allusion is not made here to mere errors, errors into which a man of great talents might have fallen; but to proofs of sheer ignorance, arising, too, not from a deficiency in the knowledge of recorded facts; but from an evident want of that sort of mind which is necessary in a profound search after causes, and in the tracing of those causes to their natural effects. In point of talent, he was, in short, exactly what Mr. Grey once described him to be : " A man of showy, but of shallow, parts."

*   *   *   *   *   *

It has been stated, in some of the paragraphs, to which I have alluded, that the loss of Mr. Pitt is a subject to regret amongst the people. This is an impudent and insulting falsehood. That he may be regretted by those who were looking up to his power for emoluments, or for *shelter;* by the numerous swarm of " blood-suckers and muck-worms : " that his loss may be regretted, and deeply regretted, by these, I am far from meaning to deny; but, that he is regretted by the *people of England,* is a falsehood which, come whence it will, never shall pass uncontradicted by me. They do not regret his loss; so far from regarding his death as an " irreparable " loss, they regard it as no loss at all; they feel and they *express satisfaction* at it; their resentment has ceased; they retain little or no anger against him; it is in their nature easily to forgive; but they look upon his death as the first dawn of their deliverance from an accumulation of danger and disgrace. They will be, as will be seen, very indifferent spectators, either of the funeral or the monument. They will be silent and so they have been under the operation of all the other long train of measures proceeding from the same source; they will coldly submit, but a cold submission is not what, upon such an occasion, wise men would be content to secure.—One person is said to have talked against raking up the ashes of the dead, and we have been reminded, that, of the dead, we should speak well, or not at all. But, surely, this maxim applies to *voluntary* speaking of the dead, and not only voluntary, but *unnecessary* speaking of them; otherwise, away goes, at one sweep, all historical truth, and, with it, all the advantages therefrom derived, whether in politics or in morals. There is a time, however, for all things; and, just at this time, one could have wished to refrain from all mention of Mr. Pitt or of his actions. But, this forbearance has been rendered impossible, without a shameful abandonment of public duty. The movers for honours, for an act that, if passed unanimously, would have given a sanction to all his and all their measures. They, it is, who have raked up the ashes of the deceased. They have challenged all men who think like me to the contest. They have compelled us to protest against this indirect censure upon our opinions and our conduct. They are the unprovoked assailants; and they ought not to complain that we have recourse to the only means of defence left us by their ungenerous mode of proceeding. Ungenerous, too, it is, in the extreme, towards the deceased as well as towards us; for, the use they make of his memory, is, to bespeak an eulogium for themselves, though thereby they expose that memory to the natural effects of our sense of the injustice of such an eulogium. Allow that Mr. Pitt was an " Excellent statesman," and you therein allow, that they were excellent colleagues; next grant that his loss is " irreparable," and you proclaim that unworthiness in yourselves which you before tacitly admitted, you having been, for the far greater part of your political lives, in direct opposition to his measures. This is the extent of their proposal; and, shall they complain that it is resisted? Shall they silence us by their whining and their cant about the ashes of the deceased? Peace to those ashes, with all my heart! Profound peace to them, as far as historical truth will permit. But, let it be real peace; peace on both sides; let them not be raked up for the purposes of annoying us; let them lie quiet; let them not be thrown either in our eyes or our teeth; for, if they are, we must, and we certainly shall, as in self-defence and in duty we are bound, throw them back again. Let him be wept by the Cannings and the Jenkinsons and the Huskissons and the Roses and the Melvilles : *they* have, indeed, *lost* by his death; to them the loss is truly " irreparable." Let that race of creatures, whom the great Lord Chatham called " blood-suckers " and " muck-worms; " let them weep; their mourning is suitable, and sincere; but, in their feelings *the people of England have no participation*. Let the City of London erect a monument to his memory, if they choose; it will become both them and him. I should be sorry if they did not do it by an *unanimous* vote. I should exceedingly regret that their conduct, in this respect, was not clearly distinguished from that of the people of England, acting by their representatives in parliament. To be "praised, wept and *honoured*" by the swarm of contractors and jobbers is due to his memory. He loved them; they were the part of the community that he selected for his own; and that man must be unjust indeed who would wish to deprive his memory of the honour of their praise. But, let them not abuse us, because we do not partake in their feelings and their acts. Let not their newspapers slander the men, who, only about seven months ago, were called upon to grant him a bill of indemnity for mis-application of the public money, and who now refuse to acknowledge that he was an "excellent minister," and that his loss is "irreparable."

India

P.R. XIII., c. 588. *India Affairs.* 16-4-08.

THE recent intelligence from India, or, "our Empire in the East," is of a gloomy complexion, in my sight, only inasmuch as it gives an account of the loss of a great number of English officers and soldiers. It may serve to make men reflect justly on the nature of the wars we carry on in India; and may lead them to the conclusion, so much to be desired, namely, that the possession of that country is a terrible evil. This, it seems, is to be *the last* war; but, we have been told the same thing for more than thirty years past. There is a constant, never-ceasing war in India. There is not always actual fighting; but, there are always going on preparations for fighting; What right, in God's name, what right have we to do this? How is it possible for us to justify our conduct, upon any principle of morality? Conquests in India are not at all necessary either to our safety or our comfort. There is no glory attending such conquests and their accompanying butcheries. We must be actuated by a shere love of gain; a shere love of plunder. I really believe, that the history of the whole world does not afford an instance of a series of aggressions so completely unjustifiable and inexcusable.

The Gridiron Prophecy

P.R. XXXV., c. 364. *To the Middle Classes of England.* 13-11-19.

THE Borough-mongers, seeing the danger of continuing a paper-bubble, as Grenville now himself calls it. Seeing that a bubble is a thing that may, at any moment, burst, have " *resolved* " to return to cash-payments; that is to say, they have *resolved,* that the nation shall, with a currency greatly diminished in quantity, continue to pay to the pawn to the former nominal amount of payment; that is to say, to make the nation pay, in fact, two, or, perhaps, three times as much in taxes as it paid before; that is to say to give to the sinecure placeman the price of two or three bushels of wheat instead of that of one which was given him before. To resolve, my friends, is an easy matter; but, as our pretty fellows will find, to *execute* a resolution is sometimes a very difficult matter; and if they execute their *resolution,* though it has now assumed the shape of a law, I will give Castle-reagh leave to put me upon a gridiron, while Sidmouth stirs the fire, and Canning stands by making a jest of my writhing and my groans. And yet, *if they do not execute it,* what a figure will they *then* make? Will any one *then* have the impudence to pretend to believe, that they are the men to extricate England from her difficulties? And will those little bands of rapacious miscreants, called PITT CLUBS, any longer dare to show their faces before the oppressed and insulted people, whom they have assisted to plunge into ruin, misery, and degradation?

Cobbett's Gridiron

P.R. XXXVIII., c. 425. *Letter II. To Mr. Peel. On the Gridiron.* 17-2-21.
Motto: " This Bill (Mr. Peel's) was grounded on *concurrent Reports* of both Houses; it was passed by *unanimous votes* of both Houses; it was, at the close of the Session, a subject of high eulogium on the Speaker's Speech to the Regent, and in the Regent's Speech to the two Houses; now, then, I, William Cobbett, assert, that, to carry this Bill into effect is *impossible;* and I say, that, if this Bill be carried into full effect, I will give Castlereagh leave to lay me on a *Gridiron* and broil me alive, while Sidmouth may stir the coals, and Canning stand by and laugh at my groans."—*Taken from Cobbett's Register, written at North Hampstead, Long Island, on the 24th of September, 1819, and published in England in November, 1819.*

To Mr. Peel.

London, 13 February, 1821

Sir,—Please to look at the head of this Register; look at the Motto; look at the *Gridiron*! And then please to pay attention to what I am about to say.

The time is now come; it is actually arrived, when I am called upon to *begin* to do justice to *myself;* and, not only to myself, but to many thousands of zealous and faithful *Disciples,* who have long adopted my political opinions, and many of whom have had to endure no small quantity of reproach, injustice and persecution on that account. Our day is, at last, come; and, please God, we will enjoy it.

It is my intention, in this letter to go back and make some remarks upon the circumstances, accompanying the passing of your BILL, which Bill was, as will be by and by seen, the very thing that I ought to have wished for, and that you and the " *Great Council* " ought to have avoided. Then, I shall make some remarks on the battle which seems to be now coming on between the Land and the Funds. And, lastly, I mean to offer you some observations; or, rather, some new predictions as to the scenes which we shall behold next Summer, if your Bill be not repealed.

As to the first topic; as to the circumstances accompanying the passing of your Bill, you, doubtless, recollect them; but that is no reason for my not stating them here. You and the " *Grand Council* " would, probably, be very glad if the world would forget them. I will take care that the world shall not; for, in every way, in which I can hold them up to the eyes of mankind, will I hold them up to those eyes. They shall not be forgotten. Justice to many many thousands of men, as well as to myself, demands that they be had in constant recollection.

This Bill was passed in direct opposition to my principles, repeatedly laid down, and to my advice repeatedly given. Between 1803 and the time of passing the Bill, I had written altogether, a large volume, from which any one of common sense might have gathered the manifest injustice as well as the monstrous absurdity of such a Bill. No longer before, than the month of July 1818; that is to say, not more than eight months before your project was broached in the Parliament, I had addressed a letter to Mr. Tierney, in which I had demonstrated, in which I had proved as clearly as any thing ever was proved, that, to attempt to return to cash payments, without a reduction of the interest of the debt and without other measures of equal importance, would be proof of downright madness. Mr. Tierney had started the idea of a *gradual* return to cash-payments, in his speech respecting the re-newal of the protection Bill in 1818. Upon this idea of his I had observed, that the very use of the word gradual in such a case rendered the speech unworthy of an answer; but, I observed, " if the paper be drawn in *gradually,* the approach of the misery and ruin and uproar will be gradual; but they will *approach*. The want of employment will come on gradually and gently; but *it will come*. The convulsion will be the end of the scene; but there will *be a convulsion*. Ruin and starvation will come by degrees; but ruin and starvation *will come*." This was written in Long Island on the 11th July 1818; and yet, in defiance of this; in despite of it, you and the " Great Council " passed the Bill. You will say, that you were not bound to listen to me; that you had a right to treat my opinions with scorn. I question your right; for you were acting for the nation, and ought to have paused, and, indeed to have stopped, when your measures were opposed to the opinions of a man of greater talents and experience than yourself. However, if you had a right to scorn my opinions then, I have an unquestionable right to laugh at you now; and at all those, be they who they may, who had a hand in producing the measure, which has now notoriously produced precisely those effects which I said it would produce.

Your Bill was passed on the 2nd July 1819. It was three months in the hatching; just double the time that a Goose sits upon her eggs. A Committee of each House of the " Great Council " sat for many weeks to inquire into the matter. You, who were Chair-man in the Committee of the House of Commons, being yourself a Privy Counsellor, and a Member for the University of Oxford, brought in this Report, consisting, together with its appendix, of three hundred and fifty five folio pages of close print. Upon this Report you brought in the Bill. The Bill passed by an unanimous vote of both Houses; and it was repeatedly stated in both houses, that this would *settle the matter for ever*! Another time, I will make quotations from the several speeches. Suffice it, for the present to say, that the Houses rang with mutual congratulations of the happy and glorious achievement. You were eulogised to the skies; and men pressed forward with anxiety to claim their share of the honour of having formerly supported the wise principles upon which your Bill was founded, at a time when those principles were brought forward in the shape of resolutions by a lately deceased and " deeply lamented " ornament of the House, whose name was HORNER, and who had been a Lawyer and an Edinbourgh Reviewer. In short, it was a day of Jubilee; " a day and such a day; the like of it, alack-a-day, Oh! Dollalolla! we ne'er shall see again! " You appear to have thought it fit, that the most should be made of such a day; for, not merely to the House themselves were the reciprocated eulogies confined. The whole House of Commons, with the Speaker at their head, congratulated the Regent on the noble achievement; and, that we may lose nothing; that old men may not forget; and that young men may have a knowledge of the exultations of that memorable day, I shall here set down the words, in which the Speaker addressed his Royal Highness, upon the subject on the 12th July 1819.

" But, Sir, of those measures, which we have completed, the most prominent, the most important, and, as we trust, in their consequences, the most beneficial to the public, are the measures which have grown out of the consideration of the present state of the country—both in its Currency and its Finances. Early, Sir, in the present Session, we instituted an enquiry into the effects produced on the exchanges with foreign countries, and the state of the circulating medium, by the restriction on payments in cash by the Bank. This enquiry was most anxiously and most deliberately conducted, and in its result led to the conclusion, that it was most desirable, quickly, but with due precautions, to return to our ancient and healthful state of currency;—That whatever might have been the expediency of the Acts for the suspension of payments in cash at the different periods at which they were enacted—and doubtless they were expedient, whilst the country was involved in the most expensive contest that ever weighed down the finances of any country—still that the necessity for the continuance of these Acts having ceased, it became us with as little delay as possible (avoiding carefully the convulsions of too rapid a transition) to return to our ancient system :—and that if at any period, and under any circumstances, this return could be effected without national inconvenience, it was at the present, when this mighty nation, with a proud retrospect of the past, after having made the greatest efforts, and achieved the noblest objects, was now reposing in a confident, and, as we fondly hope, a well-founded expectation, of a sound and lasting peace."

Here, then we find the Speaker saying that the inquiry into this matter had been most anxiously and most deliberately conducted; we find him saying that the necessity for the Bank protecting Acts had ceased; we find him saying that it was wise and necessary to return to cash-payments; and we find him asserting that the Parliament had chosen the proper time to return to our ancient and healthful state of currency.

Let it, therefore, never be said, that the thing was done in a *hurry;* let it never be said that there was not time for reflection; let it never be said, that you had not read *Paper against Gold* and my letter to Mr. Tierney. If you had not read these, you ought to have read them. They had been written for your instruction. Let it never be said that this was a party question, for the votes were unanimous. Let it never be said that it was an *experiment;* for it was declared from all parts of the Houses, that the question was *settled for ever.* A hundred times was it repeated, that this subject was now *done with.*

It was in the month of *August* that I received a copy of the *Bill,* and of the *Report,* on which the Bill was founded. It may appear provokingly insignificant to you; but it will not be uninteresting to those who have, for so many years, kept company with me in opinion, and borne up with unabated fortitude under the obliquy, which they have endured for my sake;

it will not be uninteresting to them, if I relate that this copy of the Bill and of the Report were delivered to me in a tent, the walls of which were made of *Morning Chronicles* and *Couriers,* pasted on upon laths that were a foot asunder, and the roof of which consisted of thatch, the eves being brought out six feet beyond the walls, in order to protect those walls from violent rains and winds. In this tent, with a large mahogany slab, supported by stakes driven into the ground, for a table, and with four young Oaks driven into the ground, and connected by four rails, with boards laid across upon them, having upon the boards a truss of Rye-straw in a species of sack, with a pillow of the same, and with one sheet below and another above, for bedding: with this furniture for use and for decoration, and sitting in this tent, with a shirt and pair of trowsers for dress, I received the copies of this celebrated Bill and Report. At that moment I had been anxiously looking for them; I hastily ran my eye over them; and in five minutes time I resolved to return to England the next fall!

The greatest want that I experienced at this time was, *somebody to laugh with me*. My son was at New York. I wrote for him to come and help me laugh. I bored my good neighbours with the subject. I explained to them the consequences of the measure. I told some of them that were rich, and who had property in New York, and were engaged in trade besides, how this Bill would affect even them. I told them how it would bring down House-rent in New York; I told the farmers how it would bring down the price of corn in America as well as in England. I spent a week or two in talking and laughing; and it was soon after, that I wrote the Registers, respecting this measure, and from one of which I have taken my motto to the present Register.

Never did man act more fairly than I have in this case. I not only gave my opinion at once, and without hesitation; I not only gave it in terms the most distinct; but, *I published it;* I not only published, but I pledged myself to acknowledge that I was a fool, if the opinion did not prove to be correct. In a letter to the Prince Regent, written about the same time, I said, " I appealed to *time*. *Time,* Sir, now stands, the *Palm* in one hand, and the

Fool's-Cap in the other. The nation are looking on; and the award will soon be made."

The award is not yet made; not *actually made;* but notification of it has been given; and the moment that your Bill is repealed, I shall lay by the Gridiron, and put the Palm in its place. I shall by and by have to speak of the manner, in which I and my Disciples will celebrate our victory; but, first, let me make some remarks on the battle, which now seems to be actually beginning between the land and the funds. In that address which I published upon taking my departure for America, I told my readers, that, at last, there would be an open rupture between the Land and the Funds; and, from what took place in the House of Commons a few nights ago; from what was said by Mr. LITTLETON and Mr. CURWEN, on the one side, and by Messrs. BARING and RICARDO on the other side, this rupture would appear to be at no very great distance; and if your Bill be not repealed (which I hope it will not) before the month of July, my opinion is, that the rupture will become open, decisive, and irreconcilable; and that then, and not till then, we shall have a constitutional Reform of the Commons House of Parliament.

This is the subject of real importance to the country. A bawling Speech-maker, who always ends without saying any thing, and who never thinks of attempting to *do* any of those things which he declares to be necessary, has observed that to talk of *this* matter, until a Reform be accomplished, is like *putting the cart before the horse*. If this wise person be correct, all that I can say is, that the horse must come after the cart; for there never will be a Reform of the Parliament as long as the Paper System can be carried on. We may laugh at the childish, sniveling stuff about Grampound; but these are the only Reforms that we shall see as long as the Paper System shall continue to prevail. And, though I hold it to be just and laudable to contend for a Reform; though I know that the nation never can be itself again without a Reform; still I must despise the man who affects to believe that there ever can be a Reform of the Commons House as long as the Paper System remains whole and entire; and I cannot help deeming those to be very great hypocrites, or very weak men indeed, who are constantly bawling about Reform, and who turn from the subject of Paper Money as something too small for the grasp of their amazing capacities.

Viewing the matter in this light I shall be rather particular in my observations on the speeches of the gentlemen below mentioned. These speeches were made on the 8th of February, on a Petition from the Town of *Birmingham,* presented by a Mr. DUGDALE. In this petition the distresses of the country had been imputed chiefly to the *diminution in the quantity of the circulating medium.* The persons who had been requested to support this Petition took occasion to offer their opinions upon the cause or causes of the distresses, and some of them to urge the necessity for appointing a Committee for inquiring into those causes. Mr. DUGDALE did not say much to the point, nor did Mr. LAWLEY, who followed him. Mr. LITTLETON, after describing the state of distress in Birmingham, spoke in a manner not to enable me to understand his meaning, with regard to the effects of your Bill. Indeed, his meaning, is not fully given in the Report, probably, but, I must take that Report as I find it; and I find it stated, that Mr. LITTLETON called the funded interest, " a monster of consumption." He appears to have expressed a wish that some tax might be laid upon the Fundholder, and not extended to other persons. I will take the conclusion of his speech just as I find it in the Morning Chronicle.—" He considered the depression of agriculture one prominent cause of the falling off in the iron manufactures. Any relief that could be devised, and was likely to prove effectual, he would be willing to support, and he thought that the time of Parliament could not be applied to a better purpose, than that of endeavouring to afford such relief. He had great satisfaction in thinking, that it was in the power of Government to assist by a revision of the system of taxation, as the farmer was obliged to *sell two bushels of corn,* where it was before necessary to sell only one, to pay the *fundholder,* his *landlord,* &c. while the *fundholder paid nothing* out of his resources, while he was *benefitted exactly in the proportion that the other suffered* [*hear, hear*!]. He did not mean that any part of the present system of taxation should be altered by a tax upon Income, but he thought that a Property Tax and *a tax on the Fundholders,* if properly explained, might *obviate many of the difficulties* under which the nation laboured. If this was not satisfactory to all parties, he would not press it; he did not advance it *upon any authority* but his own opinion, and he thanked the House for the indulgence with which it had heard him; but he could not avoid the opportunity of expressing sentiments, which he *felt too strongly* not to avow."

This is all pretty fair. Mr. LITTLETON, as to the state of the Farmers compared to the Fundholders; as to the cause of the ruin of the Farmers, he repeats, pretty nearly, what I have said about a thousand times over, and what I particularly dwelt upon in my " New Year's Gift to the Farmers," published on the sixth of last month, in which, for only sixpence, Mr. LITTLETON bought his doctrines, and, therefore, to which he has a fair claim, the only fault being that he bought them, *fourteen years too late*! With respect to the *remedy, too,* Mr. LITTLETON is now right enough, for, so that the thing be done; so that the *" Monster of Consumption,"* be stinted in its meals, I care not whether the operation be called reduction or tax. But, as Mr. CURWEN spoke out with regard to this matter, I reserve myself for further remarks on it till I have quoted the words of that Honourable, though rather confused Orator.

Mr. CURWEN, who, though he be a curious sort of a man, has often said some very good things, has got some very good stuff in him; and, notwithstanding his whimsical Bill about Parliamentary Reform, that bantling which he obstinately persevered in calling *his* after *Perceval* had picked out it's eyes, hammered out it's teeth, pulled out it's nails, and changed the very colour of it's skin, leaving it nothing but it's mean; notwithstanding this piece of wonderful, of incomprehensible excentricity, Mr. CURWEN has, now and then, put forth some wholesome truths, and has, upon the whole, done a great deal more than any mere bawler about Parliamentary Reform. Upon the present occasion he came to the point. He spoke manfully, though not, in all respects, so clearly as I could have wished. In the extract from his speech which I am now about to make, there is a good deal of confusion of idea; a good deal of that bouillant matter which is apt to arise from the mind when the body is fed chiefly upon potatoes. It is of the *yeasty* kind. But still, in the main, Mr. CURWEN is right; and upon the *vital* question, he is sound as a bell; solid as a piece of corn-fed beef. Pray, Sir, hear him; and I beg you to pay attention to what he says upon this vital point. The frothy matter serves merely as an ornament, in this case; and it comes first, too, like the froth upon a pot of ale. Blow it away, Sir, and dip in, with good heart, to what Mr. CURWEN says about reducing the interest of the debt.

" An Honourable Member had given him (Mr. Curwen) credit for not having expressed any alarm at what was about to be done for the foreign trade, and at the same time stated, what he had never denied, that all the interests of trade, manufactures and commerce were intimately and indissolubly connected. He (Mr. Curwen) had always thought that these interests ought not to be separated. He could have no alarm on account of relieving foreign trade from those restrictions that embarrassed it. Though, supposing that measure was accomplished, and supposing also that the agriculturalists were put in complete possession of the home market, he would ask the Noble Lord if these two measures would better the order of things? He would tell the Noble Lord, and he was convinced of the fact, that they would not. So far from it, he believed that the country would, from day to day, go on from bad to worse [*hear, hear!*] It was not by such palliatives that the present distresses of the country were to be effectually and permanently relieved. Nothing could be done till Government looked those distresses in the face in a manly way, and met them with firmness and comprehensive wisdom. He had seen it stated that the difficulties were not owing to taxation, as sixteen millions had, since the war, been taken off labour, agriculture, and commerce. But he would answer, that a sum far greater than that had been lost to the country in the mean time. The Noble Lord had stated, that the revenue arising from labour, agriculture, and commerce, had been reduced one-fourth; but he could tell the Noble Lord, that no less than one hundred millions of capital had been completely absorbed. At the time when the country was said, with reference to all those interests, to be in the zenith of its prosperity, there were 80 millions of revenue, and 400 millions of agricultural property; the former was now 60 millions, and the latter but 300; wheat had been at that time 10s. and now but 6s. so that in that article alone there was a deficiency of several millions. The honourable Member then proceeded to argue, that the return to cash payments had the effect of lowering the value of the land, by increasing the value of money; and he asked the Noble Lord, on the part of the landed interest, to inquire into the operation of this fact. It was right to call for the only remedy which could now be effectually applied, and that was the *diminution of the interest of the funded property* [*hear, hear!*]. That was the *first time they were fairly brought at issue.* This was *the remedy* which would afford relief to the immense body of petitioners, whose sufferings arose from the general depression of agriculture and trade, while the value of the fundholders' property increased in proportion as that of every body else was depreciated. The landed interest ought not to be placed in a worse condition than the other; and every measure, in this state of things, which did not take all those circumstances into consideration, would be partial, and could produce no general and permanent benefit. If he rested his case here he thought it would be a strong one; but he should ask the Noble Lord whether the poor rates were not to be taken into consideration? Things were coming to that pass, that when the Government had received their taxes and the poor their rates, the landed occupiers had better surrender their property, for there would be nothing left for them to enjoy. He would ask the Noble Lord, what prospect of relief there was on that subject? Had the landed proprietors no right to call his attention to the dreadful accumulation of the Poor Rates? Mr. Pitt had in his time stated the landed property of the country at 28 millions per annum; the Poor Rates were then about two millions. Now the yearly value of the landed property had fallen to 20 millions, and the poor rates had grown to the amount of 8 millions. The Honourable Member dwelt some time longer on these topics, and stated that on his own estate farmers had, under the pressure of the causes which he alleged, asked for an abatement of 25 per cent. in their rent; but he requested them *to wait till July next, when the property would be valued,* and according to that value a fair abatement should be made. This, which was now, perhaps, local, would soon become general; and if a new burthen was imposed on the landed proprietors, as had been suggested, in every other part of the kingdom, the lands would be surrendered to the proprietors, even to those who treated the farmers most fairly and moderately."

This is really as Mr. CURWEN says, bringing the thing to issue. It is, as he truly says, the *only remedy*, and it is a remedy that must, at last, be adopted; but, observe, to prevent uproar and confusion, it must be accompanied with other measures, on which Mr. CURWEN may, probably, have reflected, but which he did not think proper to mention. Mr. CURWEN appears to have taken it for granted, that a Committee would be appointed to examine into the matter; and he also appears to have considered this proposition for reducing the interest of the Debt as a subject whereon *for the Committee to deliberate*! This would be coming to the point, indeed! This would be doing rather more than even I expected to see done this year; though it is what I recommended seventeen years ago.

Lord Castlereagh kept silent upon this occasion; but Mr. ROBINSON, the President of the Board of Trade, who appears to be the great Political Economist of the Administration, made the following speech, every word of which is of such importance, that I here preserve it entire. "Mr. F. Robinson said, that however zealous the supporters of the petition might feel, he hoped the house would pardon him for not entering at length into the subjects introduced on this occasion. He felt the more satisfied that it would be improper for him to enter at length into the discussion, when he found that one of the means proposed by the petitioners, as calculated to revive the trade and manufactures of the country, was *the repeal* of a measure (the resumption of cash payments) which had been passed only two years ago. That measure he had been less agreeable to at first than he had become afterwards. Upon the fullest inquiry and consideration he had become a convert to the measure, and he could now see no reason or safety in abrogating it [*Hear, hear*!]. The resource which had been alluded to by the honourable gentleman opposite was one of *fearful consideration* [*Hear, hear*!]. It might be palatable to many, but it would be pregnant with the *utmost danger, forcibly, by an act of legislation, to reduce the rate of interest on the national debt* [*Hear, hear!*]. Such an expedient might give temporary relief, but it would create more evil than could be calculated. When they thought of its effects, not on the *great fundholder,* but on the small fundholder, who wrapped himself in perfect confidence, when he thought of the faith pledged for his income—when they thought of the infinite evils of *breaking faith* with the *public creditor* [*Hear!*], they could not view such a project but with the utmost possible alarm [*Hear!*]. *Great* and *pressing* as the *difficulties* and *distresses* of the country were, he did hope that the house would not be *hurried into rash measures* that might produce incalculable and irreparable mischief.—[*Hear.*] It was for this reason that he would not take on himself the *awful responsibility* of entering hastily into such subjects. Government were bound to guard against precipitate measures; they ought to feel the *awful responsibility* of preventing others from introducing measures of such *awful tendency.* It was a little hard to charge government with indifference to the distresses of the country, and reluctance, to adopt means of relief, because they opposed wild projects of undoing one day what had been done on another, and violating the national faith. [*Hear.*] If the honourable member brought forward any motion for relief to the petitioners, without doing injury to other classes, he (Mr. Robinson) was most willing to give it his best attention."

Bless us! How " *awful!* " Thrice " *awful!* " What! Are the mighty come to this! It is " *awful* " to talk about what ought to be done? Is the " Great Council of the Nation " so placed as to render any proposition made to it " *awful?* " You see, Sir, that Mr. Robinson does not speak decidedly as to the repealing or not repealing of your Bill. He hesitates a little, though Lord Castlereagh did not hesitate a night or two before. He deprecates Mr. CURWEN's project for reducing the interest of the Debt; but, he gives no hope of any relief from any other means. He acknowledges that the difficulties and distresses of the country are great and pressing; but, while he disapproves of Mr. CURWEN's remedy, he proposes no remedy of his own; nor does he give the slightest hint that he or his colleagues have any such remedy in store.

What Mr. ROBINSON says about the Great Fundholder and the Small Fundholder is any thing but logical; and is, indeed, a very barefaced begging of the question. As, however, it might be a comfort to Mr. ROBINSON to know, that there *are the means* of making a distinction and a just *distinction,* too, between different classes of Fundholders; and, that, what he calls *breaking faith* with the Public Creditor, can be (and, indeed, *has been*) clearly proved to be no breach of faith at all : as it may be a comfort to Mr. ROBINSON to know this, be so good as to assure him from me, that, whenever the measure of reduction shall have been agreed upon, I will engage to remove all his apprehensions as to these two points.

But, it was from Messrs. BARING and RICARDO that Mr. CURWEN received the stoutest reply. The former gentleman said a great deal upon this part of the subject. He " concurred entirely in the observations of Mr. Robinson respecting the sacred nature of public faith, and thought that, if there was any one question in which every *honest* mind had but one opinion, it was, that all the obligations of *morals* and of *religion* guarded as sacred the laws of *honesty* and *honour*. [*Hear, hear, hear.*] He could see no *honesty* or *honour* in a measure that would—notwithstanding the great war carried on for so many years—notwithstanding the exertions made during the war—and notwithstanding that the country had been relieved from taxation during the war by borrowing—point out *a fraud* on the *public creditor* as the means of relief. [*Hear, hear.*] He did not impute to the hon. member for Cumberland any intention, on due reflection, of proposing such a measure. But not only would such a measure be unjust, but it was perfectly clear that it would not, after all, produce the benefit contemplated. [*Hear, hear.*] In such emergencies, one species of property could not be touched without putting every kind of property in hazard; and therefore, if the hon. member for Cumberland could carry such a measure into effect, he would ask him what could be the *value of the parchment of his deeds?* [*Hear, hear.*] If, then, the point of honour were renounced, the measure would be resisted by the meaner and narrower principles of interest."

Faith! this is almost beginning with Great Guns! But, how many hundred times have I said that it would come to this? What calumny have not I had to endure for having said it? And shall I not now laugh? Yes; and I will laugh, offend whom it may.

Mr. CURWEN seems to have felt a little this rap at the *parchments;* and, begging pardon for interrupting his honourable *friend,* he said, "that his Honble friend had quite mistaken him, for, that he had never suggested that Public faith should be violated; *if* the country could, by possibility, keep faith with Public Credit." To this Mr. BARING answered, slap, that, "he knew no *other* inability to prevent keeping faith with the Creditor, but the DEBTOR HAVING PAID ALL HE HAD!"

Bravo! Mr. Baring! Stand to that! Insist upon Boroughs and all; for, indeed, why should they not give up all, as thousands upon thousands of Farmers and Tradesmen have given up their all? However, I shall speak more of this breach of National Faith, as it is called, by and by. Mr. RICARDO also pitched on upon Mr. CURWEN; and expressed his sorrow that that gentleman's attack on the Fundholders had been "received with cheers by so many Members of that House." He did, however say, and I say, too, "that the deduction from the Fundholder, if it were made at all, ought to be made *openly,* and not by stratagem."

Before I come to what I have to say about this pretended *breach of faith,* I have to notice that Mr. BARING acknowledged that your Bill was the principal cause of the distress. But that Mr. RICARDO insisted that it was not the principal cause. If we ought not to presume to decide when "Doctors disagree"; we ought certainly to keep silence when *Oracles* are at logger-heads. I must, however, venture to say, that the only remedy proposed by Mr. BARING; namely, *making silver concurrently with gold a legal tender,* is really, what it was described by that gentleman's antagonist; that is to say, a mere delusion. I must also be permitted to observe, that Mr. Ricardo's reason for believing that your Bill had not been the principal cause of the distress, was such as I could not have expected even from the illustrious inhabitant of Gatcombe Park. It was this, that wheat *could not have been made to fall one half in price by a Law which had caused the value of Gold to vary, or, rather, to fall only four or five per cent*!

There! I give that as a specimen. I give that as a proof of the extent of Mr. RICARDO's knowledge as to these matters. This Nation is suitably punished for the foul and base treatment of Mr. PAINE while alive, and of his memory, when dead. Read, Sir, almost any one of his essays on political economy; read how he went to work to extricate the American States from their Paper money difficulties; read any one of these essays and you will never more suffer your head to be bothered by men who gabble about the prices of Gold and of Silver, as criteria whereby to judge of the effects of Legislative measures on the prosperity of Nations. It is very certain that enormous issues of Paper will raise the price of Gold; and that a drawing in of the Paper will lower the price of Gold; but, Good God! are we come to such a pass of ignorance as to believe that the degree of distress is to be measured *by* a standard like this! The idea is monstrous; and, that it should have been tolerated for a moment; that it should have been suffered to escape peals of laughter, would plunge us in despair had we not something to rely on other than the wisdom of those who could listen with patience to such miserable trash.

I now come to this "*awful question*" as Mr. ROBINSON would call it, of *national faith*. This Mr. ROBINSON appears, by the by, to be both a clever and a modest man; and though I know him to be wrong, I perceive nothing of the grossness of absurdity in what he says, at any time, and I wish I could say the same of a great many others. As to the question, let me first lay before you what was said upon the subject the next day, by that surprisingly wise gentleman, Mr. James Perry, of the Morning Chronicle. You know who this gentleman is, I dare say; you remember, perhaps, the lofty panegyric which was pronounced upon him by that worthy countryman of his, Sir James Mackintosh, in a speech delivered during the last memorable sitting of the Six Acts Parliament. You remember, perhaps, Sir

James describing him as "writing under the impulse of generous feelings: acting as an *invisible, unaccountable* and *unassailable being,* exercising a power almost despotic over the minds of his readers; having all the temptations to which a man, in such a situation, must always be exposed, and only secured against greater temptations by the *integrity* of his own *incorruptible nature."* From what part of Sir James' frame, whether from the thigh, the belly, or the brain came the inspiration that produced this effusion, in praise of this invisible, unaccountable, unassailable and incorruptible being, it is not for me to say; but perhaps, when you have read the following paragraph, you will be better able to judge from which of the wondrous qualities of this most wondrous brother Scotchman, it proceeded. For my own part, I am disposed to ascribe it to the *unaccountableness* of this great personage; but, read, Sir, and judge for yourself.

"The deep distress of the country has already drawn the attention of Parliament to our financial system, and to the means of affording relief to the oppressed classes of the community. Various projects seem to be entertained by different Gentlemen; and out of doors we hear of numerous specifics, each of which, in the contemplation of its Doctor, would be a remedy. *All men are agreed that any violation of public faith must not be thought of.* Justice demands *a sacred adherence to the engagements into which we have entered,* and therefore whatever mode may be adopted to lessen the load under which we totter, it must *equally affect every class of society.* The Income Tax was not considered as a violation of public faith, though it encroached on the dividend of the Fundholder, because it equally broke into the receipt of every other person. In like manner the lowering of the standard would, by its general and uniform operation, be free from the censure of violating national faith. If silver were made the standard, and that a pound weight of silver were coined *into* 80 *shillings instead of* 65, and that each piece should still bear *the denomination and pass current for a shilling,* we desire to know what effect such a measure would have on internal circulation and on foreign exchanges? It is a question for political economists to solve. In the mean time we presume to think, that instantaneous relief might be given to the country by the measure proposed by *Mr. Maberly*. It is *idle* to say, that out of an increased expenditure of no less than 18 millions annually since Mr. PITT's winding up account in 1792, three or four millions might not be saved by retrenchment. Add to this, all that is left unappropriated of the ridiculous Sinking Fund—and immediate relief from taxation, to the amount of at least *seven millions per annum,* might be given to the Country. This would be a measure of conciliation—which would give *an impetus to agriculture,* manufacture, and commerce; the effects of which would be felt in *increased consumption* at home and *sales abroad.*—It would also afford a *breathing time* for Parliament to enter into the investigation of all the causes of our disordered state; and that great question could not be placed in better hands than those of *Mr. Baring, Mr. Ricardo, Mr. Maberly, Mr. Pascoe Grenfell,* and *others,* who have *distinguished themselves* by their knowledge of our monied system."

You see, Sir, that here there is not only an insisting upon the preserving of *National Faith;* but there are two projects broached, in the way of *remedy.* The first is to reduce the value of the coin; that is to say, to make the present shilling pass for eighteen pence or somewhere thereabouts. This is what was proposed by Mr. JAMES of Birmingham, in 1817; and it is what LORD FOLKESTONE talked of the other day at the meeting in Berkshire. Mr. PERRY, with more modesty than really was to be expected, in an " *unassailable being,*" who " exercises despotic power over the minds of his readers," has submitted this as a *problem* for political economists to solve. My dear Mr. PERRY, if, instead of foully calumniating me; if, instead of imputing my flight to the most sordid and base motives; if (Oh! thou incorruptible and unassailable being!), if, instead of this you had, as it would well have become you, carefully perused those Registers, which I sent from that country, whence you predicted I should never send any; if you had read those Registers, you would have found this question satisfactorily solved in a letter addressed to that very Mr. JAMES of Birmingham; in which letter, it was very clearly shown, that such project would, to start with, be most atrociously unjust towards one part of the community; and that, in the end, it would only widen the gulph of ruin and add to all the existing elements of general confusion and devastation.

Mr. PERRY seems to have got here four famous financiers in tow! Whoever wishes to see a mess such as never was made of a nation's affairs before, must pray for two couple of just such men to be ministers. The silly harping about *economy* here is as ridiculous as it is in every other place. Besides, is Mr. PERRY ready to recommend the reducing of Salaries, Pensions, Grants, and public pay of all descriptions? If he be not, what is the sense of this talk about economy? Mr. BARING said something about economy; but Mr. BARING took special care to observe, that he should not propose to reduce the salaries of the *Great* Officers of State. This is all empty talk, then. It has no meaning at all; and, indeed, the very idea of reduction of expense, without a reduction of the interest of the debt, is ridiculous.

Having now, Sir, swept away this childish stuff, let us come *to the point* : let us come to the question of *public faith,* two words very much used, very little understood in their application to this matter, but capable of doing an enormous quantity of mischief to the nation. I assert that, whether the Nation pay the whole of the interest as it is now paid, or whether it cease to pay any interest at all, is merely, like every other question of state, a question of EXPEDIENCY. We have so long called the thing a Debt; we have so long called the funds *property;* we have so long talked of a *mortgage* which the Fundholders have upon the Nation; we have so long called the Fundholders *Creditors;* that, at last, we have confounded a matter of State with a private transaction; two things wholly distinct in their origin, in their progress, and in all their bearing and effects.

It is pretty enough to hear Mr. BARING talk of dishonesty in not continuing to pay to the full nominal amount; it is pretty enough to hear him appeal to *morals* and *religion* in behalf of the Fundholder. It is pretty enough to hear him dash along so glibly and say that the Debtor is not to plead *inability* to pay, until he has given up his all But, if the Fundholder now receives from the Farmer two bushels of wheat instead of the price of the one bushel which he lent; if the mortgagee receives, in fact, double interest, when he contracted only for single interest; if the man who lent nine and twenty shillings in the shape of a guinea, now demands a guinea and eight shillings back in return; if this be the case, where is the *honesty,* where the *morality,* where the *religion,* of these harpies of Loanmakers; and where is the justice, where the wisdom, where even the common prudence of the government that will pass and enforce Laws for compelling the borrowers to submit to such lenders?

Even *this* might suffice as an answer to Mr. BARING. But what analogy is there between this affair of State and an affair between two private persons? And what a groveling mind must that be that can hang upon the Laws of Debtor and Creditor, while it has a subject like this before it? Take, for instance, this vulgar idea of the Debtor giving up his all. How does this apply to a Nation? Why, a Nation cannot give up it's all. The thing is impossible. And, upon the wild supposition that the present borrowers, the Landowners particularly, are to give up their all to the money lenders, is this to be done, I pray, without any consideration had for others, labourers and artizans, who may be starved during the terrible operation of the transfer? Besides, be it known to Mr. BARING, that the *land,* of itself, does not pay a fifth part of the interest of the Debt. The rest is raised from *labour* of various sorts. It is taken out of *wages.* So that to give up it's *all* the Nation must give up it's bones and it's blood.

We here see enough, at once, to convince us of the worthlessness of arguments like those of Mr. BARING. The very ideas upon which he proceeds are false; they are mere vulgar notions; but, such notions have, but too frequently, been the parents of legislative measures, as this nation has long experienced to it's cost. I say, and I desire it to be remembered that I do say, that as to this national *Debt,* as it is called, it is just and proper never to pay another farthing of interest upon it, if the good of the whole nation, taking one part with the other, require a cessation of such payment. The Fundholder is not to be thought of for a *moment,* if the prosperity and happiness of the Nation demand that the interest should no longer be paid. What a monstrous idea, that a *Nation* is to be bound to it's ruin by individuals! Suppose, for instance, that a combination of the powers of Europe, were preparing to invade England, would Mr. BARING tell me that the dividends of the Fundholders must still be paid, though without taking them, there were not a sufficiency of means for the Nation's defence? And yet what is there in this more monstrous, more brutally stupid, than to argue that the Fundholder must be paid though a considerable portion of the people be starved to death? Mr. LITTLETON's expression was not a bit too strong. It is, indeed, "A MONSTER OF CONSUMPTION." It devours the substance of the Land; and it reproduces nothing. Mr. BARING did let slip out the word drone. He should have called it wasp; for it stings while it devours; it punishes, while it starves, the industrious Bee.

We are now approaching the time, when this subject will force itself upon the country. I foresaw that it would so force itself, and I fully and boldly discussed it many years ago, in spite of reproaches and calumnies. In 1806, just about this time fifteen years ago; when the interest of the Debt was not much more than half what it is now, I insisted upon the *justice* and *necessity* of ceasing to pay that interest. I maintained that it was just and wise to cease to pay any part of the interest; this doctrine I still hold; and, I think it is high time that I receive some answer other than that of abuse, if I am to receive any answer at all. The essays which I wrote at that time were entitled " *Fate of the Funds;*" I will re-publish them now, as soon as I can conveniently. They will form an introduction, or *Preliminary Part* to *Paper against Gold.* I will then publish the Essays written in Long Island; and they will form a *Second Part* of *Paper against Gold,* a title which I highly esteem on account of the time and place and circumstances, when, where, and under which, the Essays which it contained were written. When I have got all these together, in suitable and convenient form, I will send you a copy, Sir, and will beg you to read it through patiently from the beginning to the end; and, when you have done that, if you do not throw ADAM SMITH into the fire, I shall pronounce you to be unfit even for managing the affairs of a country parish. *Paper against Gold* was deliberately undertaken by me, for the express purpose of having something to hold up in the face of those who put me into the prison where I wrote it. This is the day of my triumph, it is now that people read this book. In one of the numbers I remember saying, that I was *throwing bread upon the waters*. Thus it has proved; and if I leave any part of the ignorance of my enemies unexposed; if I do not take what is due to me upon this score, at any rate; then I will say that I deserve to be trampled upon.

The next Summer will bring to light some very curious matter. At this moment the public are pretty much divided. Some say your Bill will be repealed. Some say it will not. I hold up the Gridiron to your face in defiance. If you repeal the Bill; then we will hold the festival of the Gridiron; and we will have a Grand Dinner of broiled Geese. If you do not repeal the Bill, then the works of the next Summer will be such as almost to broil the Nation alive. Repeal it you must, or the thing must go to pieces like a wreck, long before the first of May 1823. Innumerable are the inquiries of me about what I think will be done. My answer is this, on the one side there is great and imminent danger; there is the danger of Gold being demanded at the Bank on the first of May. There is a danger belonging to that very few men see at this moment, and the particular description of which I reserve for another letter. There is, in short, terrible danger; on the other hand, there is pride; false-pride the most obstinate of all pride; and there is the stinging, scorching, scalding thought of *fulfilling my predictions;* of seeing me and my Disciples keep the festival of the Gridiron; of seeing us seated laughing, while an Actor dressed in paper with a fool's cap and bells upon his head, personifies the Pitt System for our amusement: " thoughts that heat, and words that burn," says the Poet, and if I do not utter words that shall burn when the expected day arrives, it shall be from no other cause than that of want of fire in the qualities of my mind. The feeling of resentment was not implanted in the human breast for nothing, and, surely, it may be indulged in a case like this to it's fullest extent; for in this case, while it gives pleasure to him who exercises it, those on whom it is exercised will never confess that it gives them pain.

A correspondent has given me a nice little history of the adventures of Country Banks; and has shewn me how the gentry to whom those banks belong will feel themselves on the first of

May, which it seems, is likely to be grand reckoning day with them. However, I have already filled up my paper and must reserve further remarks on the May morning for another letter.

In the hope that dear Lord Castlereagh will adhere to his *"firm resolution"* of producing payments in cash, and of not repealing your Bill,

I remain,

Your most obedient,

Most humble Servant,

WM. COBBETT.

P.S. When you write to your learned and pious constituents at Oxford, pray give my compliments to them, and ask them, whether, as a Queen's name can be left out of the liturgy, they do not think, that the *Feast of the Gridiron* may be got into the Kalendar. Ask them, whether they do not recollect, that I told them, in 1803, that, if the *"Muck Worm"* were not speedily *crushed,* it would devour both *Church* and *Aristocracy.*—Oh! infatuation! A Nobility and a Hierarchy crying aloud against imaginary Republicans, and Deists, and, at the same time, cherishing a race of men, who are actually *taking away their estates*! What! One House filled wholly with Landowners, and the other four sixths filled with their relations; and both agree in adopting and enforcing measures, which *must* make all the lands change owners! The Hindoo (I believe it is) Wife, is not a more self-devoted victim!

Gold

P.R. XXX., c. 416. *Gold! Gold! Gold!* 12-5-21.

"EH! It is, it *is,* a guinea!" Not less delighted than SCRUB was when ARCHER put the shiner into his hand, am I at this moment with a sum of sovereigns lying upon the table on which I am writing, just brought from the Bank, from the dear old Lady in Threadneedle Street! She had *numerous visitors* yesterday, and she *paid her one-pounders honestly.*—Now, then, whoever takes a forged note *after this* has himself to thank. There is no excuse for him. And, whoever circulates the paper farther than on its road to the Bank will have to answer for the temptation which brings so many poor creatures to the gallows.

Paper-Money

P.R. XXXIX., c. 509. *To Mr. Coke. On the question of Large Farms and Small Farms, and on the fall of the System out of which they have arisen. 26-5-21.*

THAT paper-money, and, indeed, that money of no sort, can *create* any thing valuable, is evident; and that it cannot *cause* it to be created, on a *general* scale, is also evident; for, all valuable things arise from *labour,* and, if an addition to the quantity of money sets labour in motion in one place, it draws it from another place; that is all that it does. If its nature and operation be such as to cause new and fine houses and carriages and " grand dinners " to make their appearance, it takes away the means of furnishing the houses of the most numerous class, robs them of their bedding, their food, their drink and their raiment. Nothing is *created* by it. It is not value *in itself;* but merely the *measure of value,* and the means of *removing valuable things from one possessor to another.*

But a *paper-money,* while it removes things from one possessor to another, *is a false measure of value.* It is *always* a false measure; but, it is, in some states of it, *more false* than in other states of it. When not convertible into gold at the will of the holder, it is false altogether.

South American Bonds

P.R. LVI., c. 553. *Foreign Loans. 26-11-25.*

WHEN the foreign loans first began to go on, Peter MACCULLOCH and all the Scotch were cock o' whoop. They said that there were prodigious advantages in lending money to South America, that the interest would come home to enrich us; that the amount of the loans would go out chiefly in English manufactures; that the commercial gains would be enormous; and that this country would thus be made rich, and powerful, and happy, by employing in this way its " *surplus capital,*" and thereby contributing at the same time to the uprooting of despotism and superstition, and the establishing of freedom and liberality in their stead. Unhappy and purblind, I could not for the life of me see the matter in this light. My perverted optics could perceive no *surplus capital* in bundles of bank-notes. I could see no gain in sending out goods which somebody in England was to pay for, without, as it appeared to me, the smallest chance of ever being paid again. I could see no chance of gain in the purchase of a bond, nominally bearing interest at six per cent., and on which, as I thought, no interest at all would ever be paid. I despised the idea of paying bits of paper. I knew that a bond, though said to bear six per cent. interest, was not worth a farthing, unless some interest were paid upon it. I declared, when Spanish bonds were at seventy-five, that I would not give a crown for a hundred pounds of them, if I were compelled to keep them unsold for seven years; and I now declare, as to South American bonds, I think them of less value than the Spanish bonds now are, if the owner be compelled to keep them unsold for a year. It is very true, that these opinions agree with my *wishes;* but they have not been created by those wishes. They are founded on my knowledge of the state of things, and upon my firm conviction of the folly of expecting that the interest of these things will ever come from the respective countries to which they relate.

The Thing is Going

P.R. LXX., c. 126. *To the Readers of the Register, And particularly those who have petitioned for the Abolition of Negro-Slavery.* 24-7-30.

THE thing is going! going! once; twice; going! going! The hammer is not raised yet, but it will be raised, and will come down too; and if uncommon care be not taken, it will come down " *with a vengeance,*" as the old Lord Chatham said it would. Men of property are not in the humour to see their families go to the workhouse; the labourers are not in the humour to lie down and die with field-sorrel in their bowels; every man is convinced that such must be the *end,* if *reform* do not take place; and, therefore, in some way or other, *reform must come and will come*!

AND, WILL THE ARISTOCRACY NOW GIVE WAY?

Never, in this whole world, was there before stated so momentous a question as that! If they yield *now,* all will be well with them, with us, and with the fame of our country : if they do not yield, and yield *now* too, be the consequences *on their own heads.* As to the Reformers, and *myself* amongst the rest, we shall have *nothing* wherewith to reproach ourselves. We have humbly and loyally petitioned, and we, for our humility, have been rewarded with chains, with dungeons, with exile, with ruin, and some with wounds or with death. Our prayers have been scorned, and we have had no hand in bringing those evils upon our country; and we are now ready to assist in preventing the natural result of the measures of which we have so long and so justly, and with voice so prophetic, complained.

SIXTEEN

EDUCATION

Learned Languages

P.R. XI., c. 36. *Summary of Politics. Proceedings in Parliament.* 10-1-07.

THE "Uti Possidetis" mean, the *learned* tell us, *actual possession;* or *the state of actual possession;* and, when they talk about treating upon the basis of the "Uti Possidetis," they mean, that the parties agree, by way of preliminary, or first bargain, that each shall retain all that he possesses at the moment when the negociators meet. But, if this be the meaning of the "Uti Possidetis," why not give us that meaning in our own language at once? Do those who make use of such phrases, which the stupidest wretch upon earth might learn to use as well as they, in a few hours; nay, which a parrot would learn, or which a high-dutch bird-catcher would teach to a bull-finch or a tom-tit, in the space of a month; and do they think, in good earnest, that this relick of the mummery of monkery, this playing off upon us of a few gallipot words, will make us believe that they are *learned?* Learning, truly so called, consists in the possession of knowledge and in the capacity of communicating that knowledge to others; and, as far as my observation will enable me to speak, what are called the *learned* languages, operate as a bar to the acquirement of real learning. I already hear some pedagogue, or pedant, exclaim : "this is precisely the reasoning of the Fox without a tail." But, to bring this matter to the test, I hereby invite the *learned* gentlemen of the two universities to a discussion upon the subject. *I assert that what they call the* LEARNED LANGUAGES *are improperly so called; and that, as a part of general education, they are worse than useless.* Two months will afford time enough for any of the gentlemen just spoken of to disprove these positions. I will, therefore, give them until Lady Day next. I will publish their defence of their calling; and, if I do not *fairly* beat them in the controversy, and, that, too, in the space of twenty columns of my Register, I will then beg their pardon, and will allow, that to be able to speak, or write, in a language which the people do not understand is a proof of learning. But, until then, I shall dissent from the opinion, that none but clear streams are shallow, and that the muddier the water the deeper the well.

Learned Languages

P.R. XXXII., c. 1076. *To Mr. Benbow, of the Town of Manchester, One of the English Reformers, now imprisoned in some prison in Great Britain under a warrant of a Secretary of State, in virtue of an Act, lately passed, lodging the absolute power of imprisonment in the hands of the Ministry. 29-11-17.*

IT is no small mischief to a boy, that many of the best years of his life should be devoted to the learning of what can never be of any real use to any human being. His mind is necessarily rendered frivolous and superficial by the long habit of attaching importance to *words* instead of *things;* to *sound* instead of sense. When you are told (a thing which you will hardly believe), that the boys at these *learned* schools are set to make what are called "*Nonsense Verses*" in Latin; that is to say, to place a parcel of Latin words in lines, so that each line shall contain a particular number of syllables, having the accent falling in a certain way, without any regard to the sense or meaning of the words : as, for example :—

Meadow when for surprize the backward
Cut finger tea-kettle coldest he again.

When you are told, that a considerable portion of a boy's time is under a grave, wigged pedant; when you are told this, you, instead of wondering, that the colleges pour forth crowds of such fools as they notoriously do, will wonder that any thing but a fool should ever come forth from such places. Is it not fortunate if half a life restore the energies of mind thus enfeebled at the outset? Must it not be a sort of miracle, if a bold thought, an original idea, ever come from such a mind? It has always been observed of these schools, that the most indolent and restive boys turn out to be the brightest men; and, in the instance of *Dean Swift* this indolence and restiveness were so remarkable, that he was actually *expelled*. The truth is, that, to a mind, strong by nature, this drudgery of nonsense is intolerable. Such a mind cannot submit to such degradation.

However, the general effect is, to accustom the mind, by slow degrees, to those trammels, in which, at last, it is not only content to remain, but for which it acquires a taste, at the same time, that it acquires a conceit, that superiority consists chiefly in the having been at a college. Hence this race of men are, at once, the most ignorant and the most conceited in the world; and, if they are of the *dependent* class, they have all the pride of the noble with far more than all the meanness of his meanest domestic servant. When you meet with one of them at a time, he wearies you half to death with his *puns,* his college jokes, and scraps; but, if *two,* they are a perfect pest. A loud tone and pulpit-like gesticulations they have learnt to great perfection, and ill-manners are the natural produce of their insolent conceit and fancied superiority. In a company, however numerous, they soon smell each other out. One or the other soon finds occasion, or makes occasion, to let it be known, that he has been at *Oxford* or *Cambridge*. The other, like gun-powder ready for the match, instantly catches, and off they both go inquiring of each other by turns after Jack such-an-one and Tom such-an-one; and then, to it they fall, reminding each other of all their college pranks; of all the drunken bouts, all the gettings out of windows; all their dances and dinners and suppers, not forgetting their duels and their amours. Now and then an empty woman, or her gaudy daughters, admire their trash; but, men of sense and of decent manners hear them with surprize and disgust.

If, however, the evil were confined to these gentry, it would not be great; but, it is far otherwise. The Aristocracy have a deep interest in the upholding of this *learned* system of cheat and oppression. There are valuable possessions of houses and lands belonging to the several great schools and colleges. The produce of these falls to the *Teachers,* under one name or another. These teachers are, in fact, selected by the Aristocracy, who have the further power in their hands of bestowing Benefices, or Bishopricks, &c. upon the teachers; and, it is a like influence that selects the *scholars,* where they are to be educated *free of expence.* Here, then, at these places, slavery is taught systematically. The noblemen's and gentlemen's sons are distinguished by a grander sort of *dress.* Here the needy learn in their youth to crawl to the rich and powerful. Here the poor expectant is early taught his dependence. Not like boys at a common school, where no one thinks about the *father* of another. Here the dependant begins to bespeak his pulpit, or his office under government, by creeping to the son of the Lord or the Baronet. The Teachers, who have the same game in eye, discover nothing but genius in the sons of the great, while they find to be dunces all who have no interest in the Boroughs or in Livings. Here are both precept and example for all that is servile towards the powerful and for all that is insolent and cruel towards the weak. Here, in short, is every thing to render the great full of insolent pride, and the poor sub-servient and base. And these are the bodies, who have the peculiar privilege (confined to them and the City of London) of presenting petitions to the king on his throne!

Mechanic's Institution

P.R. LVIII., c. 436. *Mechanic's Institution.* 15-11-23.

I GAVE my five pounds as a mark of my regard for and my attachment to the *working classes of the community,* and also as a mark of my approbation of any thing which seemed to assert that these classes were equal, in point of intellect, to those who have had the insolence to call them the "*Lower Orders.*" But, I was not without my fears, nor am I now without my fears, that this institution may be turned to purposes, *extremely in-jurious to the mechanics* themselves. I cannot but know what sort of people are likely to get amongst them. I know that there are *Rump Committees,* and I heard the name of "JOHN CAM HOBHOUSE *Esquire,*" who gave *ten pounds* to the mechanics, while his father is receiving *twelve hundred pounds a year as a Commissioner about the Nabob of Arcot's debts,* and who has received out of the public money about *five and twenty thousand pounds since I can remember;* and that, too, in part, out of the sweat of these very mechanics. "When father and son *take different sides,* lands and tenements commit no treason." Thus BURDETT is thanked at the late dinner of *"Patriots"* for his *hostility to military outrage;* while his son, in a high court regiment of whiskerandoes, is *pushing on fast in time of peace towards the* rank of *General!* So much for Rump Committees and *" free* and *independent Electors* of Westminster."

Mechanics, I most heartily *wish you well;* but I also most heartily wish you not to be *humbugged,* which you most certainly will be, if you suffer any body but REAL MECHANICS to have any thing to do in managing the concern. You will *mean well;* but, many a cunning scoundrel will get *place* or *pension* as the *price* of you, whom he will sell just as unconcernedly as a grazier sells his sheep at Smithfield. Scotch Feeloosofers are, sometimes, *varey cleever* men; but, if you suffer yourselves to be put into their *crucibles,* you will make but a poor figure when you come out. An *" Institution"* to get the *" Combination Law"* repealed would, I fancy, be the most advantageous that you could, at this time, establish. The *"expansion* of the *mind"* is very well; but, really, the thing which presses most, at this time, is, the getting of something to *expand the body* a little more : a little more *bread, bacon,* and *beer;* and, when these are secured, a little "expansion of the mind " may do *vary weele.*

On Popular Education

P.R. LIII., c. 347. *To Mr. Brougham.* 5-2-25.

YOU assume that the people : and, mind, you address yourself to the *working classes,* stand in need of what you are pleased to call *"education"*. Now, you know, as well as I, that education means, not the reading of books; not the being able to read and sing the psalms of Sternhold and Hopkins; that it means *breeding-up,* and, that people may be brought up very well, and especially to the most numerous sorts of *work,* without any reading at all. But, taking education to mean reading and writing; or, in other words, knowledge to be got from books; what knowledge, I pray you, are the people to get from those *"religious tracts"* with which you are so peculiarly gratified? You seem to have abandoned the broad sheet now; for, now, you are for "*itinerant libraries*" as a means of instruction to the working classes. We have just seen, in the former part of this letter, what pretty instruction the broad sheet is calculated to give to the working classes; and now let us see what your itinerant libraries and your "*lectures*" are calculated to do for them.

You are for treating them to the same repast which, as you tell us, your northern brethren have so long enjoyed; namely, "the profound wisdom, sustained by unbounded learning, and embellished with the most brilliant fancy, which so richly furnishes every page of the *Essays of* BACON! "

Talk of *March hares,* indeed! Cursed wild things, I, when a boy, have run after them till my legs were ready to break under me; and I am determined not now to renew the pursuit. Yet, only think of JOHN PLODPOLE, with every finger as thick as your wrist, and chaps between the finger and thumb, a quarter of an inch deep, no more capable of running over the leaf of a book than you are of turning over, with the spade, twenty rod of ground in a day; only think of poor John, coming home from hedging, with a nitch of wood upon his back, to which is appended a pair of gloves or cuffs, each as big as your brief-bag; only think of him, with a pair of shoes weighing half a score of pounds, and with jacket impenetrable by thorns; think of poor John; now pray think of him, pray do look at him, who, when he throws down his nitch is so tired that he is ready to follow it to the earth; only think what you would say even to a *March hare,* if she were capable of speaking, and were to tell you that this is the person who is to sit down over his handful of fire and his farthing or half-farthing rushlight, and meditate on "the profound wisdom, sustained by unbounded learning, and embellished with the most brilliant fancy, which so richly furnishes every page of the Essays of Bacon "?

"If," said a gentleman, upon reading this extract in the Morning Chronicle the other night, " he had talked to them about bacon *to eat,* instead of Bacon *to read,* they would have found a great deal more sense in it." Yes, Sir, that would, indeed, have been becoming in that "Education Digest " (not to pun, mind) which you promised us so long ago. It is food that is wanted, and raiment; and not reading and writing, by the class of persons to whom you have addressed your " Practical Observations." It is the want of these, in which the once happy people of England were not in want, that causes the far greater part of all the thefts and dilapidations which now prevail, and the number and magnitude of which are daily increasing.

* * * * * *

There is no man of experience in England who will not tell you, and who cannot produce you indubitable proofs, that the people of England were much more honest, more laborious, more contented, forty years ago than they are now; that servants were quite a different sort of creatures; and, in short, that all, with regard to the working classes, has changed for the worse; and, yet, Bibles, religious tracts, gospel-shops, itinerant tub-men, and national schools, stare us in the face in every village. What is the conclusion? Not, indeed, completely that these things produce the immorality; but quite complete as to the conclusion that they are unable to prevent it. The mischief has quite another source than that of a want of reading and writing. Its source, and its *only* source, is the infernal system of taxing, funding, and making paper-money. By these, all the working classes in the country parts are deprived of the means of decent existence, and almost of the means of existence at all. A full third part, perhaps, of the whole of the really good food of the country is, by these means, drawn up to the Wen. Many of the poor creatures in the country, being actually in a state of half-starvation, are tempted to commit thefts. To avoid the whip, the jail and other consequences of crime, and of loss of character, they, female as well as male, flee away to hide their shame, in this all-degrading and corrupting Wen, to smooth their way to which, to facilitate their escape and their impunity, the same system has provided them most conveniently with roads and conveyances. So that this is a grand assemblage of all the thieves, all those, in every part of the country, whom miseries have driven into the commission of those crimes which otherwise they would not have thought of. In such a state of things, how can there be morality; how can there be a regard for character; how can there be a sense of shame to prevent the crime amongst those who have not half a sufficiency of food as a reward for incessant labour and for trustworthiness?

Here, then, is the root of the evil. This root must be torn up; the trunk and the branches of the mischief must be hewed off and cast into the fire; or, the working classes will grow worse and worse, in spite of your " Practical Observations," the Essays of BACON and the Lectures of Doctor BIRKBECK.

Our Friend Brougham
P.R. LXIII., c. 114. *Mr. Brougham at Liverpool.* 7-7-27.

OUR friend BROUGHAM is, I am ready to allow, a piece of goods very different from this. He is not a dull, heavy thing, like HORNER. He has entertainment in him; and though he chops about like the wind in March, and pops in and out like the sun in April; though he be white frost in the morning, hail at ten, rain at twelve, sultry heat at three, snow at six, and black frost at midnight; though he boxes the compass and goes through all the degrees of the thermometer every twenty-four, or, at most, forty-eight hours; still he has *amusement* in him; he has *life,* and that is a great thing with me, who hate your *solemn* asses, who seem to think that their beholders will infer wisdom from the screwing up of their lips. There is, however, a *medium* in all things, except in your *professed talkers,* who are absolutely without any measure or conscience, when once they get *a-going.* Thus it appears to have been upon the present occasion. However, I shall examine this speech, as soon as I have room; and shall endeavour to give this very rank plant a " *twist down* " again.

The Society for the Diffusion of Useful Knowledge
P.R. LXIX., c. 710. *To Mr. Brougham.* 29-5-30.

SO much for your negro slavery affair; though I should not forget that Wilberforce voted for *Pitt's gagging* and *dungeoning bills,* and for pretty six acts into the bargain. So much for *the present.* I lay the negro affair by till another time;

and *now come to your society for the diffusion of useful know-ledge,* at a meeting of which you and Lord ALTHORP were, the other day, beplastering each other with praises. This, like all the rest of the "*education*" schemes, is a combination for the purpose of *amusing* the working classes, and *diverting their attention from the cause of their poverty and misery.* The methodist parsons are the most *efficient* tools in this way. They flatly assert, that when a man's dinner is taken away by the taxgatherer, it is *for his good,* and that he ought to bless God for it. The vagabonds are fat and sleek enough themselves, in the mean while. *You* are at work in *another way;* but you have the same *end* constantly in view; namely, the *keeping the cause of the poverty and misery of the people disguised from them,* and thereby perpetuating the plundering of them.

This *educating* work, this *feeding with tracts,* began, about forty years ago, under the guidance of that prime old prelate in petticoats, that choice tool of the boroughmongers, HANNAH MORE; and it has been going on ever since. Now, as *crime* is TWENTY-FOLD in amount what it was when Hannah began; as the jails, including hulks and all sorts of prisons, are ten times as capacious as they were before Hannah started with her tracts; this being undeniable, would not the *education-schemers,* if they had only common sense, cease to cry up the *utility* of their schemes? Ah! you do want for sense to perceive the *inutility* for *good* purposes; but you want the thing for the purpose before mentioned; that is to say, for the purpose of *amusing* the working classes, and of *disguising from them the cause of their poverty and misery.* It is the *will of God;* it is *untoward seasons;* it is their own *want of care;* it is *any thing* but the *taxes!* Then *some Lord* is in the *chair* of the Society! How good! How condescending! This lord *must* be a good man! The people are not told how much this lord and his family cuts off their dinner every day. In this case, to which I am now alluding, your *generous* associate, LORD ALTHORP, said, that he had read the society's tracts with *great advantage.* Indeed! They must be fine tracts! I wonder who wrote them?

"*Useful knowledge,*" indeed! If LORD ALTHORP will tell the tract-readers how it happens, that *his brother*

FREDERICK is, or was a little while ago, *Captain* of a man of war, with *Lieutenants* under him, who were *fighting at sea before the said* FREDERICK *was born;* if LORD ALTHORP will tell the tract-readers *this,* he will give them a piece of knowledge more *useful* than all that your thousands of tracts contain. And this is not only what he will not tell them, but what he will, if he can, *take care that they shall never hear of;* and this is the main object of all the "*education schemes.*"

Announcement of Two-Penny Trash

P.R. LXIX., c. 737. *New Publication.* 5-6-30.

AGREEABLY to the hint that I gave in the Register of last week, I shall on the FIRST OF JULY, publish the FIRST NUMBER OF A MONTHLY PAMPHLET, to be called

TWO-PENNY TRASH;
OR
POLITICS FOR WORKING PEOPLE.

It will be in the DUODECIMO form; each Number will consist of *one sheet,* well filled with matter; the main *object* will be, to show the working people *what are the causes* of their being poor; *what it is,* that in spite of their ingenuity, industry, and frugality, makes them unable to provide in a suitable manner, for their wives and children; and the *motto* will be,

> "Yes, while I live, no rich or noble knave
> Shall walk the world in credit to his grave."

This pretty little work shall take in the *past* and the *present;* it shall show how the public money *is raised,* and *who gets it;* it shall contain heaps of most interesting facts and *biographical anecdotes;* it shall speak *plain,* and prepare the people for that really RADICAL REFORM that is now at no great distance. It shall strip the thick mantle from political hypocrisy; it shall lay hypocrites and oppressors *bare,* and shall leave them to be dealt with as justice shall dictate; it shall inculcate industry, sobriety, conjugal fidelity, paternal care and tenderness, filial affection and duty, honesty towards employers, due obedience to the laws, devotion to the country, and *inextinguishable hatred* against its worst enemies, *those who wallow in public plunder*. In short, it shall contain matter which, when once got into the head of a working man, will remain there for the whole of his life, and be to him and to his children after him, a mass of *useful knowledge*.

It remains for me to speak of the *mode of publication*. The SIX ACTS forbid me to publish a work like this oftener *than once a month;* and they *compel* me to publish it *within two days of the first of the month,* on pain of being pretty nigh-half-killed. Beautiful " *liberty of the press!* " The publication will, of course, be at my shop, in London, No. 183, Fleet-street. The retail price will be TWO-PENCE, with the usual allowance to booksellers. I sell no books to booksellers at a distance, nor, indeed, to any body, except *at the shop;* so that booksellers in the country will please to apply to their correspondents in town, who will, of course, send the required supply in their *monthly parcels.*

WM. COBBETT.

And now, MASTER BROUGHAM, you shall see whether I am not more than a match for " *Useful Knowledge* " humbug; you shall feel your nose nipped off, if you venture to poke it out only a quarter of an inch too far. I want no " *society,*" no " *subscription,*" to send my work about. It will want no *pushing* about; it will contain a spring, in its inside, to set it and keep it in motion. I dare say that *your works* are published at *a loss;* what else is the " *subscription* " for? In short, they are *forced* about; half *given away;* and, as is natural and right, nobody but " the *society* " ever reads them. You shall see that I will send forth some stuff that people will *read,* and be eager to read, without any *coaxing,* to do it. What do you want of a " *subscription,*" if you can *sell* your tracts? What! you *sell* your tracts; you brag of the *extent of the sale;* and yet you want a *subscription* to assist you in carrying on the publication! You are an odd sort of author! Now, I shall want no subscription; and this marks the great difference between us; this shows, in fact, that your stuff is *not sold to a profit;* that you *force it about;* and that it produces no other effect than that of causing you to be *laughed at.*

SEVENTEEN

RELIGION

Religious Toleration

P.R. XXIII., c. 714. *The Trinity*. 15-5-13.

NO, no; I am for no partial repeals. I am for a general Act, permitting every man to say or write what he pleases upon the subject of religion, or, I wish the whole thing to remain what it now is.

P.R. XXIII., c. 812. *The Trinity*. 5-6-13.

My opinion is (and, I think, that no man will say openly that he differs from me here) that, upon all public matters, whether of religion, politics, or any other, TRUTH ought to prevail over falsehood. To deny this proposition would be to declare openly in favour of lies.—This point being settled, we have next to consider what is the most likely way of *ensuring the triumph of truth;* and, my opinion is, confining myself now to religion, that the most likely way is, to leave all men at perfect liberty *to say or write what they please upon the subject of religion.* To suppose, that, in consequence of such liberty, truth would not prevail, is to suppose, that truth is, in its nature, less pleasing than false-hood, or, that the human mind is prone towards a preference of the latter; which is directly contrary to all the maxims, and, indeed, all experience on the subject.—Hence it naturally follows, that I must be of opinion, that it would be conducive to the complete triumph of truth, in matters of religion, to give full and free scope to the tongues and pens of all descriptions of dissenters. But, it does not follow from the same premises, or from any thing that I have ever said, that I must be in favour of a *partial* liberty to speak and write upon the subject of religion. I know that it is said, as some say about parliamentary reform; *get what you can;* but, it has never been, that I have heard, attempted to be proved, that the getting of a little would do any good, or, that it would not tend to the *perpetuating of the evil;* and, I have no hesitation to say, that I would rather all the penal statutes on the subject of religion should remain as they are, than to see a repeal of certain parts of them, and especially at the request of particular sects.—For, observe, what, in such case, becomes the effect of such penal statutes. They are bands in the hands of the government, who, to gain the good-will of one sect, relaxes a little this time; of another sect, relaxes a little next time; and, thus, it gains the gratitude of these numerous sects by means quite distinct from considerations connected with the public and general weal. For my part, I can imagine nothing better calculated to give undue power to the government, and, of course, nothing more hostile to public liberty, than the existence of numerous religious sects, all condemning each others' creeds, and all having motives to make them seek the favour and indulgence of the ministers of the day. A religious sect, and more especially the priests of such sect, who, in fact, guide the sect, naturally think the prosperity of the sect of more importance than the prosperity of the nation at large, and, of course, their first and chief object, whatever may be their politics, is the prosperity of the sect. And, if the government, by the partial repeal of acts of parliament, or by any other means, possesses boons to toss down to them at pleasure, we may be very sure, that those sects will never take much trouble in the cause of a reform in which all the nation is interested.—We have seen the Methodists, with their roaring, raving, ranting, foaming priests at their head, pouring in thousands of petitions against a Bill which they thought would a little cramp their particular sect; and, the Bill having been given up, they flocked round Perceval, and, at the very time when he was proposing the Mary-le-bone and other new Barracks, covered him with their applause as a *friend to freedom.* Thus their gratitude was gained without any boon at all; but merely by shaking the rod at them, and then laying it aside without using it.

The Methodists

P.R. XXIII., c. 842.   *The Trinity.*   12-6-13.

I AM well aware of what a correspondent reminds me, namely, that to publish these and the like remarks is to expose myself to the " animosity and execrations of great numbers of knaves and fools; " but, being convinced of the truth, and of the *public utility* of such remarks, I am resolved to make them whenever the occasion appears to me to call for them.   There are, I know, persons who look upon the Methodists, for instance, as *friends of freedom.*   It is impossible they should be.   They are either fools or tricksters, or so nearly allied thereto, as to be worthy of no consideration.   Their heavenly gifts, their calls, their inspirations, their feelings of grace at work within them, and the rest of their canting gibberish, are a gross and outrageous insult to common sense, and a great scandal to the country.   It is in vain that we boast of our *enlightened state,* while a sect like this is increasing daily.   It would seem, that, at last, men had fallen in love with ignorance of the most vulgar kind.   The very sound of the bellowings of one of these pretended sons of inspiration is enough to create disgust in a hearer of sense.   The incoherent trash, the downright balderdash, that these *gifted* brethren send forth surpasses all description, and it really is a stain upon the national character, that they should find such multitudes to follow at their heels.

EIGHTEEN

STRIKES AND TRADE UNIONS

To the Stocking-Weavers

P.R. XXXIX., c. 102. *To the Stocking-Weavers of Leicestershire, Nottinghamshire and Derbyshire. On the Subject of their present turn-out; and on the real causes of their distress.* 14-4-21.

BUT, now, what is the cause, the primary cause, of all this turmoil; of all this unnatural strife between *masters* and *men?* For, I like these words a great deal better than the newfangled jargon of *"Employer* and *Operative."* When *master* and *man* were the terms, every one was in his place; and all were free. Now, in fact, it is an affair of *masters* and *slaves,* and the *word,* master, seems to be avoided only for the purpose of covering our shame. What, I say, is the *primary cause* of all this unnatural strife? To see bands of stockingmakers prowling about from town to town, dragging waggon *loads of coals,* as is, at this moment the case; to see bands of their *wives and daughters,* which is also actually the case, dragging waggons loaded with coals or chalk or stone, from town to town. To see these things; to see you, the ingenious and industrious people of England, prowling about in begging bands, with inscriptions and devices to call forth charity. To see fathers of families, engaged in this manner, *run over and wounded, or killed,* by the very waggon, which they themselves are dragging, as was the case only last week. To behold these things, and to suppose that the *cause* is to be removed by a turnout of workmen for an addition of wages, is to evince a symptom of stark madness.

We must look for this cause elsewhere than in the *avarice* of your masters. There must be something at work far more powerful than that.

The Combination Laws

P.R. XLVII., c. 537.   *To William Wilberforce.   On the state of the Cotton Factory Labourers, and on the Speech of ANDREW RYDING, who cut HORROCKS with a cleaver.* 30-8-23.

EVERY man's labour is his *property*. It is something which he has to sell or otherwise dispose of. The cotton spinners had their labour to sell; or, at least, they thought so. They were pretty free to sell it, before this Combination-Law of 1800. They had their labour to sell. The purchasers were powerful and rich, and wanted them to sell it at what the spinners deemed too low a price. In order to be a match for the rich purchasers, the sellers of the labour agree to assist one another, and thus to live as well as they can; till they can obtain what they deem a proper price. Now, what was there wrong in this? What was there either unjust or illegal? If men be attacked, either in the market or in their shops; if butchers, bakers, farmers, millers be attacked, with a view of forcing them to sell their commodities at a price lower than they demand, the assailants are deemed rioters; and are hanged!

The London Turn-out

P.R. LIV., c. 641.   *The Turn-out; On one of the Curses of Paper-Money.* 11-6-25.

THE present *turn-out* of the journeymen of this enormous WEN is a great evil. That every one must allow, while many have to taste its inconveniences and injuries. I have had, for some time, a journeyman carpenter at work for me, furnished me by my neighbour, who is a master of that trade. All at once this man has disappeared, leaving his tools behind him; though it is a rule, from which I never depart, to suffer no journeyman, at work for me, to quit his work, for even a quarter of a day, except in case of sudden illness, without *my leave* previously obtained; a rule arising not more from a love of regularity than from my wish to promote, as far as falls to my lot, the good of the workmen themselves. But, here comes *a cause* that sets all regularity, all proper subordination, all order, all the mutual interests of masters and men, and all the rules and the convenience of employers at defiance.

The journeymen have, what they call, *struck* for higher wages; and, surely, they are right in doing this; for, are they now to work for a day for what will purchase them only about *two-thirds* as much food and raiment as the same sum would have purchased them three years, or, but two years ago? Why is a man now to work for less than he worked for then? Then the bread was at *eightpence* the quartern loaf, and now that same loaf costs about *twelvepence.* Bacon, which then sold, in London, at 4d. a pound, now sells for 8d. The same may be said of every article of food and raiment; and, if the *pot of porter* continue at the same price, it is *weaker, poorer, worse* than it was, in the proportion that malt and hops are dearer. Is there, then, any just man, who can blame the *men* for seeking to obtain a rise of wages; and, yet the *masters* are not to be blamed. They cannot easily raise *their* prices. If, for instance, the master carpenter, whom I employ, bring in his bill, charging me more in the latter part of it, than in the former part of it, for the day's work of a man, shall I be pleased with this? As *to me,* indeed, there would be no disagreement arise out of this, because I know that it would be just; but is this the case with employers in *general*? But more, perhaps than one half of the journeymen, who work in the raising and finishing and furnishing of *buildings,* work on buildings to be erected and to be finished by CONTRACT! Is it *just* that the contractors should be compelled to adhere to *their* contracts, and that they should have to pay *one-third more* for the work done, than was the fair and regular and customary price of work at the time when the contract was made?

If, then for all this mischief; all this disorder; all this ill blood between masters and men; all this inevitable loss of time; all this loss of money to the masters; and, which is a still more serious evil, all the want and unhappiness that must necessarily accrue to the wives and families of the workmen : if, for these evils, neither men nor masters merit any *blame,* where, let me ask you, does the blame lie? Divine Providence (not to speak profanely) has a " broad back "; and has, accordingly, had to bear the consequences of thousands and thousands of human negligences and blunders. But Providence has been good enough to us : it has not visited us with scarcity of corn, of meat, of flax, or of wool. It has given us crops as abundant and every thing as good as usual.

Yet, there must be *a cause somewhere;* and, mark this, to the cause of evil, or, rather, to those who cause notorious and acknowledged evil, be they who they may, *blame* is justly due in proportion to the magnitude of that evil. There is no effect without *a cause.* The turn-out has a cause; that cause is the rise in the price of the necessaries of life; and if we discover who it is that has *caused that rise,* we have before us the objects of just blame.

Trade Unions

P.R. LXXXII., c. 624. *Rights of Industry.* 7-12-33.

IT is very well known, that the whole country is in a stir with what are called "TRADES UNIONS." This has become so formidable a matter, that it demands the attention of every one who meddles at all with public affairs. I have just received from Lancashire, and under the frank of my honourable colleague, an account of a society, of which he himself is a member, and of which he himself is one of the managers. I have long been contending that labour had not is just reward; that those who do the work have long been unfairly treated; and that, at last, it must, in some way or another, end in their being better treated. The working people have long been combining in one way or another to obtain better treatment; and at last they seem to have combined for some practical purpose. The nation has been divided very nearly into two classes, the idlers living chiefly on the taxes, in one way or another, and the industrious, who have their earnings taken from them to maintain the idlers. Lord BACON said, and the history of the world has said, that no state can long stand in peace, and maintain its power, in a state of things like this. The people hoped that a reformed Parliament would make a complete change in this respect; and they have been completely disappointed. Therefore, casting aside all disquisitions relative to forms of government, and political and constitutional rights, they have betaken themselves to what they deem the best method of insuring them

sufficiency of food and of raiment in return for their labour.
Many of the employers enter into the views of the workmen;
and we are now about to see whether a working people will
continue to live upon potatoes and salt, while so large a part of
their earnings is taken from them to be given to pensioners,
sinecure people, men and women, half-pay people, retired-
allowance people, military-academy people, and to bands of
usurers who pretend to have a mortgage upon the labour of the
child that is in the cradle. The Government newspapers have
been recommending the Parliament to pass a *law* to put an end
to these unions. Better call for a law to prevent those in-
convenient things called *spring-tides*. Were there no other
circumstance than that of the name of JOHN FIELDEN being
found in the list of these friends to the *rights of labour,* that
alone would be sufficient to satisfy me that the thing was right;
but I have been contending for these rights all my life-time; and
now, I verily believe, I shall see them recognized and established;
and that, in a very short time, we shall find not even a
Methodist parson, to tell a working man that it is right that he
should have neither bread nor meat, while those who live on his
labour are wallowing in luxury. I have no time for further
remark. The following paper will convince every man of sense
that some great change is at hand.

The Dorchester Labourers

P.R. LXXXIV., c. 47. *Dorsetshire Labourers*. 5-4-34.

TO the eternal honour of England and, indeed of Scotland and
Ireland, too, they have been roused from one end to the
other by the sentence passed by WILLIAMS (the new judge) on
the six agricultural labourers in Dorsetshire. There have been
meetings at, and pressing petitions sent from, innumerable places
throughout the whole kingdom. The working people of the
metropolis led the way by a petition from an assemblage of
twelve thousand men, which petition I had the honour to be
chosen to present to the House of Commons. The next petition
came from the town of OXFORD, signed by fifteen hundred
men in eleven hours; and it was very punctually and zealously

presented by Mr. HUGHES HUGHES, one of the members for that town. The petition to the King from my constituents of OLDHAM, I have duly transmitted to Lord MELBOURNE; and I insert it here below. At BIRMINGHAM there has been a prodigious meeting on the subject; but, if what the newspapers say be true, his Majesty's Ministers themselves have signified their intention not to cause this sentence to be carried into execution.

The whole nation has been surprised at the sentence; not one man in the whole community appearing to know that there was any law to punish men for taking oaths, or administering oaths, relative to proceedings merely connected with their own private affairs. It seems that these men have been convicted and sentenced, in virtue of an Act passed in the 37th year of Geo. III., and on the 19. of July, 1797, being chapter 123, of that King's reign. The whole of that act relates to oaths administered or taken for the purpose of seducing persons serving in his Majesty's service by sea and by land. It was passed in consequence of the mutiny in the fleet. The preamble of this act is in these words: "WHEREAS divers wicked and evil-disposed persons have of late attempted to seduce persons serving in his Majesty's forces by sea and land, and others of his Majesty's subjects, from their duty and allegiance to his Majesty, and to incite them to acts of mutiny and sedition, and have endeavoured to give effect to their wicked and traitorous proceedings, by imposing upon the persons whom they have attempted to seduce, the pretended obligation of oaths unlawfully administered." This was the preamble, setting forth the whole of the object of the law; and under this law, which was intended solely to prevent mutiny in the army and navy and conspiracy against his Majesty and his throne, these poor labouring men, for combining together for the purpose of getting *better wages,* without the smallest notion of anything political, have been sentenced by this Judge WILLIAMS, to seven years' transportation beyond the seas.

NINETEEN

THE LABOURERS' REVOLT

Distress for Ever

P.R. LXIX., c. 342. *Gin against Rum. To the Duke of Wellington. On the Cost of our "Conquests."* 13-3-30.

IT is curious to observe how *"distress"* works for the BENEFIT *of the labourers in husbandry.* In *"prosperous* times," the *commons,* even the *gardens,* were taken from them. For *twenty-five years* I have been complaining of this, and showing how it tended to the ruin of the country. I made this complaint particularly as to WILTSHIRE, where (near Cricklade) I said, that they had been driven to stick up their mud-huts in the *corners of roads, without an inch* of land to plant a cabbage. That they seemed to have been swept off the fields by a tempest, and to have dropped under the banks. Judge, then, of my pleasure, upon reading the following, in the London papers : "It was unanimously resolved last week, at a vestry meeting of the parish of *Corsham, Wilts, that land should be let to the poor upon an extensive scale,* the practice upon a small one having been found to operate most beneficially to all parties." Good! The land yields *no profit;* and now they may have some of it! *Distress* for ever! say I.

Causes of the Fires

T.T., November 1830. *The Fires*

AMONGST all the crimes that men committed against their neighbours, that which the law calls ARSON, and which is *a malicious setting fire to their buildings or their stacks,* is a crime always held in great and just abhorrence, and always punished *with death;* and so necessary has this punishment been deemed to the safety of society, that children not more than ten years of age have been put to death for it; because it is a crime so easily committed, committed with so much secrecy, and in the commission of which a very young person may be the instrument of grown-up persons. It is a truly abominable crime, because the commission of it may cause innocent persons to perish in the flames; and, at the very least, it may, in a moment, ruin whole families, reducing them from competence to beggary.

When, therefore, we hear of acts of this description being almost nightly committed *in England,* our first feeling is that of *resentment against the parties;* but, when we have had a little time to reflect, we are, if we be not devourers of the fruit of the people's labours, led to ask, What can have been *the cause* of a state of things so unnatural as that in which crimes of this horrid sort are committed by hundreds of men going in a body, and deemed by them to be a sort of *duty* instead of *crimes?* When we put this question we are not to be answered with the assertion, that the crimes arise from the *vicious disposition* of the working people; because then we ask, *what it is* that has made them so vicious? No; this cannot be the cause. The people are of the same make and maker that they always were; the land is the same, the climate the same, the language and the religion the same; and, it is very well known, that schools and places of worship and the circulation of the Bible and of religious books have all been prodigiously increasing for many years, and are now more on the increase than ever. There must, therefore, be some *other cause,* or causes, to produce these dreadful acts in a people the most just, the most good-natured, and the most patient, in the world. I know this *cause;* or, rather, these causes; I know also that there is an effectual *remedy* of this great and melancholy evil; and I need not say, that it is my duty to state them both with perfect frankness; a duty I shall perform as briefly and with as much clearness as I am able.

Fires

P.R. LXX., c. 695. *Fires.* 13-11-30.

READER, look at "*Domestic Affairs*", particularly the transactions at *Hastings,* and remember how long I have been *praying the Parliament* to repeal *Sturges Bourne's Bills,* which enabled the parishes to *hire strangers* to be "*assistant overseers.*" Look also at the declarations of the men sent to prison at Canterbury, that they "cared nothing about it, for that *they could not be worse off.*" Pray, my readers, attend to these things; and then (if you be Catholics) *cross yourselves* when you hear Peel and Knatchbull say, that the fires *do not proceed from the* "*peasantry,*" a *new* name given to the *country labourers* by the insolent boroughmongering and loan-mongering tribes. But, if it be not the "peasantry," *who* is it? Nonsense! Go, go; GET GOLD; and *make haste about it*! How I shall laugh at those who despise this warning! The *bloody old Times* newspaper, that constant tool of the Boroughmongers, which well knows that its very existence depends on theirs, has said, in form of a letter from Sussex, *that COBBETT'S going into that county had added to the mischief.* If the *advice* which I *there gave* had been followed, *not another fire would have been heard of!* And now, *even now,* if the landowners and farmers of Kent and Sussex will pay my travelling expenses, and compensate me for the use of my time, *I would engage to put an end to the violences in a month.* "Sailor, will pump?" "No: *sink first*"! This old satire, which the soldiers play off on the sailors, is brought to my mind by the disposition of these people. "Will you be saved by Cobbett"? I verily believe, that the answer of the aristocracy, without a dissenting voice, would be: "No: be d——d first".

P.R. LXX., c. 861. *Domestic Affairs.* 27-11-30.

The fires are blazing, more or less, in SIXTEEN *of the counties of England;* and the farmers appear, in a far greater part of the counties, to make *common cause* with the labourers.

Rural War
P.R. LXX., c. 876. *Recent Events of Rural War.* 4-12-30.

WHY, 'tis a war; for, if the newspaper accounts be true, *thousands of prisoners* have been taken. Two members of parliament, BARING (I mean *Alexander,* for there are no less than *four* of them in the great, big omnipotent House that "*works well "*) said, just after the meeting of the big affair, which is as pure as it is big, that the working people were *as well off now as they ever were*, and that there was *no distress in his neighbourhood*. The newspapers tell us, that *his house in Hampshire has been attacked by his poor neighbours*, and that *one Baring* (I do not know which) has been nearly killed by them! BENETT, one of the members for Wiltshire, said about a fortnight ago, that the labourers in that county *were very well contented*, and that, "so far from being tempted by bad example, and committing outrages, they would be active in putting down those who might commit them." Mr. BENETT said this in Parliament, in the big, mighty, honourable, and pure (above all things *pure*) House, on the 12th of Nov. On the 27th of that same month, the labourers (see the account) *pelted him with flintstones before the door of his great mansion in that same Wiltshire*. He was rescued by a troop of horsemen, called *yeomanry*, who, it appeared, chopped and captured some of the rural army. When BENETT said the above, I remarked upon it: "Pity Mr. Benett took upon him to vouch *so very positively;* because there is a long winter coming. The best way is to *raise the wages at once*: do that *now*, before there are any people coming in *post-chaises* to set fire to homesteads." How much better would it have been if Mr. BENETT had *followed my advice! No!* They will *never* do it! They will perish first. Well! it is their affair, and not mine!

* * * * * *

There is now before me a Report of a Committee of the House of Commons, on the subject of the Corn Laws. This Committee report the evidence of certain persons examined by them; and, amongst the rest, of a great landholder, in Wiltshire, named BENETT, who, upon being asked how much a labourer and his family ought *to have to live upon*, answered, "We calculate, that every person in a labourer's family should have, *per week*, the price of a gallon loaf, and three-pence over for *feeding* and *clothing*, exclusive of house-rent, sickness, and casual expenses."

Mark! pray mark! a gallon loaf; that is to say, not quite *a pound and a quarter of dry bread* and a *half-penny a day* for

FOOD and CLOTHING! And a SPECIAL COMMISSION is gone into Wiltshire! There is a God of justice, to be sure! That God will do justice, in the end, to be sure! Talk of blasphemy, indeed! Talk of Atheism! Who is not to be an Atheist, if he believe that there is no God to show displeasure at human creatures (and those, too, who make all the food and all the raiment to come) being doomed to exist on a pound and a quarter of bread a day, and a half-penny for clothing, and nothing for *drink,* and nothing for *fuel,* and nothing for *bedding, washing, or light*! And, what are we to think of the *Parliament* that received this evidence, and that never bestowed so much as one moment on the subject? What are we to think of that Parliament! Why, just what the people *did* think of it, to be sure.

* * * * * *

Look at the *gallon-loaf* and the *three-pence* a week, and all this sinks out of sight! Every one must lament to behold such a state of things; but yet every one must, when he looks at the cause, *wonder that it did not come before.* The important feature in the affair now, however, is, that the *middle class,* who always, heretofore, were arrayed, generally speaking, against the *working class,* are now *with them* in heart and mind, though not always in act. It will frighten Lord Gray, but he ought to know it that, amongst the tradesmen, even of the metropolis, *ninety-nine out of a hundred are on the side of the labourers.* It is not that they *approve of the destruction of property;* but they think that these means, desperate and wicked as they are *in their nature,* will tend to produce THAT GREAT CHANGE which all, who do not live on the taxes, are wishing for.

* * * * * *

Thus, then, we have the whole affair before us. Retrograde movements are impossible. The millions have, at last, broken forth; hunger has, at last, set stone walls at defiance, and braved the fetters and the gallows; nature has, at last, commanded the famishing man to get food. All the base and foolish endeavours to cause it to be believed, that the fires are the work of *foreigners,* or of a *conspiracy,* or of *instigation* from others than labourers, only show that those who make these endeavours are conscious that they share, in some way or other, in the guilt of having been the real cause of the mischief. But, if any could surpass, in point of baseness and folly, these endeavours to cast the blame on foreigners, it would be the monstrous baseness and folly of imputing the risings of the labourers and the fires TO ME! This has been done, in one shape or another, in almost every newspaper in England; and, if I were not regarded by these miscreant writers as a man *for whom there is no protection from the law,* the base wretches would tremble for the consequences. I despise the miscreants and their efforts more than anything on earth, except their baser *employers.* I will say this, however, that, if I were possessed of the power of, while sitting here in London, causing the destruction that is now going on, and if I deemed it right to render evil for evil, I should be *fully justified in exercising that power.* For what injury, what evil, what destruction, have not this ARISTOCRACY and this CLERGY inflicted, or endeavoured to inflict on me! And, when I recollect what I have suffered at their hands, and in consequence of their machinations, I must be a hypocrite indeed to say, that I do not rejoice at their troubles. When they thought they had me down for ever, their exultation was boundless; and, oh! how *shameless*! For twenty long years have I warned them of this very danger; and when I meet with scorn and punishment where I ought to have found attention and marks of gratitude, more than once I have said, and particularly to the parsons of Hampshire, "Ye have set at nought all my *counsel,* and would none of my *reproof;* I also will laugh at your calamity, and *mock* when your fear *cometh.*"

Rural War
Special Commissions.
To the People of Hampshire
and Wiltshire

P.R. LXX., c. 929. *Rural War. Special Commissions.* 11-12-30.

Countrymen and Friends,

THE BLOODY OLD TIMES, that sanguinary crew who hunted poor CASHMAN to the gallows, who bellowed for the blood of the WATSONS, who urged the King of France, on his restoration, to murder a large part of the people of France, who defended the massacre of the Protestants at Nismes; that bloody sheet, that most infamous of all the parts of the mercenary and infamous daily papers of London; that bloody newspaper bawled for SPECIAL COMMISSIONS, and Special Commissions are about to sally forth upon *Hampshire* and *Wiltshire,* in one of which Special Commissions is the name of SERJEANT WILDE! SCOTT ELDON (a name and a man to be *borne in mind!*) expressed the other day his "*infinite satisfaction*" that Special Commissions were going forth "to *expound* the law to the *ignorant* men" who were to be tried; but, then, if what SCOTT ELDON related, on the same day, were true, a set of *interpreters* ought to go with each Special Commission; for he said that he had been informed that some of the jails were *full of foreigners!*

But how comes it that these *two counties* are selected for these *Special Commissions?* And why could not the *'Squires,* by holding special sessions, as in *Kent,* have done the business? Let me stop here to observe upon this matter. Amongst the silly, or rather knavish, boastings about our "*happy* constitution," is, that all men are tried before, and sentenced by, JUDGES who are *independent even of the King;* who, when once appointed, cannot be displaced even by the King himself, unless they be first proved to have been guilty of some high crime. To keep them from all undue bias they cannot be members of the House of Commons; and though they sit in, they cannot *vote* in, the House of Lords, except such of them as are Peers. And *thus* is their purity and impartiality secured; and this is one of the great boasts of the vile knaves, who wish to uphold the present system. And while our *infamous press* is trumpetting this boast about the world, there is a *justice of the peace,* down at Canterbury, *sentencing men to transportation for life,* while he and all those who sit upon the bench and co-operate with him, derive their authority from the ministry of the day, are appointed by their sole will, and may, at any moment, and that, too, without cause assigned, be *turned out of their offices!* And these men can now *transport for life,* and that, too, in virtue of laws, which, perhaps, (as is actually the case with this Knatchbull), they have themselves *assisted to pass*! A few years ago a law was passed, and is now enforced, *to transport men for poaching;* and the *justices of the peace,* many of whom *assisted to make this law,* were empowered to *pass such sentence*! Poh! you rascally knaves, who grind the paragraphs and pamphlets about the *"independence of our* judges"! Poh! you vile Scotch and Irish rascals! Keep your breath to cool your burgoo and *taties*: you will not persuade *the people of England* to admire a state of things like this. This is one of the GREAT WRONGS that we now feel. In nineteen cases out of twenty, the common people have now *no trial by jury,* and are judged by men appointed and removeable at the absolute will of the ministry of the day. Is this what the enemies of real reform call one of the *"institutions of the country"*? This is one of George the Third and George the Fourth's *institutions.* Would a reformed Parliament leave this *"institution"* untouched?

*　　　*　　　*　　　*　　　*

But coming now to the SPECIAL COMMISSIONS, what are they to do? SCOTT ELDON says, that they are to *expound the law* to the *ignorant* people; and, indeed, it may want expounding; if it be the *law of George IV.,* the *"mild* and *benevolent* George IV." it will require a long deal to prove the *mildness* of it, as well as to explain its meaning. If the Judges go to put *new laws* into execution, those *death-dealing* laws which were the work of the *mild* reign of George IV., whose history, when I have completed it, will show what impudent liars the eulogists of this reign and regency are, it will require a great deal. But will these ministers SHED BLOOD? That is the question. Will they enforce the *new laws* against the labourers? Will they shed the blood of men made desperate by starvation? Will they shed the blood of men who saw their children dying for want of food? I hope, and I not only hope but *believe,* that they *will not.* They are not a fierce crew of hard lawyers, such as we have seen in power before. The *chief* is a mild and kind man, very fond of his own family, and who is likely to make the case of the labourers his own. There is *one man,* who is in what is called the cabinet, that *I do not like;* but his office gives him little weight. But, indeed, the whole affair, must rest on LORD GREY; and I have, as to this matter in particular, great reliance on his humane disposition. The only charge against him is, that he is *haughty,* and this charge runs through the French as well as the English papers. I once had occasion to wait on Lord Grey; I asked leave to do it; he very politely gave his consent; it was just before I fled to Long Island, to avoid Sidmouth and Castlereagh's and Scott Eldon's dungeons; he received me in the most obliging manner, and conversed with me a long while with the greatest affability. So that, as far as my knowledge of him goes, this charge is not well-founded. Then, though Lord MELBOURNE did take part against us, in 1817, he is not a ferocious fellow; he is a good-tempered man, and not inclined to be bloody. There is Lord Holland, who never gave his consent to an act of cruelty; and there is Lord Althorp, too, who has never dipped his hands in blood, nor crammed victims into the dungeon; and the Lord Chancellor, with all his half-Scotch crochets, has, at any rate, *no blood about him.* These are the principal men; and, therefore, I hope that we shall see no blood spilled upon this occasion.

* * * * * *

But, short of death, how great, merciful God, have been the sufferings of the labourers and their families! And is not the parish allowance *slow starvation?* . . . And if this be their horrible state, will this Ministry *shed their blood?* . . . The bloody old *Times* newspaper, which is the organ, and, perhaps, in great part the *property,* of this hellish crew, says, that the labourers "*are starving,* and that they have been *cruelly oppressed;* but that *some* of them must be made to suffer the *severest penalty* of the law." So that this bloody crew would have men *put to death* for using the *only means* left them to save themselves from starvation!

No: this will not be done. The course of these ill-used men has been so free from ferocity, so free from anything like bloody-mindedness! They have not been *cruel* even to their most savage and insolent persecutors. The most violent thing that they have done to any *person* has not amounted to an attempt on the *life* or *limb* of the party; and in no case, but in self-defence, except in the cases of the two *hired overseers* in Sussex, whom they merely trundled out of the carts, which those hirelings had had constructed for them to draw like cattle. Had they been *bloody;* had they been *cruel;* then it would have been another matter; had they burnt people in their beds, which they might so easily have done; had they beaten people wantonly, which has also been in their power; had they done any of these things, there would have been some plea for severity : but they have been guilty of none of those things : they have done desperate things, but they were driven to *desperation* : all men, except the infamous stock-jobbing race, say, and loudly say, that *their object is just;* that *they ought* to have that which they are striving for; and all men, except that same hellish crew, say that they had *no other means of obtaining it.* And yet this bloody old newspaper calls for the shedding of their blood. This bloody old vehicle of lies, the printer of which was *made a magistrate* by SCOTT ELDON, sees the evidence given before a Committee of the House of Commons by BENETT, stating that he and his brother magistrates of Wiltshire, calculated that every person in a labourer's family *" ought to have a pound and a quarter of bread and a half-penny a day for food and clothing; "* and yet the infamous and sanguinary vehicle calls for the *blood* of the poor men of Wiltshire !

The Special Commissions

P.R. LXXI., c. 126. *Special Commissions.* 8-1-31.

OH, yes! I " behold what has passed, and is passing, in HAMPSHIRE and WILTSHIRE "! I *behold* it; I cannot, at present, trust my pen upon the subject; but, when I forget, or neglect, *my duty* with regard to it, may the God that made me instantly reduce me to dust! I am getting together all the facts relating to it : *names, dates* and *circumstances;* and that is all that I can do at present.

The Special Commissions!

P.R. LXXL., c. 199.   *To the King's Ministers.*   22-1-31.

THE *means of terror or of punishment are not calculated to put an end to the fires.* It is an old saying that, *if you kill a fly, twenty flies come to his burying.* The newspapers tell us, and indeed we know the fact must be so, that there is scarcely a village in the counties before mentioned, and particularly in Hampshire and Wiltshire, which has not been, in a greater or less degree, plunged into a state of mourning in consequence of the late trials and their result. But, is mourning *all?* When men suffer for well-known and long-understood crimes, then there is no apology to be offered for them. Their memory is grieved, their banishment or death lamented; but the relations and friends acquiesce; the law takes its course, and no vengeful feelings are excited in the survivors. You have read the Birmingham petition for the sparing of the lives of the men of Winchester; if you have not, I beg you to read it. The question, however, is not what sort of feelings the surviving labourers *ought* to entertain upon the subject; but what feelings they are. likely to entertain; and now, then, consider the effect of screaming mothers and wives and children; think of the feelings of fathers for sons, brothers for brothers, friends for friends; and consider that there can be scarcely one single man, amongst the labourers of Hampshire and Wiltshire, unaffected in his mind and heart by these transactions. *The Morning Chronicle,* in giving an account of the hanging of Cooper and Cook, at Winchester, last Saturday, concludes the account thus:—
" There was not a crowd of more than 300 persons, and those chiefly boys. Some of the crowd we heard say they would willingly give a sovereign for a reprieve. The moment the drop fell most of them went away. The special constables were in attendance at 7 o'clock, and, in fact, composed the greater part of the crowd. Close under the scaffold, on some doors, was written in chalk—' MURDER FOR MURDER! BLOOD FOR BLOOD! '".

Now, this is what we never see and never hear of when male-factors are executed at other times. Cooper's offence was riding at the head of a mob, who *extorted money,* or *broke machines,* or something of that sort. Cook's offence was, striking BINGHAM BARING with a sledge hammer. But Baring was well enough to appear and give evidence against him; and it appears was seen immediately after the affair walking in the streets of Winchester; so that this was very far from being MURDER; and, before the passing of *Ellenborough's Act* it would have been an ASSAULT, punishable not even with transportation, but with a fine or imprisonment, or both. Now mind, the labourers are not lawyers, they know nothing of *Ellenborough's Act;* their estimate of crimes is traditionary; and it will take a great deal indeed to convince them and to produce perfect acquiescence in their mind upon the subject of this punishment. "Kill one fly, and twenty come to his burying." Accordingly the very next sentence in *The Chronicle* newspaper is in these words: "There have been eight fires in the neighbourhood of Blandford since Saturday last."

*   *   *   *   *   *

P.R. LXXI., c 199. *To the King's Ministers.* 22-1-31.

Now, King's Ministers, if you be convinced, as I hope you are, that the fires have been set by the labourers without instigation from any-body; that the means of terror or of punishment are not calculated to put an end to the fires; and that the fires, unless effectually put a stop to, may become far more extensive than they hitherto have been; if you be convinced of these truths, as I hope you are, it only remains for me to point out to you what I deem the proper and effectual means of putting a stop to these fires; and these means are as follows:—

1. To issue a proclamation pardoning all the offenders of every description, whether tried or not, upon their entering into sureties to keep the peace for a year, and bringing back those who have already been sent away, and including them in the pardon on the like terms. Oh! Gentlemen, think of the joy, think of the happiness, with which you would thus fill all the bosoms in all the villages in these beautiful counties! And think

of the gratitude with which you would fill those bosoms towards yourselves; and, above all things, think of the blessings which, coming from the hearts of fathers and mothers and children and brothers and sisters, you would bring down upon the head of your royal master.

2. To repeal Sturges Bourne's two bills, and thereby restore to the ratepayers their rights, restore the power of the native overseers, and restore to the justices of the peace their former power of ordering relief, without which the indigent poor can have no sure protection.

3. To pass an act, making it a misdemeanour punishable with heavy fine and imprisonment for any overseer or other person in parochial authority to subject the indigent poor to work like beasts of burden, to put them up at auction, or otherwise wantonly to degrade them, taking as the preamble of the bill that text of holy writ which says, " Oppress not the poor *because* he is poor! "

4. To repeal all the acts which have been passed relative to the game since the late King George the Third mounted the throne, and particularly that act which punishes poaching with transportation, which act has filled the county jails with prisoners, which has trebled the county rates, which has thrown a burden on all the people in order to preserve the sport of the rich, which has filled the breasts of all the villagers of England with vindictive feelings, which has been the cause of endless affrays between poachers and keepers, and which in conjunction with Ellenborough's act has brought scores of men to the gallows.

5. To pass an act to repeal and utterly abolish Ellenborough's act, which, by making it a capital felony to strike a man with a heavy instrument without killing him, or to use deadly weapons in your own defence against a gamekeeper, though without killing him, puts the striker in the one case, and the defender in the other, upon a level with the wilful, premeditating, cool, and cruel murderer, tends to confound all notions of discrimination in crime; tends to harden men's hearts, and weaken in them every sense of justice and humanity.

Cobbett Defends Himself

*From a Full and Accurate Account of the Trial of William Cobbett Esq.
before Lord Tenterden and a Special Jury on Thursday, July 7, 1831 in the
Court of King's Bench Guildhall 1831.*

IN the month of October, I was at Battle, in Sussex, where I
gave a lecture to the chop-sticks of the country. There was
a man of the name of Goodman, who was tried at Lewes, in the
following month of November, for setting fire to a barn. He set
fire five times to the property of one man, and was convicted;
three witnesses positively swearing to the malice; therefore he
was left, and justly left, for execution, because there was no
excuse for him. He was not in the situation of poor Cook, out
of work, and not receiving more than 4s. 6d. or 5s. per week,
and having a poor father and mother with five children at the
time. He was not in that situation, he was a cooper, and for a
long time received 15s. per week; he set fire to a barn five times
with his own hand; but Cook had the misfortune to strike a
relation of five members of Parliament! However, he was left
for execution, and then it was said, Ah! cannot we find out from
this young man, a simple young man, a something to hook on
Trevor's prosecution against Cobbett? . . . A curate of the
name of Rush, of the village of Crowhurst, not the chaplain of
the jail, not having any business to visit the condemned cells,
not belonging to the prison; this curate of Crowhurst, who lived
several miles from Battle, who had for several years been
huntsman of a subscription pack of hounds; this curate, this
sportsman, urged on by some one, went to hunt up Goodman,
and to get a confession from him that Cobbett, who had come
into Sussex to give " *lactures* " there, had instigated him to the
commission of the deed for which he was doomed to suffer the
extreme penalty of the law. The *Times* newspaper had this
confession directly; " Ah! this poor man," said they, " was the
victim of this arch-*lacturer,* this sedition-monger, Cobbett."

＊   ＊   ＊   ＊   ＊   ＊

My contradiction was rather a stinging one. I said, in the
first place, that this being the certificate of a parson, I did not
believe it; nor would any man in his senses give it credence. I

then showed, by a slight process of reasoning, that it could not be true, and in fact I denied it, in which statement I was confirmed by persons at Battle. Then the next step was, that of three magistrates of the county of Sussex visiting Goodman. I wish that the three were alive, God forgive me! but one is dead. I wish, however, that the other two were here. These three magistrates went to Goodman, who had been taken to Horsham to be hanged with another man who had set *one* stack of corn on fire. Being at Horsham, and getting nearer to the hour of death, and almost feeling the halter about his neck, they thought they could then get more from him than the curate of Crowhurst did. There he repeated his former confession, but he went a little further; ah! unluckily, went a little further! " Liars," they say, " should have good memories." . . . Now these three magistrates went to Goodman and they said, " We, the three undersigned magistrates, went to see the unfortunate person on the 30th of December." Mark the dates, gentlemen; the libellers at Westminster left off work on the 23rd December, and to keep the affair up, these magistrates commenced their operations on the 30th December. They let Christmas-day pass, and then they go at it. They go on to say,

" Who being questioned as to whether he had any enmity against the person whose ricks he had set fire to, declared he bore no malice against him, but that he would state what induced him to act in this manner; and when asked whether he would commit this to paper, he proceeded to write the following statement in our presence, without any dictation or suggestion from us—

WALTER BURRELL ⎫
HENRY TREDCROFT ⎬ Magistrates.
FRANCIS S. BLUNT ⎭

" I Thomas Goodman, once heard of one Mr. Cobbit going A Bout gaving out lactures at length he came to Battel and gave one their and their was a gret number of peopel came to hear him and I went he had verrey long conversation concerning the state of the country and tilling them that they was verrey mutch impose upon and he said he would show them the way to gain their rights and liberals (liberties) and he said it would be verrey Proper for every man to keep gun in his house espesely young men and that they might prepare themselves in readiness to go with him when he called on them and he would show them which way to go on and he said that peopel might expect firs their as well as others places.

This is the truth and nothing But the truth of A deying man.

THOMAS GOODMAN

Written before us,
30th Dec., 1830

WALTER BURRELL
H. TREDCROFT
FRANCIS SCAWEN BLUNT

Now, this was the statement of the magistrates, notwithstanding it was proved by three witnesses, at the trial, that he was influenced to the commission of the act by malice.

*   *   *   *   *   *

When I first saw the lie, I knew it all to be a fabrication, and that he never wrote one of these papers. I said, if I go to Battle and bring twenty or thirty witnesses, which I can do, to prove that I uttered no such words as Goodman has attributed to me, or rather these magistrates have made him attribute to me; if I bring evidence, which I can do, to prove an *alibi* as to Goodman being at the lecture; if I do that, they will hang him, and I shall be exonerated from all blame; but I will bear this calumny to prevent the shedding of blood. There were many respectable tradesmen and farmers, in Battle, and about Battle, who had the same notion as myself, and they were going to sign a declaration, and in fact had drawn up an affidavit expressive of their conviction that Goodman's confession was a lie. When, however, they saw my Register, in which I expressed my willingness to bear the calumny rather than the life of the man should be taken, they came to the determination not to say anything respecting it until Goodman was gone away. It is a very curious thing, that a man who, it was clearly proved, had been guilty of five fires from private malice should be pardoned, while the life of poor Cook was taken, who did nothing but strike the rim of a hat of

a man who had five relations having votes in Parliament: Mr.
Bingham Baring. They also executed a man at Maidstone upon
the evidence of the man who instigated him to the commission
of the crime! But this Goodman told a lie, and because he
belied *me,* they spared him! If they had executed him, it would
have been a proof that they did not believe his accusation against
me; but, because the Attorney-General did not put a stop to the
calumnies affecting my character; because he had plotted his
prosecution against me, Goodman was pardoned. Here was
mercy arising out of malignity; here was one of the highest
prerogatives of the Crown prostituted for the purpose of
propagating calumnies against one of his Majesty's most faithful
subjects.

*　　　*　　　*　　　*　　　*　　　*

I will not, however, content myself with a negative statement
that what Goodman said was false; for I hold in my hand a
document containing affirmative evidence of that fact; I have
here a declaration signed by 103 persons belonging to fourteen
different parishes in Sussex, the parish of Battle being one;
persons who were present at my lecture, and who have
voluntarily come forward to sign the declaration, among whom
you will perhaps not be a little astonished to find the name of the
prosecutor of Goodman himself, who was present at the lecture,
and whose barn Goodman burned.

*　　　*　　　*　　　*　　　*　　　*

I will, however, now come to the grand and obvious object of
the article; and I will put it to the Jury to say, when they shall
have carefully read it all through, whether they can entertain the
slightest doubt, that my object was to save the lives of those
unfortunate men who were convicted under the special commissions. . . , The *Times* newspaper, which has always a keen
nose for blood, which praised the massacre of the Protestants at
Nismes, and called for the blood of the unfortunate Cashman, it
was this Journal, which called for the special commission, and its
observations were sent forth as feelers. Under such circumstances,
I anticipated a great shedding of blood, and I therefore felt

myself called upon to endeavour to prevent it. Now, let the Jury read the article in question from beginning to end, and say if they can possibly come to any other conclusion than that it was written for the express purpose of preventing blood from being shed. Let this fact then be borne in mind. Now, such being my object, how is it possible to suppose that I would incite to further acts of outrage which would of course be the means of defeating the end I had in view? I again repeat, that that was my only object, and to effect that purpose I appealed to the ministers in every possible way; I even used the license allowed by Paley, by telling lies to soften them in their severe measures. I went still farther, and invited all parts of the country, and the parishes of the metropolis, to petition on this behalf. I succeeded in procuring those petitions, and particularly from the noble town of Birminham. Such was my object, and such the tendency of the article for which this " false, scandalous and malicious " indictment, has been preferred against me. His Lordship will tell you, that you are to look at the whole of this *Register* from the first to the last, and that, if you find anything there rendering it impossible to believe that I had the intention which this Whig Attorney-General has imputed to me, you are bound to acquit me; though I admit that, in so doing, you will at the same time be pronouncing a verdict of *guilty* on this Whig Government.

*   *   *   *   *   *

On my return from America, thirty years ago, I took a great interest in the welfare of the labouring classes, and wrote several papers upon their state. About ten or twelve years ago, I published for their especial use, a little work called " *Cottage Economy*," teaching them how to make bread and beer in the best manner, and otherwise to provide for their comforts. In a similar spirit, I wrote and published a book called " *The Poor Man's Friend*." Then again, in my Letter to the Luddites, in 1816, when they had been guilty of rioting, I did what I could to persuade them to be quiet and respect the property of their employers. If I were to speak of this work alone, my motives would be apparent, and these motives are known to my Whig persecutors, but I will confirm the evidence of my motives by the evidence of facts. This very publication of mine to the Luddites has been revived by the instrumentality of my prosecutors, and revived at the very time that the fires were raging in Kent. Early in December, the Lord Chancellor, Lord Brougham, applied to me to give him leave to re-publish my Letter to the Luddites, because in his opinion it was calculated to have a good effect on the minds of the people. The Lord Chancellor, applied in the name of a society with which he is connected for this purpose, and he sent to ask on what terms I would allow of the republication. The society is the Society for the *Diffusion of Useful Knowledge*, and they wished to circulate it among those very labourers whom I am now charged with inciting to acts of violence. What times are these! This *Diffusion of Useful Knowledge* Society, with the Lord Chancellor at its head, came to quiet the labourers by some of the stuff out of " *Cobbett's Sedition Shop* !" Nay, another member of that Society is my worthy friend the Attorney-General; my worthy friend who accuses me of stirring up sedition, and stirring up the labourers to destroy property, applied to me for leave to publish my writings, as a means of quieting the labourers! This is so monstrous, that it will hardly be believed. You will hardly credit, gentlemen, that the same Lord Chancellor and the same Attorney-General are now prosecuting me. . . . My learned friend has called my writings " false, scandalous, and seditious," and a Society of which he is a member, has borrowed my book with a view to publishing my book!

* * * * * *

I have little else to add, except to state what evidence I shall lay before you. The first witness I shall call will be the Lord Chancellor, and I will put in the Letter to the Luddites, and which by delivery to Lord Brougham for publication, I, in point of law, republished at the very time when I was said to be endevouring to stir up the labourers to sedition and outrage. I will then call his Lordship to prove the fact respecting the application for it, and he will tell you that I stipulated no terms, but that the whole of the letter should be published. I shall then call the Earl of Radnor, who knows me and all my sentiments well, and he will tell you whether I am a likely man to design and endeavour to do that which this "false, scandalous, and malicious" Whig indictment charges me with wishing to do. I shall also call several persons of the highest respectability from Kent, Sussex, and other parts of the country, to prove that I have not done anything to stir up disturbance, but that I have done a great deal to prevent it and to restore quiet. I shall then call Lord Melbourne to prove that the sentence on Goodman was not executed, but that he was sent out of the country, whereas Cook was put to death. When the Jury shall have heard all this, and shall have read over the various publications, I have not the slightest doubt but that they will dismiss with scorn and contempt this groundless charge of the Whig Attorney-General.

* * * * * *

Why am I now tossed down before this court by the Attorney-General? What are my sins? I have called upon the Government to respect the law; I have cautioned them that hard-hearted proceedings are driving the labourers to despair; that is my crime. If the Government really wish to avoid disturbances in the country, let them give us back the old laws; let them give the people the old game law, and repeal the new law; and let them do away with the other grinding laws that oppress the poor. I have read with horror which I cannot describe, of a magistrate being accused to the Lord Chancellor of subornation of perjury; I have read of that magistrate being re-instated, and I have shuddered with horror at supposing that a poor starving labourer may be brought before such a man, and, in conjunction with another such magistrate, may be doomed to seven years' transportation for being out at night, and such a magistrate may be himself a game-preserver! This is a monstrous power, and certainly ought to be abolished. The ministry, however, will perhaps adopt the measures I have recommended, and then prosecute me for recommending them. Just so it is with Parliamentary Reform, a measure which I have been foremost in recommending for twenty years. I have pointed out, and insisted upon, the sort of reform that we must have; and they are compelled already to adopt a large part of my suggestions, and avowedly against their will. They hate me for this; they look upon it as I do, that they are married to Reform, and that I am the man who has furnished the halter in which they are led to church. For supplying that halter, they have made this attack on me, through the Attorney-General, and will slay me if they can. The Whigs know that my intention was not bad. This is a mere pretence to inflict pecuniary ruin on me, or cause me to die of sickness in a jail; so that they may get rid of me because they can neither buy nor silence me. It is their fears which make them attack me, and it is my death they intend. In that object they will be defeated, for, thank Heaven, you stand between me and destruction. If, however, your verdict should be—which I do not anticipate—one that will consign me to death, by sending me to a loathsome dungeon, I will with my last breath pray to God to bless my country and curse the Whigs, and I bequeath my revenge to my children and the labourers of England.

The Effect of the Fires

P.R. LXXI., c. 405. *To Wiltshire Benett.* 12-2-31.

THE labourers at Wiltshire have *had their wages raised*. If I have been in any degree the *cause,* to the winds I cast all the calumnies that it has brought upon me. They now get a morsel of meat now and then; but I shall never be content, till every honest hard-working man in England has his belly full of bread and meat every day. Damned potatoes were never intended to be the food of a labouring man, and his dress never was intended to be that of the scare-crow; and until his state be changed for that which it ought to be, I, as long as I have life and health, will contend for that change.

" Here will I hold : if there be a God above, and that there is all Nature cries aloud through all her works," he must abhor the wretch who would wish the honest labourer, who raises all the meat, all the bread, and all the clothing, to be compelled to live upon a root nine-tenths of which are dirt and water, while those who do not labour, live in luxury on the fruit of his toil. I know well that the labourer cannot have his due, and, at the same time, the funds, the army, the church, and all the rest, go on in the present way. I know this perfectly well. I repeat that SOMETHING MUST GIVE WAY. Choose you what it shall be: I have suggested the remedy often and often enough: you have rejected my advice: reject it still: do what you like with your own concern: but, Benett, if I can prevent it, the labourers of England, SHALL NOT LIVE UPON POTATOES. This is my resolution; and from this all the abuse in the world shall never drive me one single inch.

The Yeomanry Cavalry and the Fires

P.R. LXXV., c. 101. *To the Yeomanry Cavalry on the Fires.* 7-1-32.

I CANNOT call you *friends,* and I will not call you *gentlemen.* This plague of the country is now raging with greater fury than ever, and I think proper to address you upon the subject. You are called *yeomanry cavalry,* though perhaps more than one half of you are loan-mongers, tax-gatherers, dead-weight people, stock-jobbers, shag-bag attorneys, bailiffs (most Scotch), toad-eating shopkeepers, who are ready to perform military duty towards the "*lower orders,*", in order at once to give evidence of your gentility and to show your gratitude towards your rich customers for their paying your long bills without scruple. A very great part of you come in under one or the other part of this description; but to those of you who are farmers; that is to say, who have land in your occupation; and who grow corn, and rear cattle, and who have barns, ricks, and other things, liable to be set fire to; to you only do I address myself upon this occasion, being well aware that my arguments would produce no impression whatever upon your comrades above-mentioned. First of all, call the roll of your corps over, and see how many of them there are who are not interested in the taxes and the tithes, either immediately or through their relations, landlords, or somebody else. When you have called the roll, and have separated yourselves from the rest, get into a plain room, pull off your hairy caps, your party-coloured jackets, and your Wellington-boots; put on you own Christian-like clothes, your high shoes well nailed; and then pick out some one with a good strong voice to read to you that which I am now about to write.

You are not *philosophers;* but you have memories; you have eyes in the front of your head, ears on the side of it, and, generally speaking, you have brains wherewith to enable you to draw rational conclusions from the facts which have been communicated to those brains by the eyes and the ears, and which have been retained there by those powers of memory with which God has been pleased to endow you.

The FIRES are blazing more furiously than they were last year at this time. You go to bed in fear, and do not ride home from market, or from a neighbour's house, without apprehension : you are compelled to have *guards* or *watches* to see to the safety of your property; in some parts of Norfolk you have entered into associations to burden your land with *a tax* at so much an acre, in order to give rewards to such men or women as shall assist in bringing their neighbours to the gallows; and, lastly, to the neglect of your business, you have enrolled yourselves as soldiers, mounted your horses which ought to be at plough, and armed yourselves with deadly weapons, in order, if need be, to wound or kill somebody or other.

This being your state, and this state being *hell upon earth,* if ever there was hell upon earth, it is worth while for you to consider a little, whether your dressing yourselves out, and arming yourselves in this manner, be at all likely to put a stop to the fires; because as to any other immediate evil, you appear not to be afflicted with it. If your swaggering about with hairy caps on your heads could possibly tend to put out the fires, even them I should despise you; but it has not the tendency, and it has a directly contrary tendency; and I am perfectly convinced, as every reflecting man must be, that the very existence of a corps of yeomanry in a neighbourhood, *in time of peace,* has a *direct and natural tendency to produce these fires;* and this you will see clearly, if you will but cast aside the instigating falsehoods of your loan-mongering and tax-eating and petty-fogging comrades, and listen to your own reason.

You have seen all your lifetime, that nine-tenths of the hostile and vindictive proceedings of men, proceed from provocation arising from words or acts of *challenge, threat,* or *defiance.*

Even a dog will let you go by him quietly, until he sees you take up a stick or a stone; and does not the very existence of your corps speak *a thrat* to the labourers? Does not the bare sight of it tell them, that you mean to shoot them or chop them down, if they do not quietly submit to live upon what all the world says is sufficient? You do not tell them *in words,* that you will shoot them, or chop them down; but your swaggering hairy caps tell them so; aye, and it has been over and over again stated in speeches in Parliament, that the object of embodying you is to repress disturbances in your counties; and have you so great a contempt for the understandings of the working people as to imagine that they do not fully comprehend the meaning of these words? Will a parcel of labourers, working in a farm-yard, see the farmer mount his cavalry-horse, and go swaggering out with pistols in holster, and sword by side; are you such jolter-heads as to imagine, that they do not ask one another *what that can be for?* They know that the swaggering blade ought to stay at home; they, better than anybody, know how much his absence will cost him; and they discuss amongst them-selves, to be sure, what can be the motive of his thus acting, at which motive they arrive by a process of reasoning, the brevity of which is not less admirable than the conclusion on their minds is impressive.

Rights of the Labourers

P.R. LXXXVII., c. 536. *The Fires.* 28-2-35.

IT is a strange thing, that none of you ever look farther than for the means of detection and punishment. You never think of looking into the cause : if you did, you would find, that to attempt to reduce the labourers to a coarser sort of food; that to propose to put them into great workhouses, and dress them in a workhouse-dress; that to punish, almost unto death, a girl for having a bastard child; you would find, that these are not the means, though accompanied with all the rewards in the world, of preventing the fires. If you be of my age, you must know as well as I do, that, fifty years ago, a single man, who was not a yearly servant in husbandry, under the statute, was rarely to be seen; and when he was seen, was considered almost as a vagrant, and treated as such. It is not the fault of the single men of this day, that they are not in farm-houses, servants in husbandry, as their fathers were : it is not their fault, that they are in the gravel-pits by day, and prowling about houseless by night; it is not their fault, that they are compelled to give up half their earnings to the tax-gather : they have had no voice in choosing the makers of the laws; God gave them life upon this land; they have as much right to be upon it as you have; they have a clear right to a maintenance out of the land, in exchange for their labour; and, if you cannot so manage the lands yourselves as to take labour from them, in exchange for a living, give the land up to them : they are not to perish, at any rate.

TWENTY

THE NEW POOR LAW

Poor-Law Commission

P.R. LXXX., c. 22. *Poor-Law Commission.* 6-4-33.

THERE has been a sort of *report* from these people, in the form of a letter addressed to Lord MELBOURNE. I always said, that the main object of this commission was, to muster up a parcel of stories from people, picked out for the purpose, to justify more severe measures against the working people; and to introduce, under pretence of protecting property, a sort of *Bourbon police* into all the villages and country towns; a police in uniform, carrying daggers and pistols, like those in London. I have mentioned this several times in the House of Commons; I saw that dirty FEELER, the base and hard-hearted editor of the *Morning Chronicle,* broaching this scheme, some time ago. I was sure that he was in communication with those who had the intention to do this thing. Why, they have had an armed police in Ireland a good while. They have had what they call a "constabulary force;" "a police force;" "a red-coat force;" and now they have got red-coat courts of justice. There are people who think, that the same thing will do in England; I see no prospect of its not being *attempted;* but I know that it will fail: that is to say, I know that it would produce confusion ten thousand times greater than that which is sought to be avoided. Already there are *watchmen* kept to guard the great mansions in the country; already do policemen scour off from London to assist these horrible vagabonds, the gamekeepers in the country. This aristocracy and country gentlemen, as they call themselves, would, I verily believe, jump with joy to get the *police-force;* for this would serve them as watchmen and gamekeepers, and be paid for by the industrious people. Thus, the *potato-diet* (and this ought to be called the potato-commission) would be, as these wiseacres think, completely enforced. The fact is this; the country labourers insist upon not being starved. They have the means of preventing their starvation, and the police-force is to deprive them of those means. Alas! it will never do! it will only bring open war; and it is truly astonishing, that the aristocracy cannot see, that the end of these things, if they should be so foolish as to adopt them, must be *destruction to themselves*. It is a strange thing, that they will not look at the *cause* of the poor-rates, and the fires. It is a strange thing, that they will not recollect what took place in France; that they will not perceive that they are marching just in the steps of the aristocracy of *Louis* XV. They had *gendarmerie* in every village; and yet, while these *gendarmerie* were in the villages, still in the villages, they were driven from their mansions, and those mansions were burnt. Is it not time for ours to begin to think of the final consequences? Is it not time for them to begin to think about obtaining security other than that which is given by daggers and pistols? The people want to live well, as they ought to live; and until they do live well, no *gendarmerie* schemes will be of any avail for any length of time. It was easy to see what this poor-law commission would be, when we saw STURGES BOURNE one of the commissioners! That which they have now published is a little beginning. It lets out, however, the scheme of the *gendarmerie;* and puts us upon our guard, and enables us to give it a *warm* reception. This I, for my part, shall not fail to do. Our aristocracy ought to recollect, that there are two items in *their affair,* which make it more dangerous than the affair of the French *noblesse* was. FIRST, they had *no church-and-poor property in their hands;* they had no lay-tithes and abbey-lands in their hands; and, what is of still more importance, they had no savings banks and paper-money. They had a *debt,* indeed; and it was that which, in fact, brought them down; but they had no bank with *a few hundred thousand louis-d'ors in its chests, with twenty-six millions of pounds afloat in paper*! They had not this terrific item; and, even only three years before their houses were in flames, their chance of escape seemed not to be so very bad. Our aristocracy has a terrible affair to deal with; therefore, it is time for them to begin to think about something besides a *gendarmerie.* I shall have plenty of occasions to return to this poor-law-commission affair; but I shall only find it that which I expected; abounding with schemes, not to make the poor better off, but to make them receive less money in the way of relief.

Brougham's Poor-Law Commission,
and
The Falsehoods laid before Parliament,
under the Signature of the Persons
Composing that Commission.

P.R. LXXXI., c. 17. *Brougham's Poor-law and the Falsehoods laid before Parliament, under the signature of the persons composing that Commission.* 6-7-33.

FROM the first moment of the appointment of this commission, I expressed my opinion, that its tendency was of a most mischievous nature. The Bishops of LONDON and CHESTER stand at the head of the commissioners. Every one must know that it is impossible that these bishops should be able to enter into any such inquiries. Next comes STURGES BOURNE, the author of those bills which have produced so much mischief throughout the country, and which have been petitioned against by so many parishes. Next comes SENIOR, a man who has written, over and over again, to maintain the doctrines of Parson MALTHUS. Next comes COULSON, who was a newspaper-reporter some time ago; who is, I believe, a relation of SENIOR, and who is a disciple of the same school. We have no written proof of HARRY GAWLER'S opinions, that I know of; and there is now another man of the name of BISHOP, of whom I have never heard before. BROUGHAM said, in 1819, " that he was prepared to defend the principles of MALTHUS to their full extent;" and that full extent was, *to refuse parochial relief altogether.* He pledged himself, the session before last, to bring in a new poor-law. I defied him to do it, the moment he gave the pledge; and, instead of bringing in a poor-law, he and his colleagues appointed this poor-law commission to obtain *information upon the subject.*

These *commissioners* sit in London, it seems, and send forth roving deputy-commissioners to collect information about the country. These rovers give in written accounts of the result of their inquiries. A parcel of *extracts* from these accounts have been collected together, printed in the form of an octavo book, and sold at *price four shillings,* " PUBLISHED BY AUTHORITY ", and, the members of the House of Commons have each of them been furnished with a copy of this book. This is a new way of doing the nation's business. We have never before heard of a published book, price so much, being laid upon the table of the House of Commons. We have never before heard of a public board turning authors, especially with a couple of bishops at its head, and selling its books. However, we have the book; and, so scandalous a thing has seldom appeared in the shape of a book. It is evident, that the book is intended to pave the way for calling upon Parliament to pass a law to do the following things :

1. To set aside the authority of the present justices of the peace, as far, at any rate, as relates to the management of the poor.
2. To make STURGES BOURNE's Bills compulsory, and to extend their effects all over England and Wales.
3. To cause MALTHUS's plan of refusal of relief to be adopted.
4. To put down the present sort of justices of the peace altogether; to supply their places by *hired* justices appointed immediately by the Government.
5. To put down all the present peace-officers of counties and parishes, and to establish all over Great Britain, a *Bourbon-police,* with commissioners, superintendents, inspectors, sergeants, and privates, just such as we have the misery to have in London.

These are manifestly the objects of this book; and to accomplish these objects, the roving commissioners have resorted to falsehoods the most glaring. I insert below, first, a petition from the town of HORSHAM, in Sussex; and, second, " An Inquiry into the merits of the Poor-law Report, by the Rev. HARRY F. YEATMAN," who is also a magistrate for the county of Dorset. In presenting the HORSHAM petition, Mr. HURST, who resides in the parish, vouched for the truth of the petition, and for the falsehood of the rovers' report. Mr. YEATMAN examines the report of another of the rovers, publishes his examination in the shape of a pamphlet, puts his name in the title-page of his pamphlet, and he exposes such a tissue of false-hoods, and such glaring instances of foul dealing, as must, one would think, make the two bishops blush at the thought of having put their names to such a book. I do beseech my readers, particularly those of the *political unions,* to read these documents with the greatest possible attention. The Whig scheme of sub-jecting England to a *Bourbon-police government,* will be blown into air; but let us, my friends, never forget the *design!* I am very much obliged to the person who has sent me the pamphlet of the Rev. Mr. YEATMAN; the whole nation is indebted to him for making this timely exposure; and it will, doubtless, rouse the people to call for an end of the expenses of this Poor-law Commission.

Poor-Law Project

P.R. LXXXIV., c. 263.　*The Poor-Law Project.*　3-5-34.

I HAVE this bill; but I will not now attempt an analysis of it, chiefly because I have not duly considered the extent of all its terrible consequences if attempted to be carried into execution. It is a sort of *Austrian* project: a scheme for bringing every thing and every body within the control, the immediate control, of the kingly part of the Government. This bill will totally abrogate all the local government of the kingdom : the gentlemen and the magistrates will be totally divested of all power, tending to uphold their character, and to secure their property and their personal safety in the country. I have talked to twenty gentle-men, farmers and attorneys; every man of them has said : " If this bill be attempted to be put into execution, there will be a revolution in England "; and I am so firmly persuaded of the soundness of their opinion, that I should look upon the result as something inevitable. The rejection of this monstrous scheme by the Lords would assuredly take place, but it would have done for the Ministry in the meanwhile; the bill would remain tied round the neck of GREY and ALTHORP to the last hour of their lives. If this bill be pushed through the House of

Commons, a thing that I can hardly believe; and if it be rejected by the Lords, it will give the Lords power to do just what they please with this Ministry. They will see their opportunity of course; and this will be the opportunity for the putting down of this Ministry for ever. The whole nation detests the bill, save and except the hatchers of it.

In the country an execution of this bill is literally impossible : every parish would be plunged into confusion immediately; men would not work, and there must be constables and jailers, or police and soldiers, stationed in every parish. The Parliament may pass the law, but it never can be executed; it would be a mere heap of rubbishy words, flung aside, while the government of parishes would be carried on without any law at all.

The Poor-Law Bill

P.R. LXXXV., c. 70. *To the People of Oldham. Poor-Law Bill.* 12-7-34.

My Friends,

This bill has now passed the House of Commons; and I deem it to be my bounden duty to lay before you the history of that passing; and also as correct an account as I am able to give you of the last effort which I made to prevent the passing of a bill which, if passed by the Lords, and attempted to be carried into effect, will in my opinion, be productive of consequences of the most fatal description, as well with regard to the people themselves, as with regard to their rulers.

    *   *   *   *   *   *

I shall not attempt to give you the report of my speech, about which, as a speech, I care not a straw; but I will state to you, as nearly as I can, the substance of the arguments and facts which I made use of. To give you more than the substance would be impossible, as it took me much about an hour to make the statement, which, I must do the House the justice to say, it heard with exemplary patience.

I began by observing, that I should not enter into any of the details of the measure; but merely confine myself to what I believed to be its *real ultimate object,* and to the showing that

that object was unjust, unconstitutional, and that it contemplated an end which, if attempted to be enforced, must prove the subversion of the Government itself. I will now proceed to state the substance of this speech in the form of propositions, which, though very dry work, is very *plain* work; and affords the best possible chance of having one's meaning clearly understood. This is the most important subject that ever was agitated in this country in my time. This bill is beyond all measure of more importance than the Reform Bill was; its provisions come home to the very means of existence of every working man in the kingdom. Already we hear the angry voices of the labourers in the fields and along the lanes. Already their menaces are heard; a dreadful convulsion I verily believe is at hand, unless the Lords shall *take time* to reflect on this bill; and if they take time, I am sure that their wisdom and their sense of justice will avert this dreadful calamity from the country. I now proceed to state the matter of my speech in the form of propositions.

* * * * * *

THAT, with regard to this most portentous bill, which was then to receive the final decision of the House, the REAL OBJECT was, in my opinion, to reduce the people of England to the state of the people of Ireland; to make them live upon potatoes, at best; and to submit to occasional famine, in order that the landlords may put into their pockets, not only the amount of the poor-rates; but the amount of one half of the wages which the labourers now receive. That I, by no means, imputed this wish to a majority of the landlords, or to any considerable portion of them, thinking them much too wise, as well as too just, to entertain any such wish; but that I most firmly believed this to be the real object of the inventors of this revolutionary project, and of its official supporters; and that, I would now, under the indulgence of the House, proceed to give my REASONS distinctly, one after another, for entertaining that belief.

THAT, in the first place, there were three countries, over whom this Parliament had to exercise supreme power: in one we found, in spite of all the fatal changes that immense taxation, and destructive monopoly, created by paper-money, had produced: we still found, generally speaking, the labourer, particularly in this reprobated south, lodged in a cottage, with a clean floor, with his bed up stairs, his little table set with a cloth upon it three times a day; that cottage surrounded by a neat garden, decorated more or less with flowers, containing a variety of vegetables, with a x x x, situated in that spot dictated by decency, by native modesty, and by purity of manners and of morals. We have another country, where the labourer has earth for the floor of his dwelling; where a few boards knocked roughly together form his bedstead; where his bed is *heather,* or straw, and his bedding the most miserable of rugs; where table cloth, knife, fork, or plate, never appears; where an iron pot, a *brose* (oats coarsely ground) bowl, and a bit of cow's horn for a spoon, are his only goods, furniture, and utensils. We have a third country, where all the household goods put together is a pot, wherein to boil the roots, upon which the family and the pig all live together, in a shed without a chimney, and covered with sods. In the first country all persons are clad from head to foot: in the second, a large part of the women and the children, have bare legs and feet; in the third, even the bodies of a large part are half-naked, and some quite naked.

THAT there is, perhaps, not another assembly in the whole world; not another six hundred and fifty-eight men, got together under one roof, who, having these three countries at their absolute command, would not set to work instantly and never cease till they had made the last two countries like the first; instead of which, we are at work to make the first country like the two last; or, rather, like the third; and professing, all the while, that we want to better the lot of its people. This is my first reason for believing that which I have stated to be true.

* * * * * *

THAT there now remains not a shadow of doubt, that the real object of this bill is, to put an end to the poor-rates, and to put money into the pockets of the landlords; and, if there were the shadow of a doubt, it would be removed at once, by looking at the monstrous provisions of this bill, which gives *six votes* to the landlord in the vestry, and enables him to vote *by proxy*. So, while he is voting for this hard treatment of the working people, without whose labour his estate would be worth nothing, he himself, like the Irish landlord; he himself is to keep out of sight, and out of reach; and throw all the odium upon his middleman, or his proctor! Ah! if there be any English landlord, who calculates thus, what an egregious simpleton must he be! It is easy enough for Scotch heritors and Irish domainowners to be absentees. This abused south of England is a place of safe refuge for them; but whither is the English absentee to go, when become uneasy in his mansion?

THAT the object is clear from the provisions which so effectually take the poor-rates out of the hands of the farmers; that this is done, because the farmer knows, that by starving his labourers he would *only add to his rent*. Take off the farmer's poor-rates and his tithes too, and the landlord demands them both, in addition to the former rent.

* * * * * *

Pass this bill and you destroy the constitution as far as relates to the necessitous. Obliterate the Act of ELIZABETH, as this bill in fact does, and the reasoning of HALE against the doctrine of GROTIUS falls to the ground: you dissolve the social compact, as far as relates to the working people. There must be two parties to an obligation: without protection on one side there can be no right to demand obedience on the other. Read the 28. chapter of DEUTERONOMY. You will there find, and in the next chapter, what is to be the fate of those who are the oppressors of the poor; amongst the number of whom I trust that this House will never stand.

The New Poor Law

P.R. LXXXVIII., c. 557. *Poor-Law Bill*. 30-5-35.

LET us set regularly to work. I will do my duty, if the friends of the working-people will do their duty; and their duty consists in the following things:

1. Wherever the Poor-law Commissioners are at work, send me word of it by letter directed to BOLT-COURT, and give me the name of the Commissioner very particularly, and the thing or things which he is about to do.

2. Give me the name or names of any lords, baronets, or such people, that are co-operating with the poor-law commissioners; and tell me the place of their residence in the country.

3. Where there is any UNION, as they call it, give me an account of the number of parishes, and the probable extent and population of them.

4. Tell me who is the chairman of any committee or body of persons who are pushing on the thing.

5. If there be any regulation about separating man from wife, or children from parents, let me have them, and particularly if they be put into print.

6. Give me their dieting scale; and give me any other particulars that you think will be useful.

Unless I be thus assisted, it will be impossible to do justice in the discharge of my duty. I desire that all statements made to me may be perfectly true; and it is desirable that the writers should permit me to put their *names,* unless they can refer me to somebody that I know.

Cobbett's Last Article—Poor-Law Struggle

P.R. LXXXVIII., c. 641. *Poor-Law Struggle.* 13-6-35.

FOR it really appears to be another " RURAL WAR," and threatens to be much more durable and mischievous than the last rural war; and there is this circumstance in addition, in this case; that is to say, that this new scene of trouble, of turmoil, and of boiling blood, has been caused by the Parliament itself; that Parliament duly warned by me of all the consequences. In this respect it is another PEEL's-Bill affair. The proposition is made in the year 1833; the projectors are then warned, and are besought not to adopt the measure; they persevere a great deal more eagerly on account of the warning and the prediction, as if for the express purpose of making the prophet a liar. Half-a-dozen counties are in a state of partial commotion; the jails are opening the doors to receive those who are called the rebels against the Poor-law Bill! No matter as to any other thing relative to this measure; here is the country disturbed; here are the jails filling; here are wives and children screaming after their fathers; here are these undeniable facts; and what is the cause? Not a desire to overturn the Government on the part of the people; not a desire to disobey the settled laws of the country; not any revolutionary desire; not any desire to touch any one of the institutions of the country. What is it then? Why a desire and a resolution, as far as they are able to adhere to it, to maintain the laws of their country, as they were settled at the time when the *present church of the country was established;* to maintain those laws which formed the foundation, the very fundamental principles of the Government; and which are of two hundred and forty years' standing.